Once a King, Always a King

Once a King, Always a King

The Unmaking of a Latin King

Reymundo Sanchez

CHICAGO
REVIEW
PRESS

Library of Congress Cataloging-in-Publication Data
Sanchez, Reymundo
    Once a King, always a King : the unmaking of a Latin King /
    Reymundo Sanchez.— 1st ed.
        p. cm.
    Sequel to: My bloody life.
    ISBN 1-55652-505-2
        1. Sanchez, Reymundo, 2. Puerto Ricans—Illinois—Chicago—
Biography. 3. Gang members—Illinois—Chicago—Biography. 4. Vio-
lence—Illinois—Chicago. 5. Chicago (Ill.)—Social conditions. 6.
Chicago (Ill.)—Biography.
    I. Title.
    F548.9.P85O53 2003
    977.3'11004687295'0092—dc21

                                                            2003004921

The author will respond to questions e-mailed to him at
mybloodylife@hotmail.com.

Cover art: Frances Jetter
Cover design: Joan Sommers Design
Interior design: Rattray Design

Published by Chicago Review Press, Incorporated
814 North Franklin Street
Chicago, Illinois 60610
ISBN 1-55652-505-2
Printed in the United States of America
5 4 3 2 1

To M.G.

You saved my life, girl. I'm so sorry it had to be you.

Contents

Introduction

IN MY BLOODY LIFE: *The Making of a Latin King*, I wrote about the street gang lifestyle and the circumstances that lead many young people to choose this lifestyle as a way to feel they have a family to belong to. In *Once a King, Always a King*, I go into how hard it is to escape gang life, and I describe the lasting damage of physical, mental, and sexual abuse. In *My Bloody Life*, I took my experiences and added parts of the experiences of those around me to create a composite character that showed what it's really like to be in a gang. Most of the mental, physical, and sexual abuse, however, was actually mine. In this book, I stopped using the composite character and began to write completely about myself. As in *My Bloody Life*, I changed the actual names and many places to protect my identity, and in this book, the order of events is accurate. I altered the situations only enough to protect my identity.

Many years of hanging out in the streets with others who secretly searched for the same love and attention I did bonded me in many ways to the gang lifestyle forever. That being said, I must clarify that this bond is based on knowing that many kids continue to suffer the way I did at the hands of those who say they care. My feelings do not contradict in any way my belief that being in a gang means wasting your life. I am well aware of the damage that gangs can do to those who try to escape the lifestyle. I know that it is a fact that gang leaders would be criminals even if gangs didn't exist. This is the reason why I keep my identity concealed.

I created a Web site for *My Bloody Life* that attempts to educate visitors about the telltale signs of gangs in a neighborhood, and how to know if a child is a member of a gang or being recruited by a gang. Via that Web site, I have received several e-mails from Latin Kings questioning my brotherhood and in no uncertain terms laying down the law of the Kings. Although my life was not literally threatened, the message was loud and clear. Had I used my real name, the retaliation I feared would certainly have happened. On the other hand, a few Latin King brothers have written to express their support without asking for details that would compromise my identity. I also received a message from a young brother who asked me if I had known his father. I did. His father is doing time in jail for a long time, and his son, although he speaks positively about his future, is a member of the Latin Kings. I hope he gets out of the gang before it's too late.

When I began to recognize the true evil behind the so-called brotherhood in gangs, I tried to get myself away from them. That task turned out to be harder than I could ever have imagined, and I unexpectedly ended up right back where I started, even though I knew it was wrong, because it was familiar and comfortable. Although the need to behave violently was no longer a part of me, I still felt scared to be alone. I'm certain that a great percentage of those who become gang members feel the same way. But there are also many people out there who will never grow up and understand that there are other things in life than dying for meaningless colors. There will always be bitterness where much blood has been spilled in the name of gang affiliation. Those who are stuck will always look for ways to keep others down there with them—this guarantees they will never be lonely.

The violence taught at home underlies the violence that is committed in the street. It creates an atmosphere where there is always something to prove, whether or not there is a logical reason. It may be easier for gang members to deal with the anger and hatred that lives inside by remaining in a place where there is never a lack of opportunity to express those feelings.

Mainly, I ignored those feelings because I didn't understand them. When I began to recognize the anger and hatred within myself, I tried to deal with these feelings in a sane manner, but it actually took two years of incarceration (which I still think was a blessing from God) to open my eyes to what being a man really means.

The complete transformation into the man I am today was not easy. The turmoil inside of me ached, but I chose to escape no longer with drugs and alcohol. What I did find was the love and understanding of a young lady—another blessing from God. Marilyn Garcia is the name I use for her in this book.

Marilyn came into my life and planted seeds of respect—for myself and others—education, and communication, and she opened up my soul so that all the harbored pain could escape. Neither Marilyn nor I, unfortunately, ever imagined how much evil would come out of me. When all my anger and hatred came raging out, Marilyn bore the brunt of it.

When it was all over, Marilyn was no longer in my life. She probably regrets the moment she ever learned of my existence. I wish I could have gotten rid of my demons in a controlled environment under professional care, but that wasn't the case. I dedicate this book to Marilyn. I hope she will read it and understand that I had no control over what happened between us. It makes me sad that I became a better person and now live a relatively happy life because I unleashed all that rage and anger upon her.

I hope and pray that other people who secretly live in pain because of sexual, mental, and physical abuse get professional help before they turn around and cause the same kind of lifelong pain and suffering on someone they love, who loves them.

Once a King, Always a King

1

Once a King, Always a King

It was prophetic that, on the day I freed myself from being a menace to the Latino community in Chicago by leaving the Latin King nation, I would walk away drenched in the blood of an innocent person.

To leave the Latin King nation I endured a brutal three-minute beating called a violation. This alone should have made me want to get as far away as I could and not turn back, but I was unknowingly still shackled to the lifestyle and to the Latin Kings. A hatred for those who called themselves King killers still burned within me. Even knowing that the main source of danger to the Latin Kings was the Kings themselves, the only evidence I looked at to fuel that fire was the event that had occurred just moments ago.

After my violation I was walking through the park on my way toward the bus stop. I didn't have to take this route, but I wanted to see how it felt to walk through the park in the Humboldt Park neighborhood with the knowledge that I was no longer a Latin King. I saw my old friend and ex-lover Loca, with her kids in tow, dealing cocaine. Also present was King Spanky, who, in a wheelchair after being shot by the Latin Kings, was dealing cocaine for the Nation. Spanky called out "once a King, always a King" as I walked past. Seconds later, shots rang out. I couldn't tell which direction they were coming from or headed. The drive-by shooter hit one of Loca's two kids. I ran to him and cradled him in my arms, but he was already dead. The cops arrived and questioned me. Then I headed for the bus.

I sat on the bus and stared out the window at Humboldt Park. The place I once thought was heaven had become a hell for many who lived in its surroundings. My clothes were drenched in blood, yet nobody seemed to notice. I cried rivers of tears, but nobody cared. Not one person on that bus looked my way, sympathetically or otherwise. No one bothered to ask about the blood on my clothes, but I did hear comments on how I should just shut up and stop crying already.

The loss of an innocent life had become too common an occurrence for anyone to react emotionally unless they were somehow tied to the victim. The death of a young Latino was seen as one less criminal to worry about instead of a horrifying reality. From my viewpoint there was nothing I could say about that careless attitude because I felt the same way.

As the bus passed by an area where Cobras and Disciples, rival gangs of the Latin Kings, hung out, I began to feel nervous and afraid. It was then that I understood what Spanky meant when he said "once a King, always a King," as I was walking away from the park. But I was determined to make my life different, to grow outside of the 'hood.

I was leaving a life filled with violence at home and on the streets. I had endured rapes, abandonment, being shot, and beatings that left me gasping for my own life. I had witnessed and/or been a part of more criminal activities in my still-short life than most people hear or read about in a lifetime.

From the time I had moved to Chicago at the age of five, the life I knew consisted of survival in gang-infested neighborhoods. The only example of life I had seen that didn't include drug use, violence, and extreme child abuse was from television. As far as I knew, everyone wore certain color clothing to represent one gang or another. I was certain that everyone used drugs.

These experiences and memories had made me the person I was. But as much as these experiences had scared me, they also forced me to try hard to survive in a peaceful world. I was trying to integrate myself into a world of hard workers, students, and peaches and cream. So much in my life had begun to change that I accepted the invitation of a gay coworker and friend to be his roommate. For a person who grew up in a gang-centered family, this was the ultimate sin. It was hard for me to accept this invitation, but as I'd made many decisions before, I accepted it as a matter of survival. I did wonder what others would think about me and the possibility that my friend might eventually want more than just friendship, but I decided to cross that bridge when I came to it. I took this as an opportunity to have shelter away from the 'hood.

My friend's name was Phillip. He was a white boy slightly taller than I was, with dirty blond hair and blue eyes. Phillip had been disowned by his middle-class parents because of his sexuality, and had only recently been accepted back into their lives and home. Phillip was a college graduate who was openly gay. He kept to himself and had obvious feminine traits. He was a sharp dresser and had a tendency to be flamboyant.

Even with the mixed feelings I had, I continued to live with Phillip. I felt comfortable with him. Living there offered me a chance to stay out of trouble as those who lived nearby assumed I was gay, too. I continued to grow into a hardworking member of society, working as a data entry clerk at the University of Chicago while attending classes. Suddenly everyone in my circle of friends was a coworker or university student. I was slowly but surely making myself a distant memory to those involved in gangs. I still, however, had nightmares, which were so horrible and vivid that I became afraid to fall asleep. All the bloodshed I had witnessed or caused awaited me every night for days and sometimes weeks at a time. I began having moments of terror during the day, too. I would drift away into a daydream and see the bloody souls of my past and begin to sweat, shake, or both. At these times many people asked what was wrong, but I couldn't answer. I didn't think anyone in my new circle would understand if they found out that I was having flashbacks of bullets entering and exiting bodies.

Phillip became a constant comfort when I awoke screaming in the middle of the night. He'd come from his room to my bedside and shake me gently until I awoke if I hadn't already. Often Phillip would bring me a glass of water. He was always compassionate about my ordeal and never seemed bothered that I woke him in the middle of the night. I'd share the details of my nightmares and he'd listen, which would allow me to fall asleep peacefully, at least momentarily.

I knew he was gay and I also knew that he was very aware of my heterosexuality. The respect that we had for each other's way of life allowed us to function well in spite of social taboos. Eventually, however, he started to interpret the emotions created by my nightmares as weakness, as an indication of desire for him.

He crossed the line. One night as Phillip held me to comfort me and assure me that everything would be OK, he attempted to kiss me. When I rejected him, he left the room angrily. The next day he told me that we would no longer be able to be roommates. I could have tried to talk it out—a move that could have saved our friendship—but my manhood seemed more important to me at that moment. Instead of trying to talk about the misunderstanding, I told him that I would kill him if I ever saw him again. I was on my way to being homeless yet again. With nowhere else to go, I returned to Humboldt Park.

There's something about that park, that neighborhood, that tugged on me and never completely let me get away—something there that made those I tried to get away from, those I needed to get away from, the only ones I felt I could could really count on. I showed up at Humboldt Park on a Wednesday afternoon five months after Loca's son was killed. There I found Spanky, still selling cocaine as if the tragedy had never taken place.

Spanky had become one of the main dealers in the area. He no longer made the exchanges of drugs for money with customers himself; many others did that for him. He couldn't, however, get over his desire to be present in the middle of Humboldt Park's gang society. It was by all accounts one of the hardest habits to break. Thirteen- and fourteen-year-old kids who lived on the streets were among Spanky's dealers. I looked at them and saw another lost generation of kids just like me. I didn't agree with him using the kids in this way, but I learned to live with it. Spanky offered me a new place to live. Speaking up against his juvenile workforce would certainly ruin that.

I moved into the basement apartment of Spanky's house that weekend. The house was located on the corner of Cortez Street and Kedzie Avenue, across from the westernmost edge of Humboldt Park. In essence, I was back home.

I CONTINUED TO work at the university, but I started to shy away from the friends I had made there. I lived in constant fear of anyone I met at the university finding out about my past and, even worse, about my present. Eventually, I thought, someone would offer me a ride home or want to come by and visit. I didn't want to risk my new friends being robbed or shot because of their friendship with me. I don't know what they thought about me once I began to distance myself, but it was obvious that they got the message.

LIVING AT SPANKY's made old problems resurface. Every so often, rival gangs of the Latin Kings would chase me as I got off the bus at North Avenue and Kedzie. I hadn't been away from the 'hood very long, and I was still recognized. Of course, the Kings would come out of the park and out of the side street along Kedzie Avenue and retaliate by throwing bricks, bottles, and any other objects they could get their hands on. And there would always be someone with a gun.

Although I was no longer officially a Latin King, and I was no longer called Lil Loco (my old nickname), I was still targeted by the Cobras, Disciples, and Gangsters. Once a King, always a King.

The feeling of sanctuary that going to work had once offered me started to disappear. On several occasions, carloads of Cobras would wait at the exit of the Damen and North Avenue station, knowing I would be getting off the train there. I again began to fear leaving the area where the Latin Kings protected me. I felt safest when secluded in the eight or so square blocks that made up the Humboldt Park section of the Latin Kings' territory. Four months after I moved into Spanky's basement, I quit my job at the University of Chicago and once again became a regular in Humboldt Park gang society. Becoming an elite member, however, was not so easy the second time around.

My integration back into the 'hood happened practically overnight. I hated it there, but at least I felt equal to everyone around me. My past was known, my intentions—good or bad—expected and accepted. It was the one place in the world where I didn't feel inferior due to my limited vocabulary and education. Gang society required absolute ignorance, a violent nature, and ruthlessness. I was known to have all of these qualities.

2

Career Change

MY BASEMENT apartment at Spanky's became a Latin King hang-out. The only part of that apartment that remained truly mine was the bedroom. The Kings often held their meetings there, which meant that I had to vacate the apartment since I was no longer a Latin King. The new generation of Latin Kings knew me as Rey Rey. I became close to Spanky's new wife, Imelda. She was a small, fragile twenty-five-year-old Puerto Rican woman with no education at all. She seemed like everyone else in the neighborhood—very street smart but with no skills to survive outside Humboldt Park.

Imelda introduced me to her sister Josefina; we called her Josie. Josie looked like a carbon copy of Imelda, but she was three years younger and a member of the Latin Queens. Josie had a reputation for being a party animal with an itchy trigger finger. Most of the Kings thought I was crazy when I started dating her. She had shot her last boyfriend one day when he tried to stop her from drinking more than she had already consumed.

My relationship with Josie started four days after I met her. She showed up at the apartment high as a kite, drunk, and reeking of stale cigarette smoke. She flirted with me, then got physical, and finally insisted that we have sex. She was beautiful, and I had not had sex for a while, but I wanted her to take a shower first. Josie was persistent. She said she was horny and wanted to have sex first and shower later. I tried to lead her toward the bathroom and she began stripping her clothes off as I did so. Once she was naked I forgot all about the shower and her bad smell.

The next day and from there after, Josie called herself my girl-friend. She practically lived with me. Josie did all her drugging and drinking at my apartment with the Latin Kings, and—just like that—I went back to my party animal ways.

I began helping Spanky with his cocaine business. I'd cut, weigh, and bag the product for him in return for free rent and five hundred dollars a week. Often I did these things on my own. Known as Lil Loco when I was a hardcore gangbanger, I would get high on a daily basis to cover up my true feelings. I reestablished these old habits. Unlike the old Lil Loco, however, I no longer sought out violent confrontations or felt the need to prove myself to anyone. In this sense, at least, I had grown.

The new Rey Rey became sort of a sex freak when under the influence of drugs and alcohol. Once I got high, I became obsessed with sex. Luckily, Josie was always ready and willing to please me. When she wasn't around I would masturbate, since other girls in the neighborhood were afraid of Josie—all of them except for Spanky's wife, Imelda.

Spanky was paralyzed from the waist down, which left him sexually dysfunctional. He was in a wheelchair because, years earlier, the Latin Kings had suspected him of ratting me out to the law. They called a meeting with the intention of talking to him but shot him in a drive-by instead. They planned to kill him as a means of discipline by setting an example to others, but he didn't die, and he didn't even quit the Latin Kings, even though he knew they were the ones who'd shot him. Spanky could only sexually please Imelda orally or with his hands. She secretly desired more. Imelda came looking for me one evening so I could help her count out the money to purchase two kilos of cocaine. It was one of the very few days that I was alone in my apartment. She walked into my bedroom to find me lying on my bed, naked, in my own sexual world, masturbating. I don't even know how she came to be in my room. I heard her voice saying something, but I didn't acknowledge it. Then the voice got louder. "*Espera que llegue Josie* (Wait until Josie arrives)," the voice said. I opened my eyes, startled, and stared at her as she looked at me with a devilish grin on her face. Imelda did not take her eyes off me for one minute. Her reaction to my nakedness and self-pleasure turned my initial embarrassment into excitement. I got up, grabbed her by the back of the neck, and gently pulled her toward me to kiss her. Imelda turned her face so I wouldn't kiss her and said, "*no puedo* (I can't)." "*Si puedes* (You can)," I whispered in her ear. I placed my hands on her waist and spun her body so her back faced the bed as I kissed her ear and neck. I laid her gently on the bed and after a few more weak "I can'ts," Imelda became my willing partner. That was the start of our affair.

My sexual involvement with Imelda became both a blessing and a curse. Imelda began to look forward to our sexual encounters, and she got upset with the lack of opportunity, due to Latin Kings hanging around in my apartment all the time and Josie's presence. Imelda grew jealous because Josie was spending nights with me, but she was only getting quickies here and there that, more often than not, left her with the desire for more. Her frustration led her to have Spanky ban the Latin Kings from using any part of the house as a hangout. I was happy that she had talked him into taking that action. I finally had some privacy within my own apartment, and Imelda and I enjoyed extended sex time. Suddenly it was I who wished it were Imelda spending nights with me instead of Josie. Imelda didn't get high, she drank very little, and she always smelled so good and clean, while Josie was always under the influence of drugs and alcohol and reeked of cigarette smoke even after having freshly showered. I wanted Imelda for myself.

My desire for Imelda got me closer to Spanky. I grew more involved in his drug business. I advised him on purchases and got him involved in the growing heroin business. Spanky's profits doubled. My knowledge of the drug business from my former time as a dealer in the Latin Kings, and my reputation for loyalty when I was a King, were the only reasons Spanky kept me around. I knew this, and I also knew that it was just a matter of time before I would no longer be needed, and therefore dispensable, but I didn't care. As long as I was a commodity, I was going to get all I could and then some.

I was now driving a beautiful Pontiac Bonneville and attracting the attention of the opposite sex. Even with Josie's reputation for violence, girls were now willing to get involved with me. My money seemed to remove all fear. The new generation of Latin Kings, however, was not impressed. Most of them felt as if I were raining on their parade. My presence kept them from getting closer to Spanky, and therefore considering themselves second, or third, in command and so forth. Because of that, they routinely requested that I prove myself worthy. My Lil Loco reputation did not carry me with this crowd. According to them I was just Rey Rey—unproven, untested, and not a Latin King. My return back to my violent ways became more and more inevitable.

A little over a year had elapsed between the day Loca's son died in my arms and my becoming Spanky's right-hand drug man. I wondered sometimes if the friends I'd made at the university ever thought about me, but I made no attempt to contact any of them. I certainly didn't want them to know about the turn my life had taken since they'd last seen me.

With my increased drug use and lack of sleep, my nightmares became less frequent. When they did appear, they contained just as much violence as before, only now I had no one to comfort me, nor did I want anyone to find out what my nightmares consisted of. I had taken a step backward in life. I knew this, but could do nothing about it.

13

Josie's Way

THE LATIN KINGS had completely evolved. They were now nothing more than violent street thugs. The memory of the first Latin King brothers, those who had fought for the survival and pride of their race, had long been forgotten even among those who'd been part of the struggle. The Latin Kings were now about nothing but crime and destruction, and they seemed to be very proud of their social stature. The older Kings were now at the mercy of a new, more aggressive, money-hungry generation of Kings. Word from inside penitentiary walls was no longer official law. The leaders on the inside (those imprisoned) came to terms with the brothers on the outside being the source of their comfort. They could still certainly get anyone severely beaten or maimed or even killed at any given time, but they began to overlook any problem that didn't directly concern them. It was now all too common to have one Latin King faction be the enemy of another. This new way of demonstrating brotherhood created challenges for me.

My growth within Spanky's clique led to unwelcome requests for me to be reinitiated into the Latin Kings. It also brought constant demands for me to prove myself by making a hit. Most of those around me didn't know me as Lil Loco, and didn't believe or care about the stories they heard about my past. They wanted to see for themselves if I was actually the guy who would go into rival gang turf by himself simply for the pleasure of inflicting bodily injury. They wanted me out there with them every day getting drunk, getting high, and putting my life on the line for the benefit of the Latin Kings. No one, including myself, seemed to remember that at one time the Latin Kings had wanted me dead for the violence I had enacted on one of my own and that I had gotten violated out because I believed they were the scum of the earth. I had shot a Latin King because of the barrage of insults he threw my way about a girl I was dating being impregnated by a King in the penitentiary. I was aware that she carried in drugs for him (a mule), but I hadn't known she was screwing him. The Kings had put a price on my head, but later downgraded it to a severe beating. I'd had to be hospitalized after the beating. As time went on, when I began to notice the favoritism given to some brothers and carelessness shown to others, I began to vocally disagree with many of the leaders. I also became vocal about my perception of the Latin Kings being a disease of the Puerto Rican community.

My reluctance to become the totally out-of-control gang-banger I'd been in the past led fourteen- and fifteen-year-old kids to challenge my manhood on a consistent basis. I knew the rules. If I knocked the shit out of any one of them, as I really wanted to, I would become a punching dummy for all the Latin Kings. Spanky intervened as much as he could, but kids in gangs, with or without guns, are still ignorant. Basically I would just walk away from the shouts of "punk," "pussy," "coward," and so on, being directed at my back, and go have sex with Imelda or someone else to make myself feel better. That was my way of retaining my sense of manhood—having sex with as many women as possible. But I knew that, sooner or later, I would have to participate in a violent act.

One Friday night Josie showed up at Humboldt Park drunk and pissed off about rumors she'd heard that I was sleeping around. It didn't help that she arrived just in time to find a pretty sixteen-year-old sitting on my lap flirting with me. The girl's name was Jessica; her nickname was Lady J. Jessica was being recruited by the Latin Queens and had taken a liking to me. Lady J looked very physically mature for her age. With her made-up face and her big breasts and ass, she looked older than Josie, though she was really six years younger. Lady J had a natural tan look, with long black hair and brown eyes. She was Puerto Rican, born in Chicago, and spoke very little Spanish. Lady J liked material things. She gravitated to people with money, and I was the one she had chosen to cling to from the first day she saw me, about a week earlier. I knew her age, knew she was jailbait, but went for it anyway.

Upon Josie's arrival, Lady J immediately got off my lap and began to walk away. I remained sitting on the park bench and watched Josie come toward me. All the folks standing even remotely near me immediately distanced themselves. They could see that I was in some deep shit, and they didn't want to be in the way if Josie pulled a gun and started shooting. Josie, however, went after Lady J instead. "You fuckin' bitch! What are you doing all over my man?" Josie shouted as she walked rapidly toward Lady J. Lady J didn't respond. She just continued to walk away. I knew I wanted to have sex with Lady J eventually, so I went to her defense. "Leave her alone," I shouted at Josie. "It was my fault." Josie turned to me, shouting every curse word imaginable in Spanish and English. She tried to slap me, but I was able to deflect her swings. She persisted in trying to hit me, but I dodged her swings, all the while laughing uncontrollably. Josie backed me up against a parked car and threw a kick to my groin. I lowered both my hands to stop her kick and got slapped on my face twice. The second slap left two fingernail scratches from my left ear to my lip. My laughter stopped and I became enraged. Josie didn't care about my anger and continued to fight me. I stepped away from the car and punched her in the face, bloodying her nose and mouth. Josie fell but immediately got back up and came after me as I tried to walk away. The Latin Kings gathered around, waiting for Spanky's approval to defend a Queen, but Spanky told them to leave us alone, that it was a personal problem. I wrestled Josie to the ground, pinning her, and asked her to stop. "I'm going to kill you!" she screamed. I asked Spanky to have someone hold her so I could leave. He gave the order and it was done. Several Kings helped Josie while I got into my car and drove away. Lady J, understandably, had already left the scene.

I drove around the park smoking a joint, then headed back to Spanky's place. I was still pretty angry when I walked into my apartment. I lit up another joint and downed a beer. I was opening a second beer when Imelda walked into the room. "My sister can sure be a bitch sometimes," she said. I walked over to Imelda and kissed her hard. She responded in the same manner. Within seconds we were half naked, having sex on the kitchen table. Our sex was violent, more violent than it had ever been. I treated Imelda as if I was beating her up, only sexually. After five minutes it was over. We were both exhausted. "I love you," Imelda said as she caressed my face. I got off her, grabbed my pants, and headed for the bathroom. I showered, got dressed, and went out to find Imelda had left. I got another beer, lit up another joint, and sat down to watch television. After a few minutes I heard a commotion outside.

I went out to witness Josie trashing my car while the Kings, Queens, and the rest of the neighborhood cheered her on. She had a baseball bat and had already put several ugly dents on the front hood and broken the front windshield and the driver's side window. When she saw me she started swinging the bat faster and wilder. I ran to stop her, and she swung the bat at me. I ducked under the swinging bat and grabbed hold of her before she could swing again. I held her really tight and made her drop the bat. I looked at a laughing Spanky and asked him why he let her damage my car. "Because you're a punk," another King answered before Spanky could say anything. That same King stepped toward me, jeering. "Hit me punk, hit me." "Back off, leave him alone. It's personal," Spanky yelled. The King backed off. I picked Josie up, threw her over my shoulder, and took her inside.

Inside, Josie continued to attack me. I hit her again, this time with the back of my open hand, across her face. I carried her into the bedroom, threw her on the bed, sat on her, and pinned her down as she screamed her lungs out. Spanky and several other Kings came and watched what was going on. They found me on top of her, pleading for her to calm down. Spanky laughed and instructed everyone that we be left alone. I told Josie I was sorry for hitting her. I assured her that I loved only her, and that she was the only one for me. I caressed her hair and face. Her screams became whispers but they were still obscene. I bent over and started kissing her face. Josie began softly kissing me back. We ended our fight with an all-night sex session. In the morning, Josie was gone. I walked into the bathroom, and there on the mirror written in lipstick were the words "I love you, Rey Rey."

Josie took my car to have the damage she had caused fixed. From that day forward, she became obedient to my every word. She seemed to become obsessed with my beating her. It was as if she liked it, and she looked forward to getting into confrontations with me that would result in my beating her one way or another. She would seem loving and caring, and then out of the blue begin fighting with me. She knew that the one way to get me to hit her was to hit me first. We always ended up having passionate sex and forgetting about it until the next time.

Our fighting and making up became the talk of the neighborhood. Spanky joked that we should stage pay-per-view events for our fights. Other Kings used it as a way to look for confrontations. It frustrated them that Spanky protected me even though I wasn't a King. I was a valuable commodity to his business, though, so I was untouchable.

I started pursuing Lady J again about a week after my first fight with Josie. She felt safer to mess around with now that I had some sort of control over Josie. Lady J and I began having some very heavy petting sessions that we both knew would eventually lead to our having sex. Her fingers sparkled with the gold rings I gave her that I had collected from junkies in exchange for drugs. I felt sure she was convinced that being my lover would get her more.

Lady J was sixteen years old and using her body for profit without actually becoming a prostitute. It didn't bother her that the first time we had sex was behind some bushes at the Montrose Avenue lakefront. Her ultimate plan seemed to be to have me for the long term. My plan was to have sex with her until I got tired of her, or until another young woman just like her took her place.

I made arrangements for Lady J to come over to my apartment on a Sunday evening. Of course, this would depend on whether Josie was around or not. Josie spent Saturday night and most of Sunday with me before leaving, saying she'd be back later that night. As soon as Josie left I paged Lady J with a special code that signaled her to come over. I told her that I would leave the side door into the basement unlocked for her. I proceeded to prepare the bedroom for her arrival.

I made the bed and cleaned up a little. I then stripped to nothing except a pair of bikini briefs and a tank top. As I was folding my pants to put them away, Imelda walked into the bedroom. She kissed me deeply, then grabbed my briefs and pulled them down as she knelt before me to perform oral sex. I completely forgot about Lady J. I just enjoyed the moment for all it was worth. Several minutes later we heard Lady J scream, "Oh my god, Spanky is going to kill you!" Imelda jumped up and told her to shut the hell up as she ran back upstairs. I pulled up my briefs and went toward Lady J. Lady J looked at me with a shocked expression and headed toward the door. I put my pants on and went after her. When I caught up to her, I talked her into believing that it was the first time that had happened. I told her that Imelda had initiated the act, and that I felt I had to comply because she threatened to have Spanky kick me out. "I'm kind of glad you walked in," I assured her. "Maybe now she'll be too scared to do it again." Lady J seemed to believe every word. She came back inside with me, but we did not have sex. I had to deal with Spanky.

"Hey, Rey, come up here," Spanky shouted from the top of the stairs leading down to my basement apartment. "Bring Lady J with you." Lady J and I looked at each other as if to say, "Oh, shit!" We worked our way slowly up the stairs and into Spanky's place.

The top of the stairs ended in a hallway that led to the kitchen on the right, and the dining room and living room on the left. I glanced toward the kitchen and saw Imelda sitting at the kitchen table with her face in her hands. In the living room, Spanky and three of his Latin Kings sat facing the television. Spanky's house was nicely furnished with expensive and beautiful objects. He wanted his place to serve as an example to younger Kings as to what they could accomplish by investing in the drug trade. He had a projection television, various stereo components, VCRs, a soft Italian leather sofa, loveseat, and recliner, and a big portrait of himself sitting on a throne, with Imelda sitting at his feet holding his hand.

I held Lady J by the hand and led her past the dining room into the living room. I was scared out of my mind, and I could feel Lady J's nervousness, too. "*Estás caliente* (You're hot)," one of the Kings said as we walked into the room. "You fucked up, fruitcake," Spanky said. "Why don't you lock that door from your side when you got bitches down there?" I didn't know how to respond. I just sat there staring at Spanky, waiting to be sentenced to death.

"I don't want my wife walking in on you while you're fucking some bitch," Spanky commanded. "We weren't fucking," I told Spanky. "But you were getting ready to. Why else would you be half naked, punk?" Spanky responded. Lady J looked as if she had seen a ghost. She was perspiring and didn't even know where to look.

Imelda had told Spanky that she'd walked down the stairs and saw me, in my underwear, coming out of the bedroom with

Lady J. She'd told him that Lady J had been startled by her angry reaction, and that's why she had screamed the way she did. Lady J and I just stood there, not believing what we were hearing. We had been convinced that Spanky was going to have me shot for having sex with Imelda. Instead, Imelda had protected me with her lie. Spanky ordered me to take a three-minute violation (beating), to be administered by two of the Kings present while the other kept time. He also ordered that I take part in a hit on the YLO (Young Latino Organization) Cobras with the Kings later on that night. I agreed to his decision—I had to. I felt I had no choice. I felt relieved. "If my wife ever walks in on you again, I'll kill you," Spanky said as I walked toward the basement door with Lady J and the three Kings in tow. "*Amor, brother, amor* (Love, brother, love)," I responded.

I glanced toward the kitchen just before I entered the basement and made eye contact with Imelda. She looked worried for me. I was thankful for her quick thinking. We both knew that our affair would now have to stop. Imelda called Lady J into the kitchen; I headed down the stairs with the Kings.

In the basement we cleared an area where the beating ceremony would take place. Surprisingly, I felt no fear. I just wanted to get it over with. The two Kings who were there to do the honor were about my size or smaller. They didn't look like they would pack a big punch, and they didn't. The beating was the typical Latin King three-minute violation, in which no punches could be thrown to my face or groin. Knowing this, I wasn't worried. It was over rather quickly. I was hurt, but not to the extent I'd been hurt in previous beatings. While I was an active member of the Latin Kings, I had been beaten for disciplinary purposes twice. The first time, I was in so much pain from all the bruises on my body that I was bedridden for several days. The second time, I had to be hospitalized for broken and bruised ribs. I compared the current beating to the one I got when I was initiated out of the Kings, when the King brother in charge had shown me pity.

The Kings went back upstairs to Spanky's house. I put all the furniture we had moved back in its place and went upstairs too. I walked up to Spanky and shook his hand Latin King style. "*Amor*, my brother," I said. "*Amor*," Spanky responded. "I'm sorry, Imelda. It won't happen again," I shouted toward the kitchen. "I hope not. My eyes still hurt," Imelda replied. Everybody laughed. It was all over.

"What time we taking out those YLOs?" I asked Spanky, referring to the hit. "Around nine tonight," he responded. "I need you to fix up an ounce of girl for me," Spanky said, referring to heroin. "Get it from Imelda." "Cool, bro," I said as I started toward the kitchen. "Why don't you get one of these brothers to go on a beer run? You know I do my best work with a Lowie (Lowenbrau)," I told Spanky. "Alright," he said as I walked away.

I walked into the kitchen where Imelda still sat in the same chair, with Lady J sitting to her left. "I need the H," I told Imelda. "It's already cooked and cut; all you have to do is bag it," she said as she got up from the table. Imelda walked toward the front of the house. I sat at the table with Lady J and reached for her under the table. "You're fuckin' crazy," Lady J said to me when I grabbed her leg and pulled her toward me. "That's OK," I said. "You like me like that." I leaned toward Lady J and kissed her. Lady J tried to kiss me deeply, but I didn't want Imelda to see us. I didn't want Imelda to get upset with me. I respected her.

Imelda came back into the kitchen with a box and handed it to me. "Let's go downstairs," I told Lady J as I took the box from Imelda. Imelda looked into my eyes but didn't say a word. I knew what she was feeling. I was feeling the same thing—a strong desire to be together. "Spanky, send me some brew when it gets here," I shouted as I headed toward the basement with Lady J behind me. "Be careful with that shit," Spanky responded.

THE HIT ON the YLO Cobras did not take place. Apparently there was an unusually high amount of police activity that night, which wouldn't have allowed us to make the hit and a clean getaway. That was a relief. I was scared to death of the prospect of pulling the trigger with the intension of killing someone. I wasn't as gung-ho about shooting a rival gang member as I had been in the past. In my present state of mind I was totally against gang violence, but I certainly would have not been accepted at all by Spanky and his boys if I said so. I bagged the heroin, gave it to Spanky, and secluded myself in the safety of my drugged-up little world with Lady J for the rest of the night.

I hated Spanky passionately, but it was convenient for me to act otherwise. I'm certain that, deep down, Spanky hated me with the same passion, but it was convenient for him to have me around. I managed my hatred for Spanky by knowing that I was fucking his wife. That made it all better. I knew, however, that my peace of mind, based on this betrayal, would one day come to an end. I began to worry about how Spanky would satisfy his hatred for me. But I wasn't worried enough to get the hell out.

4

Fear

EVEN WITH JOSIE'S constant attention, Imelda and I never stopped being lovers. Our encounters occurred less frequently, but we both looked forward to them. Imelda's desire to be with me made her bolder. I was scared Spanky would catch us. I'd been hanging out with Spanky for almost six months, and for four of those months Imelda and I had been lovers. If Spanky ever found out I was screwing his wife, the consequences would be disastrous. I knew how non-Kings were treated if they had no protection. What we were doing meant a certain death sentence if we were caught, even for a member of the Latin Kings; nevertheless, I couldn't say no. I was also afraid that if I rejected Imelda, she would certainly turn against me, and turn Spanky against me, too.

Imelda acted as if she wanted to get caught. She would come down to my apartment and have sex with me while Spanky sat upstairs in the company of other Latin Kings. I don't even know what excuses she gave Spanky to explain her visits. She always wore dresses, but now she would go without panties so that she could be ready at every opportunity. She even went so far as having sex with me in her kitchen while Spanky ate dinner and watched television in the living room. She just called me into the kitchen to help her clean up. "It's the least you can do for the delicious meals I cook," Imelda said. Spanky was no fool; he suspected something was going on. He just didn't have proof. On several occasions he questioned me about my friendship with Imelda. I assured him that our friendship revolved around my loyalty to him. "That's your wife, bro," I told Spanky. "I love her and respect her because of you."

Spanky's suspicions made it harder for Imelda and me to get together. He began to require that I hang with the King brothers more, to watch over them. He now also pressured me to take part in a hit so that I could earn my respect (prove my toughness) with the new generation. I became a target of verbal abuse from Spanky and his Kings. Spanky's suspicions bred hostility, which in turn lessened my importance in his drug business. I no longer played such a big part of his business. He no longer trusted me to collect and handle the thousands upon thousands of dollars of profits, nor was I trusted to oversee the packaging and dealing of the drugs that brought in those profits.

Josie also began to question me about sleeping with Imelda. Only she did it in a dramatic fashion, of course, for the whole world to see. That infuriated Spanky. It got the whole neighborhood talking about his wife getting screwed by me. I denied everything, blaming the rumors on Spanky's jealousy. Josie believed me, but she insisted that I take part in a hit, which would put all rumors to rest. "Get your respect back and they (the new generation of Kings) will shut the fuck up," Josie told me. I didn't want to make a hit, but I knew she was right.

I tried to convince her that I had no reason to prove myself, hoping that she would convince the Kings as well. "You know how many *crusaos* (traitors) I took down for the nation? Mention the name Lil Loco to any of the elite brothers and they'll tell you of a righteous brother who threw down for the nation," I told Josie. "This is not about you being a down brother, Rey, and you know it," Josie answered. "This is about you fucking my sister. Besides, you gave up the Lil Loco legacy when you decided you didn't want to wear the crown anymore. It's time you get it back." Then she left.

I sat in my apartment and thought about what she said. I began to question my own manhood. I realized that the drunken, drug-crazed, violent legacy of Lil Loco had carried me throughout my years as a gang member and that I had no place within gang society without it. Reclaiming the identity of Lil Loco was the one and only way I could get myself out of having to prove myself to the new generation of Kings. The only problem was that Lil Loco had been all about reaching violent peaks on a daily basis, and he was all but dead within me. The circumstances, however, made me reach deep inside in an attempt to resuscitate my past glory.

Spanky had me join a meeting held in my apartment and announced that I would be taking part in a hit on the YLO Cobras. "This is a down brother, and he'll prove it to you, won't you, Rey Rey?" Spanky said as he looked at me with an evil grin. Where Lil Loco would have been elated to be included in a hit, Rey Rey sat there, expressionless. The nervousness, the desire not to be part of the inevitable, and the fear were clearly noticeable.

The YLO Cobras were the newest in a long line of new gangs popping up in opposition to the Kings. They hung out around California Avenue and Cortland Street, an area that had once been part of the Latin Kings' 'hood. The YLO had started out as a non-gang-related group. They were more into the party scene, and preached nonviolence toward Latinos. As the structure of the neighborhood changed, the YLO fell under the influence of the Spanish Cobras, and the YLO Cobras were born.

Fearful of saying anything else, I agreed to take part in the hit. Besides, it wasn't like I was going to do something I had never done before. The hit was to take place that night. As soon as the meeting adjourned, I began drinking and smoking weed. Getting high had carried me through times of trial in the past. I was hoping it would still have the same effect. By nightfall, I was pretty damn high and anxious to make the hit. The Lil Loco of old was present, talking shit, looking for danger. Josie showed up and decided to go with us. She stashed her drugs and money in my apartment and gave me her gun to use in the hit. "If you're gonna take out a *crusao* it will be with my piece (gun)," Josie said as she wrapped her arms around my neck and kissed me.

Josie—who lived for this kind of violence—two Kings, and I got into a car, and another four Kings got into a different car. We headed toward the YLO Cobras' 'hood. Josie drove; I sat in the back seat. As we neared our destination, I realized that I no longer had the old feeling of wanting to kill. I did not look forward to pulling the trigger. The influence of drugs and alcohol, which used to carry me in and out of battle successfully, were now putting thoughts of my own death in my mind. Drugs and alcohol had always made me think of death, but never of my own. I had headed into hits with visions of my rivals bleeding to death at my hands and at the hands of my comrades, but it felt different this time. I was nervous. My hands trembled. I wanted to jump out of the car and run fast and far. Nobody else in the car seemed to notice my fear. They stayed focused on the mission at hand. They were just as I used to be.

Josie dropped us off about half a block from where a group of YLO Cobras gathered. There were twelve to fourteen guys and girls hanging out on the front steps of a house on Cortland Street about a quarter block from California Avenue. Josie would circle around and pick us up on California after we made the hit. I thought a drive-by shooting would be more appropriate and safer for my own sake, but the Kings had a different idea. They wanted to show other gangs, especially the newer ones, the consequences of being rivals of the Latin Kings. That meant showing extreme bravado while making hits, so there would be no mistaking where the violence was coming from and who should be feared.

We met up with the Kings from the other car in the alley just behind the house where the YLO Cobras hung out. The plan was for three of us to go around the front and three of us to come out through the gangway. I was one of the three who would go around the front. I was shitting bricks. I couldn't for the life of me conjure up the Lil Loco mentality to go through with the crime without being noticeably terrified. My heart pounded. I was sweating profusely, and my legs felt weak. My fear was obvious. It went unnoticed only because I followed slowly behind the two Kings as we headed toward the front of the house. We got to the corner and prepared to charge the YLO Cobras. They were about fifty feet away around the corner. We could hear them talking and laughing. They were just like us, only in a different neighborhood.

We heard gunshots and footsteps racing in our direction. The two Kings with me jumped out and began firing in the direction of the YLOs. As soon as I heard the first shot, I got the hell out of there by running in the opposite direction. I didn't think about the consequences of not taking part in the hit. It didn't occur to me that what I was doing would be considered an act of cowardice and I would be dealt with as an enemy by the Latin Kings. Fear had taken control of my body. As I ran, I put the gun in my pocket, and I didn't stop running until I was safely on the Latin King side of Humboldt Boulevard. I walked back to my apartment not once thinking about what the Kings would do to me.

"Where are the brothers at?" Spanky yelled from the top of the steps when he heard me come in. "I don't know," I responded. "I made it back on foot." Nothing else was said for about an hour. I lay on my bed smoking a joint, oblivious to what had happened. I was startled by the sound of a herd of footsteps coming down the stairs into my apartment. "You fuckin' pussy," Josie shouted as I sat up on the edge of my bed. She charged at me, trying to hit me. I spun her around, held her in a bear hug, and pushed her back out of the room. I walked out to see Spanky and four other Kings looking my way. "I don't have to prove anything to anybody," I said as I tried to make my way toward the door. "Move out," Spanky said.

I hesitated momentarily, thinking Spanky was asking me to move out of his house. I instantly realized that he was actually giving his boys the order to move out on me. Fists, feet, and all kinds of objects began flying. I defended myself the best I could, but they soon overpowered me and wrestled me to the ground. I knew the only way I would be able to survive was to fight my way out the door and get into my car. Somehow I managed the strength to get back on my feet and fight my way outside. That turned out to be both a blessing and a curse.

The commotion caused a group of Kings and Queens to gather outside Spanky's house. As soon as they realized what was going on, they also began to kick my ass. I had nowhere to run. I was taking the same type of beating I had witnessed Slim taking many years before. Slim was a small, puny member of the Latin Kings, whose addiction to cocaine caused him to burn the Kings out of the cocaine he had been entrusted with to sell. He was given a violation out of the Kings that left him critically injured, then was further beaten out on the street by Kings who once closely hung out with him.

Luckily, I was bigger and stronger than Slim had been and was therefore able to withstand more. I fought back enough to keep from being cornered and possibly killed. I didn't really know where I was or what was happening around me. I just started swinging and kicking in every direction while trying to fend off all the fists and feet flying my way. Fortunately, so many blows were thrown at once that they obstructed each other and therefore did not land with enough force to knock me to the ground.

"Freeze! Put the gun down," I heard a voice say over a loudspeaker. I knew it was the cops. I had never been so happy in my life to see police officers arrive on the scene. The violence suddenly stopped. I could hear people running away. After a few seconds I was finally able to make out where the cops were. There were three squad cars in the alley where I was being beaten. One had come in from one direction; the other two were at the mouth of the alley, blocking it. All but four Kings, two Queens, Spanky, and Josie had gotten away. Spanky was about four feet from me, staring at Josie, who slowly lowered her gun at the order of the police officers. Imelda watched me from the mouth of the alley near a police car.

Once Josie laid the gun on the ground, she was instructed to move away from it. As she did so, the cops closed in with guns pointed directly at her. "You fuckin' pussy," Josie turned to me and said. The cops took the gun and proceeded to search and handcuff Josie. They searched Spanky, too. They questioned me about the incident while a paramedic cleaned and dressed my wounds. My mouth and nose were bloody, and my left eye was slightly swollen. What hurt most were my ribs whenever I took a breath. They decided to take me to the hospital for further treatment. Spanky and Josie were taken into custody along with the other Kings and Queens as I was led to the ambulance.

At the hospital the police continued to question me. I continued to say that I was OK and that nothing had happened. The cops became frustrated at my stubbornness and finally left me alone. My ribs were not broken, but they were badly bruised. I was wrapped in an ace bandage, given a prescription for pain medicine, and released.

Without hesitation I headed back to Spanky's; my clothes were there. So was my car. I was scared, but I had to go there. Luckily, when I arrived there were still police around. I was able to get into my apartment without being harassed. Imelda came in as I picked up my things and stuffed them into plastic garbage bags. Spanky had been released after questioning, but he was still at the police station waiting to be picked up. Imelda helped me pick up my things without saying a word. "Wait here," I told her, and went to put two plastic bags in the car. I went back inside and immediately began having sex with Imelda. My ribs hurt like crazy, but I was able to overcome the pain by fucking Imelda violently with the thought of avenging Spanky on my mind. "You're hurting me," Imelda said as I pulled her hair, fucking her from behind. I didn't care, and actually pulled harder. She pulled away from me and turned around to tell me that I was hurting her. "I'm sorry," I said as I turned her back around to continue what I was doing. Imelda finally complied with my desire. She positioned herself to receive me. I took advantage of her willingness and sodomized her. Imelda tried to pull away when she realized what I was doing but I pushed her flat on the floor, held on to her, and continued until she gave in and let me do what I wanted. "Are you happy doing that?" she asked. I didn't answer. Happiness wasn't my priority. Getting revenge on Spanky by doing what I wanted with his wife was what drove me. I felt an orgasm coming, so I got up and had it all over Imelda's face. This was not about sex. This was about power. Then I got dressed, took the drugs that Josie had stashed, and left. No good-bye, no see you later. I didn't look at Imelda. I didn't even take the time to wash myself. I just left. I had no clue as to where I was going, but I felt content with the revenge I had enacted upon the Kings through Imelda.

Imelda was probably the only person left in the whole city I could turn to for any kind of help, yet I chose to use her as an avenue of self-preservation. I overlooked her feelings to recover my pride and my sense of manhood. I was a different kind of animal now, yet an animal nonetheless.

5.

Cocaine Again

As I DROVE away from Spanky's house, several bottles were thrown at my car. The bottles missed their intended target, but their message was loud and clear. I could not, should not, ever set foot anywhere near the Latin Kings' portion of Humboldt Park again. And I knew that I would have to watch my back every second of every day while I lived in Chicago.

The nine months or so I had spent back in Humboldt Park made it perfectly clear that I didn't belong there. I'd gone from living a peaceful life of meaningful work and intellectual growth at the University of Chicago to almost being killed by my girlfriend. I knew I couldn't return to the university, and was too embarrassed even to attempt it. My life was just as it had always been—one bad decision after another. I felt scared, lost, and hopeless.

My feelings of hopelessness got me thinking about my ex-lover, Loca. I hadn't seen Loca since the day her son had been killed in Humboldt Park. She had stopped dealing in the park, and I thought maybe she had finally gotten out of the Latin King bullshit and was out on her own. With her on my mind, I drove north toward Kedzie and Lawrence, hoping to find her. I figured I could rekin dle our friendship, if not our romance, long enough to get a job and a new place to live. I didn't even know if Loca still lived in the area, especially after sacrificing her son to the gangs, but I couldn't think of any other options. (There were Kings on Kedzie and Lawrence, but I knew there was no way that news of what had happened between Spanky's Kings and me could travel so fast. Besides, different Kings' sections weren't as united as they had once been.) It seemed likely that the Latin Kings of Kedzie and Lawrence would have a good laugh at Spanky's expense, but do little about it. Luck seemed to be on my side that day. Not only did I manage to leave Humboldt Park with my life, I was also able to locate Loca. Although she didn't live in the same place anymore, a King from Kedzie and Lawrence who hadn't heard about my dishonor recognized me and pointed me in the direction of Loca's new home. She now lived roughly half a block away from her previous residence.

As I parked my car and walked to Loca's building, I started to recall the loving relationship we had once had. It was Loca who had inspired me and led me in my pursuit of education by helping me obtain a General Equivalency Diploma. She had also been instrumental in getting me out of doing jail time when I was arrested for possession of cocaine.

Although Loca had once been the only good thing in my life, she had also turned her back on me when I decided to quit the Kings and attend classes at the University of Chicago. When I started making new friends, she thought that meant I would abandon her for a college girl, and it destroyed our relationship. At the end of our relationship, she was the one having sex with another man while I slept on the sofa because I had nowhere else to go. I had held Loca's dead son in my arms because she refused to leave the life of the Latin Kings and Queens Nation. And yet I now thought of her as my only hope.

Two guys and three girls were sitting on the steps of Loca's building. A skinny, frail-looking, well-dressed, and jeweled girl asked me what I wanted. "I'm looking for Loca," I told her. "She's not here. ¿*Qué quieres?* (What do you want?)" she asked me. "Loca is my friend; I just want to see her," I responded. "You look familiar," the girl said. "What's your name?" "Reymundo," I replied. "Loca knows me by Lil Loco." "So you're Lil Loco. Loca has told me all about you. My name is Lilly," she continued. "Loca is out right now, but you can wait for her here with us or in my apartment."

Lilly spoke softly and with confidence. Her neck and fingers were covered in gold. She had a sweet smile and beautiful long hair. Her perfume intoxicated me, even while it competed with the smell of cigarettes.

Lilly led me into her first-floor apartment without introducing me to the others sitting there with her. Loca lived on the third floor. "Sit down. Do you want something to drink?" Lilly asked. "Yes, please," I responded. Lilly walked toward the back of the apartment. I sat on a loveseat near the door facing the back of the apartment. Lilly's apartment was neatly furnished and included an entertainment center that housed a television and stereo, living room and dining room sets, and a few pictures on the walls. The windows were covered in curtains that matched the earth-tone living room set, and the floors were hardwood. The apartment was very conservatively decorated and had a certain classiness that was missing from any other apartment I had ever been in before.

"I think you should know," Lilly said as she walked up to me and handed me a beer, "that Loca is living with someone. He's not a King brother or anything but he gets his respect from the nation." "It's cool. I just need a favor from her," I told her. Lilly asked me about my wounds. She thought that maybe I had gotten jumped by Disciples or Cobras. I let her think that was the case, but I knew it was only a matter of time before she heard the truth.

"Loca's told me a lot about you. You're a pretty crazy character," Lilly said. She went into a room on the right side of the apartment and came back out with a shoebox cover in her hand. Lilly sat down next to me and handed it to me. It contained about a dime of marijuana, a pack of rolling papers, and a small round mirror with a small mound of cocaine, a razor blade, and a small straw. Lilly took the mirror and began making lines of cocaine with the razor blade. I started filtering the seeds away from the marijuana and began to roll a joint. "Let me put some of this on it," Lilly said, referring to the cocaine. I held up the rolling paper filled with marijuana just above the mirror so that Lilly could put the cocaine in it. Then I finished rolling it. Lilly made four lines out of the remaining cocaine. She snorted two of them and then handed me the mirror. "Here, let me have the joint," Lilly said as I took the mirror from her. She took the joint and walked to the living room table where she had a pack of cigarettes and a lighter. She came back and sat next to me, put the whole joint in her mouth, and turned it in a circular motion as she pulled it slowly out of her mouth. "You do that very well," I told her. "Much better than you think," Lilly said with a wicked smile on her face but without making eye contact with me.

Lilly began to heat up the joint with the lighter. The wetness from having put it in her mouth kept the paper from burning, while the heat from the lighter melted the cocaine on the marijuana for easier smoking. I stared at the cocaine on the mirror, having second thoughts about whether I should do it or not. I had not done cocaine for about a year and half, and I was afraid I'd get hooked on it again. Lilly lit up the cocaine-laced joint and reached for me, saying, "Come here, let me give you a shotgun." She put her hand gently on the back of my neck and pulled me toward her while she inserted the lit side of the joint into her mouth and held it with her lips. Lilly blew the smoke into my mouth and nose. I sucked it all in and held it in my lungs as long as I possibly could. Lilly pulled the joint out of her mouth and continued to smoke it.

The cocaine-laced joint had a distinct taste. It was kind of mellow and seemed to allow me to take more smoke into my lungs without gagging and gasping for air. Within minutes I felt a slight numbness around my lips. After taking several hits from the joint and eliminating my worry, I snorted the two lines of cocaine and handed the mirror back to Lilly. "*¿Quieres más? Esperame* (Do you want more? Wait for me)," Lilly said as she got up and walked outside. She said something to her friends on the front steps, then came back inside. I finished the beer she gave me and helped myself to one of her cigarettes.

"*Traite eso y vente* (Bring that with you and come on)," Lilly said when she came back in and headed toward the room where she had gotten the marijuana and cocaine. I followed. She waited for me to enter and then closed the door behind me. It was her bedroom. Lilly had a huge canopy bed with a nightstand on the left side and a dresser with a large mirror directly across from the foot of the bed. The bed was made up with fancy ruffled pillows and a comforter with a flower pattern. There was nothing in that room, or in Lilly's entire apartment, indicating she was involved with the Latin Kings.

"*Sientate* (Sit down)," Lilly said, patting her bed. I sat at the foot of the bed and watched her go into a closet directly on the right side of the bed. I began to roll another joint and pictured myself having sex with Lilly on her giant bed. Lilly came out of the closet holding a metal tackle box that had a plastic sandwich bag full of marijuana on top of it. "Do you like my bed?" Lilly asked. "Only if I can sleep on it," I responded. Lilly laughed and mentioned that Loca had told her I was a womanizer. I didn't comment and just smiled shyly as I pushed my way up her bed and against the pillows with a joint in my hand. Lilly sat down facing me and opened the metal box. From the box she pulled out about half an ounce of cocaine and used a teaspoon to shovel a good amount of it onto the mirror. She put the cocaine back in the metal box, set it under the bed, and began to work through the cocaine on the mirror with the razor blade. I lit up the joint I had, grabbed the bag of marijuana, and began removing the seeds. "The ashtray is over there," Lilly said, pointing to the nightstand. I got the ashtray, took another puff of the joint, and passed it to Lilly. "You go ahead," Lilly said, "I only like it with *perico* (cocaine)."

I prepared another joint and laced the marijuana with cocaine. Lilly asked me to prepare two more joints the same way. As I did what she asked, Lilly prepared the first one by wetting it in her mouth and then heating it up with the lighter to melt the cocaine. When I was done, Lilly set the marijuana under the bed and handed me the mirror and straw so that I could snort the several lines of cocaine she had prepared. While I snorted, Lilly lit up the cocaine-laced joint. She got up and walked over to a boom box that sat on the dresser and played an Eddie Santiago CD. Eddie Santiago was very well known for his romantic salsa tunes, and the CD Lilly played was one of his classics. I asked if I could take a shower. I sensed there would be something more than just getting high between Lilly and me. Lilly led me to the bathroom and showed me where the soap, shampoo, and towels were. As she left the bathroom she said to make sure and call her if there was a spot I couldn't reach.

I showered and returned to Lilly's room with only my pants on. Lilly was sitting on the bed but got up when I came in. She asked me to sit down as she got the mirror with cocaine on it and a joint. Lilly handed me the mirror as she sat next to me and asked me to snort some cocaine as she lit up the joint. I snorted a line of cocaine into each nostril, then handed her the mirror. Lilly in turn handed me the joint. That went on until two more joints were gone, along with the cocaine. While we got high I flirted sexually with Lilly. She did the same with me. Once the drugs were gone we immediately started kissing.

Lilly pushed me back against the pillows in a sitting position and sat on me. We kissed wildly and passionately. The marijuana and cocaine served as a pain reliever for my sore ribs. I worked my hands under her blouse and pushed her bra above her breasts so I could fondle them. Then there was a knock at the door. Lilly tried to get up to answer it while I buried my head under her blouse. She said something I couldn't make out and began to get up. I held her tightly, pulled her toward me, and told her not to go. Lilly pulled my head out from under her blouse and said, "*Llegó Loca* (Loca arrived)." I let Lilly go and started fixing myself up. I thought about what Loca would think when I walked out of the room with Lilly. But I suddenly didn't care. I quickly devised another plan; now my new goal was to live with Lilly.

"Spanky's boys fucked you up pretty good, huh," Loca said when she saw me. "You heard about that?" I responded. "I can't believe you let yourself get caught up with that shit," Loca said. *"Especialmente con Spanky después que te ratió* (Especially with Spanky after he ratted on you)," Loca continued. I went into the living room and sat on the loveseat. Loca sat on the sofa to the right of me, and there was silence for what seemed like an eternity. "How have you been?" I finally asked Loca. "Doing good," she said. "My kid is in Puerto Rico with *mami* (mom)," Loca told me. "*¿Para que me buscas?* (Why are you looking for me?)" Loca asked. "I need a place to stay," I told her. "*Ya encontrastes adonde quedarte* (You already found where to stay)," Loca replied as she looked at Lilly. "You can stay here," Lilly said. Loca got up and said she had to go. She had things to do, but would come back later that evening so that we could talk. "I'll be here," I said as I walked Loca outside. Loca went upstairs without saying another word or looking my way. I went back inside Lilly's apartment, found her in the kitchen, and led her back into the bedroom.

Loca didn't come back to talk to me that day after all. Lilly and I spent all night getting high and having sex. Just like that, I was Lilly's official live-in boyfriend. Just like that, I was addicted to cocaine again. I quickly learned that Lilly was Loca's mule. Picking up and delivering packages of cocaine into prisons and to street vendors was her main source of income. As a mule, Lilly enjoyed the respect and protection of the Latin Kings without actually being a member of the Queens. In return, she put her freedom in danger and often degraded herself by carrying drugs past prison security guards inside her vagina to get past security checkpoints.

Lilly also received a monthly check from the Social Security Administration for a learning disability she supposedly had. I didn't notice the disability; Lilly seemed pretty smart to me. The work she did for Loca gave her a steady supply of cocaine, which she was also addicted to. Lilly helped me become hooked on cocaine-laced joints, too.

My first three days at Lilly's were spent in her bedroom, naked. I only came out to use the bathroom or to take a shower. Lilly told me all about herself in between our sessions of sexual activity. Lilly had been getting high since she was fourteen. It was her mother who introduced her to drugs, alcohol, and sex. Lilly's mother was a bartender who started taking her to the bar where she worked after her husband left her. Her mother thought that it was the best way for Lilly to learn about the "real" world. When men began to proposition Lilly, her mother told her that it would be better to be with an older responsible man than with a little boy who couldn't take care of her. At the age of fourteen, Lilly was having sex with men over twice her age. She became more of her mother's double-dating partner than her daughter.

At the age of eighteen, Lilly became pregnant and had a miscarriage. The miscarriage left her unable to ever have kids. While she was still eighteen, her mother left for Puerto Rico and left Lilly in the hands of her then forty-year-old boyfriend. The man was insanely jealous and constantly beat her. After two years she left him for a guy closer to her age. Unfortunately, that only got her someone younger to beat her up. This new boyfriend was a Latin King nicknamed Psycho. His name explained his personality. She couldn't get away from him even when she tried. That is, until he butchered his uncle over ten dollars and was sentenced to life in jail. Lilly went to the penitentiary to deliver drugs, but never to see him. He knew this and swore to kill her if he ever got out. Now it was my turn to be Lilly's boyfriend.

Unlike me, Lilly didn't feel her mother was responsible for the way her life turned out. My mother beat me and allowed me to be beaten by the men in her life. I held her responsible for planting the root of what became my evil nature. Lilly believed that she did the drugs at fourteen because she wanted to. She hung out at the bar where her mother worked because she liked it. And she had sex with men much older than she was because she loved it. Lilly did have an incredible hunger for sex. In that way, Lilly and I were the same. Always waiting, always willing. We were great together, and soon began to develop feelings for each other that were deeper than just sexual feelings.

My relationship with Lilly also rekindled my loyal relationship to cocaine. It felt so natural to just spend days and nights smoking cocaine-laced joints and snorting cocaine. Cocaine became a significant part of our sex life. We got high before, after, and sometimes during our sexual intimacy. Often we snorted cocaine off each other's bodies. This practice often resulted in the numbing of our sex organs, which allowed us to have sex for hours on end without once feeling the growing sensation of an orgasm. Our groin areas would be sore from the activity, which we thought was the coolest of all things.

Lilly and I were pretty happy in our big lie of a life. We denied our addictions by pointing out those in others. We certainly confused the difference between addiction and homelessness. We didn't think we were addicted because we weren't homeless. We were our own suppliers, had money, food, and a place to live, therefore we couldn't be junkies. In our minds we were much better off than those who lived on the street and begged, robbed, or stole for drug money even though we probably had a worse habit than most of them.

In the year I had been away from the 'hood, from drugs, and from the Latin Kings, I had gained weight and looked rather healthy. My new lifestyle, however, had me losing weight quickly without realizing it. Cocaine again became my food, my drink, and my life.

IN MY FIRST month as Lilly's live-in boyfriend, I rarely saw Loca. She had yet to introduce me to her boyfriend, and she hardly ever came into our apartment even though her transactions with Lilly were frequent. Lilly and I thought that it had something to do with my being Loca's ex-lover and her boyfriend not being comfortable with that. Whatever the cause, that situation began to change.

On a late Saturday night, while Lilly and I were into our usual cocaine-induced sex frenzy, there was a knock on the door. We were in the living room and decided to ignore the knocks. Then we heard Loca's voice. "Lilly! Lilly!" Loca shouted. We quickly scrambled for our clothes. Within seconds we were dressed, very haphazardly, yet dressed. Lilly let Loca in. Loca's boyfriend came in right behind her. "Rey, this is Cheo," Loca said. "What's up, bro?" I said as I reached out to shake his hand. Cheo shook my hand without saying a word and handed me a case of Lowenbrau beer. Loca asked Lilly to get the domino set so we could play and hang out for a while. I headed to the kitchen with the beer; Lilly went into the bedroom for the dominos. I opened the case of beer, put the bottles in the refrigerator, took four bottles with me, and headed back.

Lilly, Loca, and Cheo waited for me in the living room. Lilly sat at the far end of the table, mixing up the dominos. Cheo sat silently, watching Loca as she cut into a small mound of cocaine with a razor blade on a mirror. Loca divided the mound into eight thick lines of cocaine. Lilly finished mixing the dominos and pushed them toward the center of the table. We all grabbed seven domino pieces each and arranged them in front of us as we patiently waited for Loca to snort two lines of cocaine and pass the mirror on. She handed the mirror to Cheo, who then handed it to me, and I in turn handed it to Loca so she could hand it to Lilly. As Lilly snorted her lines, I went into the bedroom and retrieved five joints, a pack of cigarettes, a cigarette lighter, and an ashtray.

Cheo seemed quiet. He was a black Puerto Rican with a thick accent. He spoke broken English and therefore spoke mostly Spanish. Cheo was tall, around six-three or six-four, with a very thin build. Cheo wore a small afro and a goatee. He also had an ugly scar that started just below his neck and disappeared to the right side of his chest. Cheo had become an honorary Latin King in prison and carried his respect and loyalty out to the streets of Chicago. His cocaine connections in Miami made him a valuable commodity to the Latin Kings.

"Spanky's boys are looking for you," Loca said as we began playing dominos. "Tell me something I don't know," I responded. "I talked to Tino and he said he's going to look into giving you back your crown so you can't be touched," Loca explained. Tino was the incarcerated leader of the Latin Kings, often called the Inca. He had been in jail since the age of seventeen for killing two Vice Lords, and his word was supposed to be law as far as the Latin Kings were concerned. Giving me back my crown meant that I would again be a Latin King without having to go through the process of initiation.

Loca's words surprised me. I don't know what made her think that I wanted to be a Latin King again. I certainly couldn't see Tino having any say in how personal street business was handled.

I didn't comment, but the expression on my face told the story. "You don't trust Tino?" Loca asked. "His word is not what it used to be," I responded. "No disrespect to the brother, but it's all about money now. The brothers in the street go along with his claim as Inca so they'll be taken care of if they're locked up." "We're going to need you to work for us, and so you'll have to go to Humboldt Park once in a while," Loca continued. "We're going to make sure that you are not fucked with. Tino is going to put the word out that you're a King under him, and anyone who fucks with you will face the consequences. Let someone fuck with you and you'll see if Tino's word doesn't carry any power anymore."

I stared at Lilly across the table. I didn't know what to say. I was again being forced into situations I wanted no part of, but didn't have the courage to say so. It was clear to me that this was the only way I could save my life—reenter the life or die a coward's death. I also knew that I had a bad cocaine habit I needed to support, so regardless of how I really felt, I knew I would become Cheo and Loca's employee. In a way I has hoping and praying for Lilly to say that she didn't like the idea so that I could back off. Lilly, however, was excited about the job I was being offered. "¿*Qué vas a hacer*? (What are you going to do?)" Lilly asked. "We just need you to make dropoffs and pickups," Loca said. "*Te vamos a confiar con dinero y mercansia* (We're gonna trust you with money and merchandise)," Cheo told me. "*Te vas a ganar mucha lana chico* (You're going to make a lot of money, dude)," Cheo said. "Are you cool with that, Lil Loco?" Loca asked. It was the first time I had been called Lil Loco in over a year. Hearing the name made me mentally reminisce about the old days when I was King of the streets. Nobody messed with me, everybody loved me, and I was feared by friends and foes alike. I was popular and looked up to. "Yeah," I said. "I'm cool with that." "*Amor de Rey* (King Love)," I said. I was back.

MY NEW JOB required me to take cocaine packaged in various sizes to street dealers who then sold it. Basically, I was a mule on the street. There were two locations in Humboldt Park where I made deliveries—an apartment on the Near North side of the city, and one in Cicero, Illinois, an adjacent suburb of Chicago. I was also supposed to collect money from previous sales at those locations. I would get seven hundred dollars a week, discount prices on quantities of cocaine if I found new buyers, and the honor to again call myself a Latin King.

The trips to the apartments were uneventful. I was usually in and out within seconds. The Humboldt Park transactions, however, were always more dramatic. I feared the police would stop me and search the car. I usually met the dealers at a location away from the park, but sometimes I had to go there looking for them. One of the dealers was positioned on the Folks' side of the park. The Folks, were a group of affiliated gangs who were rivals to the Latin Kings. But these divisions were being ignored when it came to the supply of large amounts of drugs. The dealer was a member of a gang called the Latin Jivers. Although word was given through Cheo that I was not to be touched, I was still nervous every time I went into the park. My Latin Jivers contact, who dealt on the Folks' side of the park, was named Manny, a tall, lanky Puerto Rican with light skin and cleancut black hair. Manny was all business when I went to see him. He understood the dangers I faced going there, and often agreed to meet elsewhere. Every so often, however, I had to go to him. I was spotted many times by Cobras and Disciples who had it in for me. I could see their angry expressions at not being able to do anything while I was there on business. Somehow it didn't surprise me that the drugs being supplied to the Latin Kings and to their enemies came from the same source, but I was surprised about Cheo having power enough to make it safe for me on both sides of the line.

On the Latin Kings' side of the park, my connection was a Beach and Spaulding King called *Gato* (cat). Gato was a muscular Puerto Rican with a medium build, green eyes, and light brown hair. Gato's dealing spot was near Spanky's. I tried to avoid going there, but sometimes it was inevitable.

After the last incident I had had with Spanky and his Kings, some new events had taken place that made me a sure target. Because she had gotten caught with a gun, Josie had been sent to the penitentiary for violating her parole. She would have to do the two years remaining on her parole plus two more for the gun charge. Spanky was cleared of all charges, but he found out about Imelda and me. Once I had moved out of the neighborhood, Lady J, in an attempt to show her loyalty to the Latin Kings, told Spanky that she had walked in while Imelda was performing oral sex on me. Spanky became enraged that Lady J had lied the day we were confronted, so he ordered the Latin Queens to beat her. Lady J was badly hurt and had not been heard from since. Imelda's punishment was a lot worse. Because Spanky was in a wheelchair, he couldn't just grab Imelda and beat her. He had a couple of Kings hold her while he beat her mercilessly with a leather belt. Imelda had no choice but to stay in the house until she recovered from the beating. There I was, screwing my brains out day and night with Lilly and getting rich, while others were being punished because of my actions. I felt no remorse. I felt damned lucky.

After all that had taken place, it seemed as if there would be no more repercussions. Spanky went back to treating Imelda as his wife. He swore that I would die for betraying his trust, and he put a price on my head. Spanky made several pleas to Tino to lift the order of protection Tino had put out on me, and Tino had told him that our problem was personal and had nothing to do with the business dealings of the Kings. As far as I was concerned, that gave Spanky the go-ahead to take me out at any opportunity as long as I was not where the Kings sold their drugs. I took precautions not to be seen, and I also carried a gun.

Being a Latin King felt nothing like it had before. I was a King again for the purpose of making drug deals and nothing more. In a way, I was better off, because I wasn't as expendable as the Kings who just hung out on the corner. My value to the Latin Kings was much more than that of a foot soldier who killed and took chances on getting killed for the colors. I wasn't just a body deflecting the law from the ones who profited from the existence of the Latin Kings. I was indeed one of the profiteers.

I had been the best gangbanger, the best source of pain and suffering, and I was now the best drug dealer and the best addict. Whatever role I had to play to get what I wanted, that was the role I was best at. Through it all, I knew that getting out was just a step away. But I didn't want to be alone. Of all the things I was, and all the roles I perfected to suit my cause, being man enough to be true to myself and survive on my own was not one of them.

6

The First Blessing

THE RELATIONSHIP I had with Lilly really blossomed, but that wasn't exactly a good thing. We were very much alike and complemented each other well. We went out dancing often and became almost inseparable. As our relationship grew, so did our addiction to various vices. We both chain-smoked cigarettes, snorted cocaine constantly, drank heavily, and smoked cocaine-laced marijuana religiously. But we never argued. Many considered us to be the perfect couple. Lilly was the first woman that I could truly say was loyal to me in every way. And I was the same with her.

The drug business was going well. Lilly and I wore designer clothes and lavish jewelry. I had three gold necklaces that I wore all the time, each one thicker than the next. One chain had a pendant shaped like the island of Puerto Rico with Lilly's name engraved in the middle. On another was the same kind of pendant but with my name. The last had a pendant of Jesus on the cross and was the most prominent. Lilly already owned a pretty good collection of gold jewelry when I came along. She now upgraded to diamonds and rubies. We were living well, but we were also very addicted to cocaine.

One evening we took a trip into the park in Humboldt Park to buy some of the ethnic Puerto Rican food sold in portable food shacks. These shacks provided visitors to the park with a variety of Puerto Rican delicacies at very reasonable prices. They truly represented Puerto Rican culture—hardworking people who were proud of their culture, and willing to share it with others by offering the popular foods of Puerto Rico. This contrasted with the drug dealing, gang violence, vandalism, and cultural destruction that surrounded them.

Our favorite shack was on the inner park drive, near Humboldt Boulevard, on the same side of the park where Spanky dealt his drugs but a little distance away. We bought our food and sat down on a bench to eat and talk. At that moment, a carload of Spanky's boys drove by, headed toward their dealing spot. When they saw us sitting there, they slowed down to a crawl and looked at us maniacally. "Fuckin' punk, you ain't no King," the driver yelled. "It's just a matter of time, faggot," yelled one of the Kings sitting in the back seat. I clearly knew that I was fair game for Spanky, if I wasn't in the park doing business. We watched the car drive away slowly, ate our food quickly, and headed toward our car.

As we pulled out of the parking spot, I saw through the rearview mirror the same car headed back our way. I turned north on Humboldt Boulevard and stopped at the red light. From the rearview mirror I saw the Kings turn in the same direction we did and noticed that the guy behind the driver had a gun in his hand. "Oh, shit, they're coming after us," I said to Lilly, and sped into the intersection of Humboldt Boulevard and North Avenue while the light was still red. Several cars came screeching to a halt to avoid slamming into us. Luckily, we made it across the intersection without causing an accident. I looked in the rearview mirror and saw that the Kings were not pursuing us. Then I saw an unmarked police car turn toward us from North Avenue with its headlights flashing. "Oh, fuck, *la hada* (the cops)," I told Lilly as the police approached us and turned on the siren. They pulled up right next to us, and the detective on the passenger side yelled and motioned for us to pull over. "*Tengo un paquete ensima* (I have a package on me)," Lilly said. "*Escondelo* (hide it)," I told her.

We pulled over and waited for the police to approach the car. Lilly pulled a package out of her purse that contained half an ounce of cocaine bagged in quantities of an eighth of an ounce each. But there wasn't time to do anything with it. The two detectives quickly approached the car, one on either side, with their guns drawn. "Both of you put your fuckin' hands where we can see them!" one of the detectives yelled. We saw their guns pointed right at us and did as we were told. "Driver, turn off the car slowly," the detective instructed. I did as he asked.

The detective on my side opened the door and held his gun inches from my head. "Get out slowly and lie on the ground facing away from me," he instructed. "You make a wrong move, you're dead." I got out of the car slowly and lay facedown on the concrete. The detective put his knee on my back, near my neck facing toward my feet, then he grabbed my arms, one at a time, and handcuffed me. He stood up, put his foot on my back, and began giving Lilly the same instructions.

By the time Lilly was handcuffed and we were picked off the ground and sat on the curb, there were dozens of police cars on the scene and the road had been blocked off. Two uniformed police officers stood beside each of us as the detectives thoroughly searched the car. They found a nickel-plated nine-millimeter semiautomatic gun I had hidden under my seat for protection should I ever need it. It was a brand-new gun that had never been used, but it was loaded. I looked up at the sky, trying to ignore the detective who had found the gun as he walked toward me unloading it.

"OK, Rey, what's the story?" the detective asked. "Why are your own King brothers chasing you?" I didn't say a word. "He fucked Spanky's girl," another detective answered. "Oh, shit, you fucked Imelda. Ha ha, she is a hot little number," the detective said. "So much for Latin King loyalty." His partner knelt before us and said, "Rey, we got you for a weapon and your girl for possession of cocaine. Both of you are going to jail anyway, so tell us if there is anything else in the car." "There is nothing else in the car," I said, "and the cocaine is mine also." "So you want to save your girlfriend's ass?" the detective asked. "That's my shit," I told him. "I didn't get the chance to dump it, and it ended up on her lap." "Hey, you won't get an argument from us—if you want to take the rap for everything, we're happy," the detective said.

They stood me up, searched me again, and sat me in the back seat of their car. A policewoman searched Lilly and, once it was determined that she didn't have anything illegal on her, they removed the handcuffs and let her go. "Where are you taking him?" Lilly asked. "Good ol' thirteenth district, Shakespeare and California," the detective shouted as he got into the car. "I'll get you out," Lilly motioned with her lips as we drove off.

These detectives, who were from the Gang Crimes Division in the Chicago Police Department, made it their business to know everything that happened within and between gangs. That's how they knew about Imelda and me. They also knew about my past and about all the things I tried to do about my past.

"Lil Loco, where have you been?" the detective on the passenger seat asked. I didn't respond. "Tell me, Lil Loco, how do piece-of-shit gangbangers like you get such good-looking girls?" he tried again. Again I didn't respond. "Stupid bitches," said the detective driving. Nothing else was said to me until we reached the police station.

At the police station I was taken into one of the gang crime unit rooms. There were four desks in the room and a bench. I was placed on the bench by one of the detectives, who sat at the desk nearest me. He put a form into a typewriter and began asking me questions. His name was Detective Garcia. He was a short, stocky, balding man with absolutely no Latin accent. While he filled out the form, the detective made comments about the gun they had taken from me. He mentioned how he hoped that a ballistics test would find that someone had been killed with it so that I could be pinned for the crime. "At least we'd drop the drug charge if we could get you for murder," the detective said. I wasn't worried about that happening. Cheo had given the nine-millimeter to me from a stash of brand-new weapons he had purchased to sell to gangbangers for profit. But I couldn't be certain it had never been used before.

Another detective entered the room with the gun in his hand and placed it in front of Detective Garcia. "The gun is clean, but we have some questions for him about where it came from," the detective said. Detective Garcia got up from behind his desk, stood me up, and led me out of the room following the other detective. I was taken into another room. This room had only two desks. White detectives occupied both desks.

Detective Garcia removed the handcuff from my left hand and put his right knee hard into the back of my right knee, making my right leg collapse to the ground and the rest of me right along with it. While I was on the ground on one knee, he handcuffed me to a radiator. Detective Garcia left the room and came back with the gun. He handed it to one of the detectives sitting behind a desk, and the detective got up and walked my way. The detective was a big, burly white guy, about six-five, two hundred and fifty pounds, with white hair and glasses.

"Where did you get this gun?" he asked as he looked down at me menacingly. "I bought it from a junkie," I told him. "Don't give me that shit!" the detective screamed, grabbing me by the hair, tilting my head upward, and putting his face inches from mine. "There were over a thousand guns stolen from a gun shop out in Niles, and this gun is one of then," the detective said, as he put the gun against my left temple. "You little motherfucker, where did you get the gun?" The detective pushed my face hard against the radiator. The heat was not turned on so the radiator was cold, but nevertheless it was painful. "I told you, I got it from a junkie,"I said. The detective let me go, walked away, and stood near his desk.

Detective Garcia got up and walked my way. "Rey, hey, Rey, come on, man, don't make this hard on yourself," he said. I was getting ready to repeat my "I got it from a junkie" line when he lunged at me and kicked me in the stomach. "I'm sure you're remembering now, right?" Detective Garcia said as he punched me in the back. "I got it from a junkie for an eight ball (eighth of an ounce of cocaine)," I gasped. "Listen, you fuckin' punk, we're gonna charge you for anyone killed with any one of those stolen guns, so you better talk," Detective Garcia said while he pulled my head backward by the hair with one hand and grabbed my neck with the other. I just stopped talking. I didn't have the information they wanted, so I didn't say a word until Detective Garcia kicked me in the ribcage. "So you're not going to talk, huh, motherfucker!" he shouted as he kicked me. "I don't know anything about any fuckin' stolen guns!" I shouted back when I regained my breath.

All the detectives walked out. About half an hour later, a uniformed police officer came and took me to the lockup area. I lay on one of the metal benches in a fetal position, nursing the pain in my ribs. I spent the night there and was transferred to Cook County jail in the morning to face a judge. That morning I limped in front of the judge, holding my midsection. I was charged for possession of twenty-three grams of cocaine with the intent to deliver. I was also charged with resisting arrest (a charge added by the cops to explain my beat-up condition). That charge was eventually dropped. No charges were ever brought for the possession of a gun. My bond was set at one million dollars, and I was taken to the infirmary right away.

THE SERIOUSNESS OF what had just happened didn't even dawn on me. I guess the pain I was in numbed me through the whole procedure. I came to learn that I had two fractured ribs along with a badly sprained wrist. I didn't even realize the consequences of the day's proceedings until I was cared for in the infirmary and then transported for processing into general lockup. I was taken into a room where I was stripped of all my belongings and thoroughly searched and examined. I was given a pair of beige pants with the initials D.O.C. (Department of Corrections) on the left leg, and a beige button-down shirt with the same D.O.C. on the back and on the left chest area. I was given the basic necessities, which included a bath towel, a washcloth, toothpaste, a tooth-brush, and bath soap. I was also given a blanket, a bedspread, a pillow, and a pillowcase. I was allowed to keep the gym shoes I had on with the laces because I wasn't a suicide risk. I was taken into Division One cell house where I would await my court date.

It was the middle of the day when I arrived at the cellblock. I was twenty-one years old and didn't know how long I'd be calling this place home. Because of my injuries, a guard asked the inmates in the television room to help me take my things to my cell. No one volunteered to help. No one even looked my way. But then I said, "*Amor de Rey* (King love)," and five guys sitting at a table playing cards got up and walked my way. Two of them grabbed my things while the others introduced themselves and shook my hand in the manner all Latin Kings did (slap each other's right hands and come up forming the Latin Kings hand sign, which is identical to the "I love you" gesture in sign language). We walked past the television room and into a hallway with doors on either side. My cell was the third door on the left. I was relieved to find out that I had the cell all to myself. The Kings helped me get set-tled, and then we all went out to the television room to play cards.

Division One is one of the oldest cell houses at Cook County Jail. The cellblock I was in had solid metal walls down the hall-way that divided the cells, and it had metal bars on the outside walls. On the other side of the bars was a corridor that allowed guards to look into each cell. The cells consisted of a steel bunk, welded to the wall, layered with a thin twin-size mattress. There was also a toilet and a sink with a piece of stainless steel attached to the wall above it and used as a mirror.

There were twenty-two inmates in that cellblock with me. All of us were either Latino or African American. Nine of the inmates were Peoples (Latin Kings and associates)—five Latin Kings and four Vice Lords, and the rest were Folks (Disciples and associates). The Kings' leader in our cellblock was called *Guero* (White Boy) because he looked Caucasian, but he was Puerto Rican. He was in his late twenties with a medium build, black shoulder-length hair, and hazel eyes. Guero was one of the very few Latin Kings I ever met who didn't have a tattoo. He was fighting a rape charge. The other Latin Kings were Macho, Flaco, Junior, and Dice. Macho was nineteen, with a chip on his shoulder. He was tall and muscular and always seemed to be looking for some kind of confrontation with the Folks. Macho was waiting to be tried on a murder charge. Flaco was a tall, skinny older King. He was in his mid-thirties, and his body was covered with tattoos. Flaco was a veteran of the prison system. Flaco's charge was attempted murder and strong-arm robbery. Junior was also in his thirties. He was short and fat and had joined the Latin Kings while incarcerated in Cook County Jail. Junior was a Colombian who had been caught transporting a large amount of cocaine into Chicago. Dice was a quiet, low-key eighteen-year-old. He was very muscular for his slim build, and had a big lion's head wearing a crown tattooed on his back. Junior was charged with the murder of two fourteen-year-olds killed in a drive-by shooting.

In Division One, most if not all inmates were being held on charges that required a large sum of money to bond out, or they were being held without bail. Because of that, there seemed to be a mutual respect among them, even if they were from opposing gangs. Most of the Folks in our cellblock were in their twenties and thirties. Out of the twenty-two inmates, only four us were first-timers.

Near dinnertime we were locked up in our cells. Guero lived two cells down from me, and began talking to me through the bars. "We'll be in here until they bring chow," Guero said. "*Ponte hacer sit-ups o push-ups para matar el tiempo* (Do sit-ups or push-ups to kill time)," he advised. I sat on my bunk, staring at the steel walls. They were a depressing gray color. It was obvious that they had been painted over and over without the old paint ever being removed. Even with the sounds of different styles of music and conversations blaring in the air, it seemed silent.

I stared into nothingness with no thoughts or feelings. For a brief moment it was as if nothing existed; even the pain in my wrist and ribs went away. But finally it all came crashing down on me. I was incarcerated with almost no chance of getting out unless I could beat the charges against me when I went to trial. A $1 million bond meant that $100,000 would be required to bail me out. The possibility of anyone I knew putting up that kind of money was nil.

The loud clanking and simultaneous opening of cell doors woke me from my empty daydream. Guero opened my door. "Chow time, brother, come on," Guero said. I silently followed everyone into the television room. Flaco had already gotten six food trays and put them on our table. The trays were the stackable kind, made of solid plastic with built-in food compartments. That evening's meal was baked chicken with mashed potatoes and corn. The food was tasteless and bland, but we ate it as if it were gourmet fare.

After dinner we were locked up again so the trays could be collected; then we were let back out. This was the usual routine, day after day, for breakfast, lunch, and dinner. At all of our meals the Kings' routine was to wait for everyone to be present, say a prayer that was half religious, half Latin King–related, and then eat.

At the front of the cellblock there were two telephones, one on each side of the entrance door. The phone on the left was used exclusively by the Peoples, the one on the right by the Folks. Exceptions were made, but only with prior permission. This rule, like all other jailhouse rules set by the inmates, was enforced by intimidation and violence. The Peoples and Folks knew to respect each other's boundaries or risk an all-out gang war that would likely spread to all cell houses. Those not associated in any way with a gang had to pay for the privilege to use the phone. These payments came in the form of food, cigarettes, arrangement of outside jail favors, or sex, although sex as payment did not apply to the Latin Kings as they had strict rules against homosexual activity, which resulted in extremely severe punishment. Inmates not affiliated with a gang who did not follow the jailhouse rules were severely beaten. Those who were tough enough to fight back usually ended up joining the gang opposing the one that had beaten them. The jail administration and the guards supposedly overseeing the inmates were powerless to stop or even curb the enforcement of jailhouse rules. It was a way of prison life, and nothing could be done about it.

Since I had just arrived at the cellblock that day, I was allowed first use of the telephone that evening. Only collect calls could be made from those telephones. I called Lilly.

Lilly was anticipating my call and sounded relieved to hear my voice. "How are you?" she asked in a very happy voice. "I'm alright," I responded. "Have you seen Loca?" "She's right here." "Put her on," I demanded. I don't know how Lilly felt about me asking for Loca immediately, but at that moment Lilly's feelings were the furthest thing from my mind. Loca was the only person who could help me regain my freedom and I knew that.

"Hey, Lil Loco," Loca said. "There will be a lawyer coming to visit you soon. You tell the brothers in there who you are and that you are a King under Tino." I sat silently, listening to her, waiting to hear that she was coming to bail me out, but I knew those words would never come. When Loca finished talking there was a long silence between us, as if we were both quietly praying that there was something else that could be done.

"Do you want to speak to Lilly?" Loca asked, finally breaking the silence. "Yeah," I responded. "I'm so sorry," Lilly said when she came on the phone. "It's not your fault," I assured her. "It was that fuckin' Spanky." Both of us went silent for a moment. Since we had become a couple, we had not spent any time apart until now. Our lack of verbal communication had never been as evident as it was at that very moment. The fact that our six-month relationship was based on sex and drugs became clear. "I'll call you tomorrow and give you visitation information so you can come see me," I finally said. "I love you and miss you so much," Lilly responded. "I do, too," I said in a whisper. "Good-bye." I heard Lilly's quiet good-bye as I hung up the phone. I walked straight to my cell and lay down.

I twisted and turned on my bunk, thinking about my situation. I wanted so much to smoke a joint, to snort some cocaine. I got up and walked toward the cell door, only to turn around and lie on my bunk again. I was losing my mind. "Hey, dude, come on out of there, man," I heard Guero say as he walked past. I didn't respond. I just got up and sat at the end of my bunk with my face in my hands. "*Oye, chico, vente aca* (Hey, dude, come over here)," Flaco said, as he opened the door to my cell. "*Toma, bro* (Here, bro)," he said as he handed me a pack of cigarettes. "*Me voy a quedar a aqui un ratito* (I'm going to stay in here for a little while)," I told Flaco. "*Gracias por los cigarillos* (Thanks for the cigarettes)." I got up and shook Flaco's hand with the Latin King handshake. He gave me a book of matches and left my cell. I sat on my bunk with my back against the hard, cold wall and lit up a cigarette.

BEING IN JAIL didn't bother me as much as not being able to get high. I was a Latin King, and the gangs ran the prisons, so in that sense I was safe. I didn't have to worry about being beaten up, raped, or taken advantage of in any way. Even if I ran into any of Spanky's boys in jail, I didn't have to worry about retaliation. In fact, they would have to back me up if it ever came to a conflict. Within a few short hours, I had a clear understanding of what "doing time" meant. Time just crawled by, allowing an inmate to think things through or go completely crazy. My thoughts were directed at things I could do very little about. Mostly, I thought about the whereabouts of my mother and sisters. I had not seen nor heard from them since my mother had sent me to live with her drug-dealing stepson. Maybe my sisters had become objects of abuse since I wasn't there any more. More likely, all was well for them because I was no longer a burden. I wondered if I would ever see them again. I also wondered how long it would be before I would see the streets again.

After a while Guero came into my cell and sat next to me. "Are you, alright, King brother?" Guero asked. "I'm cool, just need a *pase* (snort of cocaine)," I responded. "You'll get over that feeling soon enough. Just don't let it get to you. What are you in here for?" Guero asked. "Possession with the intent to deliver *perico* (cocaine)," I told him. "I got a million-dollar bond, bro, a million dollars! I'm a million-dollar man," I added. We both laughed weakly at that. "No shit, man, it's that RICO shit they came up with," Guero said. "I don't know about no Rico but I hate his ass already," I said. In the fight against drugs, RICO (Racketeer Influenced and Corrupt Organizations), made drug users and dealers a higher priority in the courts than even murderers, rapists, or other violent criminals. RICO enabled judges to hand out high bail requirements and mandatory sentences, and allowed the law to seize everything owned by offenders. I found it quite ironic that I was subject to a law whose name sounded like a street nickname.

"What did you do?" I asked Guero. "I'm in for rape, man, but I didn't rape that bitch," Guero responded. "That bitch wants to get back together with me now," he added. According to Guero, he was a victim of his girlfriend's vindictive nature. She was teaching him a lesson by falsely accusing him and having him incarcerated. Guero explained that they had broken up because of a one-night stand he had had with her cousin. She didn't accept his "I was drunk" excuse and kicked him out of their apartment. After a couple of weeks, she finally allowed him to come back to the apartment to retrieve his property.

He went there and found her getting high. Supposedly she offered him marijuana and booze but he turned her down. She led him into the bedroom so he could get his things and then began seducing him. Guero said he could've, but didn't resist, and they ended up having sex. During their sexual encounter she suddenly reached up and scratched his face and neck. She then began screaming loudly for help. Guero said he slapped her in an attempt to calm her down, but that only made her scream louder.

The neighbors heard the commotion and called the police. The police arrived as Guero was leaving the apartment and arrested him. He had been in jail ever since. He had been in Cook County Jail going on eight months when I arrived. His bond had been set at $100,000. He was certain that on his next court date, which was less than a month away, he would finally be released. "The court doesn't even know that this bitch is talking to me on the phone saying she is sorry and that she wants me back," Guero told me. "She has already talked to my lawyer about dropping the charges. It's up to the state now." I thought he was lying and making excuses to convince himself of his innocence. After all, even I considered myself innocent, knowing very well that I was involved in criminal activity.

The next couple of weeks were pretty uneventful. Lilly visited me a few times. We pretty much just reminisced about our drug-induced sexual frenzies. I called her every so often on the phone, but we never had much to say to each other. Our conversations always revolved around things we had done and declarations of love for each other. I passed the time by playing cards and doing push-ups and sit-ups in my cell. The jail food was doing me some good. When I was processed into jail, I weighed a mere 128 pounds, mostly because of my cocaine addiction. I hadn't even realized I had lost so much weight until I was incarcerated. After only two weeks of incarceration I was already gaining weight and feeling better physically.

At the beginning of the third week, my street problems caught up with me, and my relationship with the Kings in the cellblock took a turn for the worse. That Monday, Macho had a court date. While he waited in the courtroom lockup to be taken in front of the judge, he met and talked to one of Spanky's Kings, who was also waiting to be taken in front of a judge. Macho learned about my outside relationship with some of the Latin Kings and the reasons behind their desire to take me out. He also learned that I had been violated out of the Kings and since then had chickened out on a hit. After that, as far as Macho was concerned, I wasn't a King and should be violated in jail for what I had done with Spanky's wife. Macho also became convinced that I was a coward because of the time I had chosen to run instead of murdering someone on a hit. Macho brought all this information, and his feelings about it, back to the cellblock and shared it with the other Kings. My stay in Cook County Jail suddenly became uneasy.

After dinner lockup was over, Guero asked me to come to his cell where he confronted me with Macho's story. I gave Guero a brief history about my tenure as a Latin King. I told him why I got violated out and admitted having an affair with the wife of a Latin King brother. I also told Guero that King Tino still considered me a Latin King and had given me the blessings and respect reserved for a senior member. I explained that the only Kings on the street that had a problem with me were those that hung out with Spanky. About the hit, I told Guero that I had done my part for the Latin King Nation and therefore should not have to be forced by other Kings to go out and prove myself.

Guero, surprisingly, took my side. He said as long as Tino had given me back my crown then I was indeed a Latin King regardless of what anyone else said. He also told me that he had problems with the new street soldiers expecting senior brothers to continue setting themselves out by committing hits. Guero agreed with my opinion that I shouldn't have to continue proving myself worthy to be a King for new generations of members. "We did our part—they need to do theirs and respect us," Guero said. He told me to stay in his cell while he made a phone call, then walked out.

About fifteen minutes had elapsed when Guero walked in with the rest of the Kings from the cellblock. My first thought was that they were going to try and take me out right there and then. I stood up, put out my cigarette, and mentally prepared to defend myself any way I could. "I just spoke to King Papo," Guero began. "For those of you who don't know who King Papo is, he is King Tino's second-in-command on the streets. King Papo made it clear that this brother should be respected as the Latin King he is." Guero pointed at me. "Regardless of what happened, King Tino respects him enough to give him back his crown, and that's all I and everyone else here needs to know."

I scanned the faces in the cell, looking for reactions. Everyone remained expressionless except for Macho, who stared at me, shaking his head in disbelief. "Does anyone here have a problem with that?" Guero asked, looking directly at Macho. "Break it up in there!" a guard yelled as he walked up the corridor toward the cell. Before we exited the cell, the guard stood on the other side of the bars. "What's the problem, guys?" the guard asked. "Guero, come here." Guero walked over to the guard. The rest of us left slowly, one at a time. "Punk ass," Macho whispered, as I walked past him. I went back to my cell, and Guero assured the guard that he was putting a disagreement to rest and not starting one. For the remainder of my stay at Cook County, Macho went out of his way to discredit me. Life went on.

THAT FRIDAY, GUERO went to court, and, just as he had predicted, his girlfriend dropped the charges against him and he was set free. That morning after breakfast, Guero came into my cell and gave me a Bible. "I'm going home today, bro, so I won't need this," Guero said. "Read it. It will help you out." The following week, the Latin King leaders in Cook County Jail assigned Macho to be the new leader of our cellblock.

I spent the next eight months in relative seclusion. Macho continued to try to draw me into confrontations but did not succeed. It crossed my mind to just get it over with and fight him, but I decided against it. It wasn't because I was in jail. I knew the worst that could happen was that I would be sentenced to solitary confinement, then placed in a different cellblock. It would be a fight between two Latin Kings, so it was unlikely that new charges would be filed against either of us unless it was a one-sided beating. More likely, we would be left in the same cellblock and Macho would have newfound respect for me. Either way, the harassment would stop. Other inmates made remarks about my manhood as Macho's comments became louder and bolder. He made everyone in the cellblock believe that I was using the Latin Kings as my protection because I was a coward. (My membership meant that anyone putting his hands on me would possibly set off a riot throughout the jail.) In a way, Macho had a point. I did use my relationship with Tino to my advantage, to keep myself safe. But I knew that if I really had to, I would fight anyone who posed a real physical threat to me. As for Macho, I didn't see him as a threat. I saw him as an ignorant young buck. I decided that he wasn't worth my trouble and that there was no one in that cellblock I needed to prove myself to.

I spent most of my days in my cell reading the Bible, sketching, and writing poetry. Every so often I would go out and watch television, or play chess or cards. After a while the older inmates in the cellblock gained respect for me because of the way I chose to deal with Macho. Some would come into my cell and read my poetry, comment on my drawings, or discuss the Bible with me. That kept me at peace and helped me overcome the desire to attack Macho.

Lilly continued to visit me every week. She was still taking drugs when she first started to visit, but then things began to change. We began to have conversations that had nothing to with sex or drugs. We talked about religion and our future. We began to see the mistakes we had made and discuss ways of changing. The attorney Loca hired never showed up to visit, but he did show up in court. I would go in front of the judge once a month to have my case heard, only to be taken back to Cook County to await another trial date. It was just one frustrating continuance after another. I never said a word, nor was I asked to say anything. The assistant district attorney would ask for more time to gather evidence, or my attorney would ask for more time to prepare his case; the judge would agree and I would be taken back to my cell. It was a sham if ever I saw one.

After four months my attorney began asking for more money. Loca had disappeared. Lilly tried to raise money for the lawyer, but she couldn't quite come up with all of it. For my last two court dates I was represented by a public defender. Finally, in the eighth month of my stay in Cook County, I was taken to court and my case actually went to trial. At the advice of my public defender, I optioned for a bench trial as opposed to a jury trial. He said that if I were found guilty, the sentence would be much harsher if I took a jury trial. With a bench trial, the decision over my guilt or innocence would be totally up to the judge.

I was found guilty on the charge of possessing cocaine with the intent to deliver, and sentenced to four years in a State of

Illinois correctional facility. The eight months I had spent in Cook County Jail would count toward that time, so I would actually do forty months. With good behavior I would do half of that, and I could be free in less than two years.

The seclusion I had been in—both by being incarcerated and by keeping to myself as much as possible—became my saving grace during this time. I started to realize that being there was actually a blessing in disguise. I drew that conclusion from reading the Bible in its entirety, praying, and learning how to count my blessings. If I were still on the streets, I reasoned, I would be either dead by drug overdose or dead at the hands of Spanky's boys.

My nightmares had also noticeably decreased. While I was living with Lilly, they had decreased due mostly to the drug use. Once I was incarcerated, they stopped almost completely, and those I did have weren't as horrifying. Maybe it was because I was finally paying for a crime I had committed. Maybe it was because I had started to consciously accept my wrongdoings. Whatever the reason, I was relieved by the infrequency of my nightmares.

I had spent a birthday, a Christmas, and a New Year's Day in Cook County Jail without once feeling depressed or angered about my situation. When I was convicted, I wasn't shocked or disappointed. I had come to terms with the possibility of being found guilty and had prepared myself to do the time. I concluded that serving two years in the penitentiary was a small price to pay for the crimes I had committed or been involved with in my life.

A week after I was convicted and sentenced, I was transferred to Joliet State Penitentiary to await processing into a medium-security prison somewhere in Illinois. I took the Bible Guero had given me along with an odd feeling of peace.

Because all my life I had felt I was cursed, I never knew what a blessing was. Being at peace allowed me to begin to understand. I remembered guns pointed at me at point-blank range that never fired. I recalled bullets shot at me that did less damage than a bad fall or the beatings at the hands of my own gang. I compared them with the events that had taken the lives of so many others but had somehow spared mine. Then I thought about the huge amount of drugs I had poured into my body, yet I was still alive. It was these thoughts that made me realize the meaning of a blessing. It was then that I started to consider my conviction as a blessing. It was actually the first blessing I counted.

7

Doing Time

I ARRIVED AT Joliet Correctional Center on a cold, snowy day. There were thirty inmates on the bus with me. We were taken directly into the processing unit and then to our cells. A portion of Joliet served as a temporary holding facility for those just entering the Illinois Department of Corrections (IDOC) from Chicago and the surrounding area. Most inmates sent there would eventually be transferred to other IDOC facilities throughout the state. We arrived at Joliet under lockdown conditions, which meant that inmates in the processing unit and the regular prison population were not allowed out of their cells except to shower once a week. Even then, only a handful of inmates were marched to and from the shower area at any given time.

Four days before I was transferred to Joliet, a fight involving the Latin Kings had broken out, and a rival gang member was fatally stabbed. Apparently, the Latin Kings had walked into the cafeteria to find two members of a rival gang occupying tables used by the Kings. In the penitentiary, that is a major sign of disrespect. All inmates know which tables belong to which gang. If you sit at a table belonging to your rivals, you are pretty much calling them pussies. If the disrespected gang does not respond with an appropriate retaliation, that gang is then targeted for similar acts and more disrespect by the other gangs.

Three Latin Kings left the chow line and attacked the two inmates sitting at their table. One of the Kings had a homemade knife and used it to stab one of the inmates. The prison guards know very well that specific gangs occupy certain groups of tables. For whatever reason, nobody said anything to the two rival members, and nobody paid any attention to the Kings until the actual attack took place. Knowing the way gangs operated, the guards must have or should have known something was going to go down. They saw the steps leading up to the inevitable confrontation and did nothing to stop it.

In Joliet my cellmate was a black guy called Smokey. Smokey was a member of the Four Corner Hustlers, a gang connected to the Vice Lords. He was about six-one, muscular, with a small afro and countless gang-related tattoos. It was Smokey's second time in the prison system. His current charges were aggravated assault with a deadly weapon and violation of parole. He had been sentenced to two years on the new charge, plus he would have to complete the year he had left on parole in prison. Smokey and I had one thing in common—we both kept to ourselves. This made for a good cellmate relationship.

After a week and a half of being locked down, we were finally let out of our cells on a routine basis. We were allowed daily visits to the cafeteria, the yard, and church services. The inmates who had participated in the brawl had been moved out of Joliet. The remaining Latin Kings gathered all the new arrivals in the yard and gave us a quick rundown of the rules. They made us aware of which section of the yard and the cafeteria was ours and which belonged to our enemies. We were also told that the

King brother who had been the leader of this portion of the cell block in Joliet had been shipped out during the lockup. We had to decide who our next leader was going to be. The vote was scheduled for the next day in the yard.

The next day, about seventeen of us gathered in the yard and introduced ourselves. Surprisingly, and luckily, as it happened, for me, several Kings not only recognized but also respected the name Lil Loco. (News from Spanky and his gang wouldn't have mattered—there are different rules of respect in the penitentiary.) That notoriety got me nominated for leadership. I turned it down but agreed to serve as advisor—to help make decisions in matters where action needed to be taken, but not to make the final decision. I thought that this would allow me to try to keep the peace without being judged on my choice not to break the peace if it came to that. The first thing I advised was that those Kings who wanted the leadership position should provide us with brief backgrounds of themselves, and we would wait until the next day for the actual vote. One nonmember among us said his brother was a Latin King from Maywood. I advised that he hang out with us so we could look out for him, but he would not be allowed to voice an opinion on any decision made by the Latin Kings. For the most part, we all agreed.

Just as on the streets, in prison there is always at least one guy in the crowd who wants to be chief at all costs. This guy is always very vocal, aggressive, and usually makes decisions based on promoting his ego. In our group, that guy was Tarzan. Tarzan was a heavyset guy with shoulder-length hair. From the beginning, he thought there was no need for a vote for leadership; we should automatically appoint him because he had been there before, and had been a leader before. But very few in our group were first-time offenders, and furthermore, no one liked Tarzan's attitude. Tarzan didn't like the idea of taking the nonmember under our wing. Tarzan thought that the guy should be initiated into the Kings if he wanted to hang with us; otherwise he'd have to be on his own. "For all we know, he could be lying," Tarzan said. I disagreed with him. "You don't know shit about him," Tarzan replied.

As it turned out, we did find out from another inmate that the guy's brother was not a Latin King. Since I had been so vocal about taking him under our wing, I had the uncomfortable task of approaching him about it. Of course, it was expected that some kind of violence would be inflicted on him for lying to us. The guy confessed that he had lied. He explained that he lived in an area of Chicago that the Latin Kings controlled, and that he had been locked up for three counts of grand theft auto he had committed with a Latin King. He also told me that he was afraid to hang out by himself in prison and that he wanted to be a King. At that point, all I could think about was the reputation I would carry while I was locked up in the penitentiary. How I handled this situation would probably become the foundation upon which I would be judged by the Latin Kings as I did my time.

All the inmates milled in the corridors of the cell house, preparing to go to chow, creating a shield from the guard's view. I made sure that I wouldn't be seen, then threw two punches at his face. The first punch hit his eye and the second hit his nose. When he reached up to cover his now-bloody nose, I kicked him in the groin with all the force I could muster. He fell to the floor, holding his groin in pain, as many looked, laughed, and turned away as if nothing had happened. "Don't you ever betray the Latin Kings, punk. *Amor de Rey*," I growled, as I stood over him.

The chow line finally started moving from the cell house toward the cafeteria. Inmate after inmate walked past the guy lying on the floor; nobody said a word to the guards. Finally, when the cell house was almost empty, the guards found him. By this time, I was halfway to the cafeteria, a good distance away from him. The guy never told the guards who had hit him. I guess he knew that the consequences would be worse if he did. There was no lockdown or any other repercussion after that incident. It just went away. Coincidently, I was shipped out of Joliet to Shawnee Correctional Center two days later.

After breakfast one morning, a group of inmates, including myself, were shackled and loaded onto a bus to be transferred to other correctional facilities. Our first stop was Lincoln Correctional Center. We had lunch there, and some inmates were unloaded to begin doing their time there, while others were picked up to be transferred elsewhere. Next we stopped at Menard, a maximum-security prison, where we had supper and spent the night. Menard was famous at the time for being the prison where serial killer John Wayne Gacy remained on death row.

At Menard, King Jawbreaker greeted me. He recognized me from a shootout that had taken place at his house years before. Jawbreaker and his family were one of the last Latin King families in the Maplewood Park area of Chicago. The shootout at his house had been part of a gang war in which the Disciples were attempting to take full control of Maplewood Park and the Kings were trying to hang onto it. The Disciples had won. Jawbreaker had been incarcerated ever since that shootout. He took me around and introduced me to the other Latin Kings. Then he gave me a shank (handmade weapon) for protection, saying, "This is yours, my brother. Use it if you need to. There are some punk-ass motherfuckers in here." "They may strip-search us before we get on the bus tomorrow," I told Jawbreaker. "I may get caught with it." "Bus, what bus?" Jawbreaker asked with a surprised look. "I'm just here overnight; they're taking me to Shawnee tomorrow morning," I explained. "Oh, man, give me that," Jawbreaker responded as he took the shank from my hand. "You won't be needing this there, bro. That's a country club. You go there and chill, little brother. Don't get caught up in nothing that will get you sent here."

That was the best news I had heard in a long time. If Jawbreaker, a veteran of the Illinois prison system, said I was going to a country club–like facility, then that's where I was going. I felt more at ease, as if I could do my time without a speck of trouble. But then again compared to Menard, most prisons throughout the country did feel like country clubs.

The next morning, right after breakfast, we were loaded onto the bus and taken to our final destination, Shawnee, a medium-security correctional facility. We were taken to the new inmate holding cells, where we waited to be integrated into the general prison population. By the time I joined the regular prison population, most of the inmates knew that I was a Latin King. The Latin Kings in turn knew that I was Lil Loco, a King who had been given a crown directly from the Inca (Tino). In the penitentiary, that carried a lot of weight; in a medium-security prison it meant even more.

Once I entered the regular population, I became close to the Shawnee leader of the Latin Kings. At his request, I became his advisor and the Kings' treasurer. I was in charge of merchandise. I kept items—such as food, toiletries, and cigarettes—in my cell that the Kings gathered and that we used to supply our new incoming brothers and to purchase things within Shawnee like good haircuts and extra-clean, neatly folded laundry. New Latin Kings would get soap, toothpaste, a toothbrush, shampoo, and a pack of cigarettes, if they smoked. They had no need for the state-issued toiletries. That was one of the perks of being a King that other inmates admired. We did not expect the new King inmates to repay us for the initial merchandise. Anything beyond this, however, they had to pay back. We also required the Kings to donate at least one item on every commissary day. Any inmate who was not a Latin King could borrow merchandise from us in return for double payment of the same item. Payment was due on commissary day, and we accepted no excuses. Because inmates knew they were borrowing from the Latin Kings, payments were rarely, if ever, late. These practices ensured that the Latin Kings always had an ample supply of merchandise to trade.

I was determined to stay out of trouble and kept myself occupied with nonviolent pursuits. I spent most of my nights writing poetry and sketching. I used some of the sketches and poems I wrote to create postcards, which I sold to other inmates. The postcards I made were tailored "Hallmark moments" for the occasion. I made dozens of them, with different drawings, but waited to include the poem until I knew the occasion. For the holidays I made generic "happy this" and "merry that" cards, but I would also make a few original cards for those who wanted something unique and were willing to pay extra. I charged a pack of cigarettes for generic cards, two packs for the specialty cards. My card service allowed the inmates to get a handmade card that they could customize for their loved one for a much lower price than the mass-made commercial cards sold at the commissary. Although other inmates also created cards, I was the only one who provided original drawings and poems. The others usually traced cartoon characters onto a card and left the inside blank. Had I not been a Latin King, my little card business would probably have been frowned upon and most likely stopped.

What made me the designated card supplier was that I extended credit. I did not demand payment upon delivery and would often allow one or two commissary days to go by before collecting payment. For those inmates not fortunate enough to have an outside cash supplier, this was the way to go. I also gave the cards that didn't sell away to these same individuals. The Latin Kings, however, had first crack at any cards I made or gave away.

When I wasn't making cards or writing poetry, I read nonfiction books, especially autobiographies, and books that taught me something new about the world such as *An Original Man: The Life and Times of Elijah Muhammad*, *Chariots of the Gods*, and *Uncle Tom's Cabin*.

All Shawnee inmates were given the choice to go to school or take a daily job within the prison. The daily jobs included kitchen duties, floor detail, yard detail, laundry, and more. For the most part, inmates chose work details instead of school. They worked during the day or night, depending on their assigned duties, and hit the weight pile during gym or yard time. I chose to go to school. I had no intention of ever coming back to the penitentiary, so I took the opportunity the State of Illinois Department of Corrections offered me to get educated in some form or another.

At Shawnee I learned how to operate various computer software programs. I learned how to type and how to use WordPerfect and Lotus 1-2-3. In the evening I would go to the yard and read or have my daily conversation with Shawnee's leader of the Latin Kings.

King Leo was fifty-two years old. He had been in jail going on twenty years, most of which he had served at a maximum-security prison. His many years of good behavior had earned him a transfer to a medium-security facility. The prison personnel knew very well that Leo was the Latin Kings' highest-ranking officer at Shawnee and respected him as such. Leo was Puerto Rican, about five-four, and weighed about one hundred and fifty pounds. Although he was a small man, Leo, a former Marine and Vietnam vet, was serving a life sentence for killing two men with his bare hands. His crimes got him recruited by the Latin Kings while in the penitentiary. Leo had no possibility of parole.

By the end of my first month at Shawnee, Leo had taken me under his wing. He valued the fact that I was using my jail time to grow as a person intellectually, and that I had no desire to become muscle-bound. Leo enjoyed reading the poetry I wrote for myself, which was a far cry from the trite crap I put on cards. The poetry I wrote for myself was dark and filled with pain and anger. Even love poems became dark when I expressed my true thoughts.

Roses are red,
But only when soaked by the blood of a victim of some
    desire.
Of the desire to be in the spotlight.
Roses are red,
But only when painted by the blood spilled for freedom
    of inconspicuous needs.
Of the need to spread the wings of freedom and fly away.
Roses are red,

When beating and being beaten is a passion.
Of the feeling that the passion received is deserved.
Roses are red,
When all is right and nothing is wrong.
When the blood spilled by all colors is for the assurance
    of attention.
For whatever it takes,
Roses are red.

Leo advised me to continue writing this way, as it would heal a lot of the pain and anger I carried around within me. With King Leo's support, I was able to explore this outlet for my feelings, and for the first time I connected my writing and drawing with my inner sense of peace.

"Look at those brothers over there," Leo told me one day, looking in the direction of the weight pile. "All of them short-timers, a couple of years and they're back on the street. *Son pendejos, mi pana* (They are idiots, my partner). *En ves de enfuerzar sus mentes, enfuerzan sus cuerpos* (Instead of strengthening their minds, they strengthen their bodies). They leave just as stupid as they came in, only stronger." Leo turned to face me. "Most of them will come back, some of them as lifers like me. *No seas haci de pendejo* (Don't be an idiot like that)," he concluded. I understood, and I stayed on the course I had chosen to reinvent myself.

After four months into my stay at Shawnee, I got a letter from Lilly with surprising news. Lilly had not been able to make the trip to Shawnee to visit me and could not afford constant collect phone calls since she was no longer dealing, but we wrote to each other regularly. In this particular letter, Lilly announced that she had found my mother and sisters and that she had become my mother's friend and companion. The news took me by complete surprise. Sadly, I had not even thought about my mother or sisters in quite some time. Even then, although I began to wonder how they were and if Pedro was there with them, the desire to see them never surfaced.

My mother had returned to Chicago from Puerto Rico about two months after I was convicted, and moved near Humboldt Park. There, one of my sisters began to date a Latin King. She coincidentally ended up at the apartment of a Queen who showed her pictures of the old crew from Kedzie and Armitage Avenue. My sister recognized me in several pictures and began asking for me and about me. Shortly after, somebody introduced her to Lilly, who filled her in on where I was and why I was there. There wasn't a flood of mail between us trying to make up for lost time. The extent of our communication consisted of Lilly writing, "your mother and sisters said this," and me writing back, "tell them I said this." "Your mother asked how you are doing," Lilly would write. "Tell them I'm fine," I would respond. "Your sisters send hugs and kisses," Lilly wrote. "Give hugs and kisses to my sisters," I'd respond. I guess the separation had been too long for any of us to know where to begin. Or maybe we just didn't care. From my end, I anticipated a "How are you, my son?" letter that never arrived. I was clueless how to open a line of communication with my own family. I was happy that they were OK. I was happy to know that my mother had finally left Pedro, my stepfather, who had brutally beaten me. Otherwise, nothing changed; they were still missing pieces from my life.

AFTER SIX MONTHS of my stay at Shawnee, the tensest moment of my incarceration took place. Guards caught a Latin King called Ghost with a homosexual in his cell. The fact that they were each given a week of solitary confinement made it obvious they were doing something other than just visiting. Although homosexual activity is common inside prison walls, for a Latin King, getting caught participating in a homosexual act is a death sentence. Most inmates and prison officials knew this about the Latin Kings. It was also a known fact throughout Shawnee that eventually the King they caught would be dealt with. We, in turn, tried to play down the incident and denied that the brother had been caught in a sexual act.

While Ghost did his solitary time, the rest of us decided his fate. The overwhelming opinion was that we had to take him out in order to restore respect for the Latin Kings, which he had destroyed by getting caught with a homosexual. One of us, maybe two, would face a murder rap for doing so, but would forever live in prison comfort as an elite member of the Latin Kings. There was no doubt that whatever maximum-security prison the killer ended up at, other King inmates there would show him ultimate respect for restoring the pride and honor of the Latin Kings. This was a matter of who was willing to take the honor of spending the rest of his life in jail. Surprisingly, many volunteered. Whether their hearts were really in it, I will never know, but Leo felt differently.

All this talk took place in the yard. Leo asked me to walk with him. As we walked and discussed the situation, the other Kings spread out into the weight pile and into the basketball and handball courts. Leo was not at all impressed by the show of hands willing to do the job. He thought that most of those Kings volunteered only to make themselves look tougher. He could not believe that so many guys were willing to spend the rest of their

lives in jail over some homosexual bullshit. He asked my opinion. I thought that if we did not assert discipline, the Latin Kings
would be sending a message that the gang and homosexuality
went hand in hand. This reputation would stay with the Kings at
Shawnee long after we were gone, I told Leo. Leo said he understood, but he did not want to be responsible for another Latin
King brother spending the rest of his life in jail. "If you can keep
that from happening, go for it," Leo told me. "Cool, brother.
Nobody knows about this decision but you and me," I responded.
We both lit up cigarettes as we walked back toward the bench
where we had been sitting. Leo motioned to a couple of Kings
to join us. "Tell all the brothers to chill until we hear Ghost's side
of the story, then we'll decide," Leo told them. Minutes later, it
was time to return to our cells.

The homosexual involved in the incident requested authori-
ties to keep him in solitary—he feared the Latin Kings would take
him out. Ghost could have requested the same thing, but he chose
not to. When he was released from solitary, we met in the yard
to hear his side. Ghost begged the Kings for forgiveness and
assured us that he had not committed a sex act. Most of the
Kings present expressed their feelings of disbelief and contempt
for Ghost's actions, and they let him know in no uncertain terms
that they thought he was bullshitting.

Bear defended Ghost. Bear was not just the biggest Latin
King; he was one of the biggest inmates at Shawnee. Because
Bear was in his thirties and a veteran of the prison system, I
thought we could entrust him with the task of disciplining
Ghost without anyone else knowing. "You brothers better not
touch this brother," Bear said as he stood next to Ghost. "You
all don't know this brother like I do; he's righteous." At Bear's

urging, Ghost began walking away from us with him. I went with them and asked Ghost to stay to himself, away from the other Latin Kings, until tempers cooled off. "Hang out with this brother, Bear," I told Bear as I looked Ghost in the eyes. "You'll be alright," I assured Ghost. "This brother is righteous, listen to him," Bear told Ghost as he put his massive hand on my shoulder.

Over the next few days, instead of coming to the yard, Ghost went to the gym. Bear went with him on some days and came out with us on others. Often he would spend a little time in the gym with Ghost before coming out to the yard with us. Throughout this time, Bear made it clear to the rest of the Kings that he was on Ghost's side and would fight along with him. Leo and I advised the other Kings to let it be for a while. That's all it took to keep the majority of the Kings away from Ghost and for Bear to gain Ghost's trust and confidence.

A week to the day after Ghost's release from solitary, it was time for Latin King discipline to take place as King Leo and I had planned. As always, Bear went to the gym's weight pile with Ghost. The weight pile in the gym was located at the far left end where the basketball/volleyball floor ended. On this day, the wall of inmates watching the games going on and waiting to play was denser than usual, thereby obstructing the view of the guards, who stood by the gym's inside entrance. Ghost prepared himself to do a chest-press exercise. Bear stood at the end of the bench to serve as a spotter. When Bear observed Ghost tensing up to lift the barbell, he picked up a twenty-five-pound plate and dropped it on Ghost's head. Ghost was knocked out cold, so there was no screaming or sudden inmate reaction to alert the guards to what had happened. Bear worked his way out of the gym and out into the yard as he always did.

The inmates in and around the weight pile slowly and inconspicuously walked away. The guards did not find Ghost until it was almost time for the inmates to head back to their cells. Ghost survived the attack. He didn't say who had hit him. It took over a hundred stitches to close the wound in his head. Ghost chose to spend the rest of his time under protective solitary confinement. After the incident, Shawnee was in lock down for almost a week. Our cells were thoroughly searched on two different occasions during that lockdown. Leo was taken to see the warden and was questioned about the incident. The warden threatened to send Leo to Menard if he didn't disclose information about the attack on Ghost. It was only after Leo made it clear that the Latin Kings did not plan any retribution for Ghost that the warden left Leo alone and the lockdown was terminated. Leo later told me that the administration worried that if the Latin Kings did not inflict justice on one of their own then there might be a riot. He assured the warden that the Latin Kings had disowned Ghost. He was on his own. Nobody was charged with the attack on Ghost. The Latin Kings' respect was restored at Shawnee, and therefore so was the peace.

Two months after the attack on Ghost, I received notice that, due to my good behavior, I was being transferred to Stateville's minimum-security unit, to await placement in a work-release facility. Only Leo knew of my impending transfer until just a few days before the actual date. I turned over all the King merchandise except for two packs of cigarettes to a Latin King in my cell house. I gave all the cards I had left over to Leo. "You're a good brother," Leo said. "You're going to make it." "I hope so, man, I hope so," I responded as we shook hands Latin King–style and embraced. The next day I was off to the Statesville Correctional Center.

BEFORE I WAS convicted and sent to prison, I didn't understand why so many people I knew went in and out of such a terrible place as if there were nothing to it. After my own experience, I realized that going to prison was really nothing to worry about, especially if you were in a gang. Aside from child predators, abusers, and some rapists, most inmates can do time relatively easily if they play by the rules. The rules are very simple. Don't fuck with nobody and nobody will fuck with you, and if someone does fuck with you, take matters into your own hands. There is nowhere to run and nowhere to hide, so you have to stand up and be counted. The easiest and safest way to do that is to align yourself with a gang. Latino inmates in Illinois with no gang affiliation align themselves with the Latin Kings, Latin Disciples, Spanish Cobras, or one of their Latin affiliates. Blacks align themselves with the Black Gangster Disciples or the Vice Lords. Whites run with the North Siders or the Aryan Nation. Protection from victimization is available for all who are willing to live and possibly die for a cause.

Although the freedom to do the simplest things on your own schedule is no longer an option, little else is missing from life in prison. Drugs, alcohol (homemade), and sex (usually homosexual, but heterosexual sex is possible with the right connections) are readily available. And of course you get three meals a day and free medical and dental care. The only deterrent I found for coming back was convincing myself that I didn't have to be there to begin with. I did just that.

I used my prison time to gain the self-confidence and common sense I had been without for so long. I took advantage of the educational programs offered by the Illinois Department of Corrections and prepared myself for my release back into the world. I guess that if my plans had been to return to gang society and climb up the leadership ladder, then my best bet would have been to hit the weight pile and build up my body to endure the punishment that lay in store. But I planned on never again being part of any correctional system. I went through a process where I thought about and regretted everything I had been involved with in the past. I started to piece together memories and recollections that made me aware that I should have been, and still could be, a different person. I realized that in order to achieve this, it was in my best interest to strengthen my mind.

THE ADVICE LEO gave me that day in the yard at Shawnee has made me wonder over the years why inmates with short sentences are not required to successfully complete some kind of educational goal as a condition of their release. I, for one, am convinced that if I had not taken it upon myself to gain even a minimal amount of education while incarcerated, I probably would have returned to gang society instead of integrating myself into normal society. The fact remains, however, that I may not have had the opportunity to do my time in peace and on my own terms if I hadn't been a member of the Latin Kings.

8

Almost Free

STATESVILLE MINIMUM-SECURITY facility was a work camp for inmates who were either waiting to go on work release or at a very low risk of escaping. At Statesville, I woke up at five-thirty in the morning, ate breakfast, and then hit the road with the streets and parks clean-up crew. It was hard work, but that didn't bother me as much as being seen on the side of the road, with a Department of Corrections jumpsuit on, picking up garbage. Citizens drove past us, staring at us, laughing at us, scared of us. It was a humbling experience. "This isn't for me, this isn't for me," I kept saying to myself. While other inmates liked the idea of looking passersby in the eyes and making facial expressions in an attempt to make them nervous, I chose to give my back to onlookers. I was not at all proud to be out there, nor did I have anything to prove to any of these strangers.

Since Statesville is located just a couple of hours' drive from Chicago, Lilly was able to visit me there. The facilities were somewhat comfortable. Although there were two inmates to a room, the beds sat across from each other as opposed to the customary bunk bed setup. The room was a bit more spacious than your typical prison cell. Just about every inmate at Statesville

was a step away from freedom; therefore the atmosphere was
very relaxed, even with the presence of many gangbangers. In
fact, I was surprised how well rival gang members got along at
Statesville.

There was a Latin King named Cuco who shared a room with
a Latin Disciple. Cuco's roommate was in fact a menace and an
enemy to the Kings of his section. The vision of freedom such a
short distance away made even this odd couple of roommates see
the best in each other. They got along so well that Cuco actually
set the Disciple up with his sister-in-law. This action would have
gotten Cuco seriously hurt in just about any other Illinois correctional facility. It didn't help that Cuco's sister-in-law was an
incredibly attractive woman. There was certainly talk among the
Latin Kings regarding Cuco's actions and what should be done
about him, but not one was willing to risk losing his chance at
freedom over it. A few, however, did swear to take care of Cuco
once they got out onto the streets.

I spent most of my evenings playing cards with and talking to
older Latin King brothers. I gathered in particular with five older
inmates, all in their forties and fifties, who had been Latin Kings
from the beginning. They felt bitterness over what the Latin Kings
had become—street thugs. They cursed the current social status
of the Latin Kings and blamed the new generation of Kings for
the social ills that afflicted the Puerto Rican community in
Chicago. They did acknowledge, however, that it was the greed
and criminal mind-set of a few of their comrades that had set the
Latin Kings in this direction. They acknowledged that the drug
dealing and weapons stockpiling had begun during their generation, but in the same breath they quickly clarified that even those
few misdirected brothers never intended that the criminal activi-

ties of the Latin Kings be directed at other Puerto Ricans. They
put the responsibility of the Latino-against-Latino gang wars on
the ignorance and lack of education of the new generation. Not
surprisingly, these older Kings shied away from ones like Cuco,
cocky brothers who they felt had no sense of loyalty. They tried
to take brothers like me under their wing and give them advice.

From these men I received daily advice on how to keep myself
from being a repeat offender. They bombarded me with the con-
cept of self-improvement through education. They felt that they
had sacrificed their futures to ensure that future Puerto Rican
generations could take advantage of opportunities to succeed
without fear of harassment due to their race. It angered them to
see so many brothers choose to be criminal statistics rather than
become educated individuals who could help with the prosperity
of the Puerto Rican community. All their rhetoric made a lot of
sense, but I felt compelled to question why all the leaders of the
Latin Kings were incarcerated and running a criminal empire
from the inside. Repeatedly they pointed out that it was my
choice, not anybody else's, whether I continued to be a convict
or not. They explained that I must be a leader, not a follower,
and that meant knowing which leader to follow and what leader
to dethrone. The present state of the Latin Kings was one where
all the leadership was based on fear, not on intelligence. Of all
the times I had heard the "be a leader, not a follower" phrase
spoken, this was the only time it actually made any sense to me.

It became clear to me that for all the years I had used violence as a way to be accepted, I was following blindly. I realized
that if I were really tough, if I were a real King of the Latin people, I would have rebelled and stood up against the destruction
our so-called leaders inflict on our neighborhoods. Of course, I

also realized that I would probably never have joined the Kings had it not been for the abuse I had suffered at home. In any case, the whys and how comes that revolved inside my mind were beginning to get answers.

I looked into the faces of these older brothers and saw their regret for allowing themselves to follow the thankless paths they had taken. I saw a deep sadness in their eyes that told all who cared to see how all the sacrifices they had made were all for nothing. Their expressions clearly said that if they had to do it all over again, they wouldn't. Suddenly I started to recognize this same regret whenever I looked in the mirror.

Because these men were veterans of the Illinois correctional system, they had many connections that allowed them to know, do, and have things most inmates didn't. They knew which guards were on the Latin King's payroll, where they were stationed, and their work shifts. It turned out that two guards employed by the Latin Kings routinely worked the visiting room on days I was allowed to have visits. The older Kings arranged it so that I could have sex with Lilly during visitation in exchange for her carrying drugs into the prison for the Kings. She would also have to bring along a family member of one of the other Kings for visitation.

The visiting area at the Statesville work camp did not have partitions separating inmates from their visitors. Inmates sat at tables across from their visitors. Although holding hands across the top of the table, and hello and good-bye hugs and kisses, were routinely allowed, all other touching was prohibited.

On Lilly's first visit, she did not have to bring in any drugs because of the short notice. That day Lilly surprised me by showing up with my mother. My heart fell into my stomach when I saw her. I fought tears as I stared into the eyes of the person I blamed for all my tragic memories. There in front of me stood the woman who gave birth to me and then allowed me to live a life filled with abuse. After a few seconds of silence, we hugged each other tightly.

I thought about how she left me at age four in the care of an aunt whose eighteen-year-old son raped me. I thought about how she allowed the men who came into her life to physically abuse me. How she left me in the care of her drug-dealing stepson when she returned to Puerto Rico with my stepfather. And how she left me to fend for myself on the streets of Chicago at age 13. I realized that I had no memory of her ever telling me she loved me.

When we hugged, I didn't want to let her go. I wanted to be cradled and caressed. I wanted to hear her say that she loved me, that she missed me, and that she was sorry for what she had allowed my life to become. The hug lasted forever, but not a word was spoken.

After the guard broke up our long hello, we walked to a table and sat across from each other. After only a few minutes of staring at my mother, I felt indifferent about seeing her again. It was as if nothing significant had happened in my life. I didn't feel that we had a lot of catching up to do or that I never wanted her to leave my life again. To the contrary, I wished she had stayed in Puerto Rico and never found out how my parentless life had turned out.

I was at a loss for words throughout that visit. I just sat there nodding in agreement to whatever Lilly said. I waited patiently for my mother to declare her love for me. She updated me on the current state of various members of my family. She told me that she had left Pedro and returned to Chicago to get away from all his ranting and raving. Hearing that, I found myself phasing out her words. What she talked about from then on were things that I couldn't have cared less about. I wanted to hear why she let things happen to me the way she did and why she hadn't protected me. Ever. I wanted to know why she didn't decide to leave Pedro's ranting and raving years ago when he had beat me bloody or when he had pointed a gun at me with the intention of killing me. I wanted to hear her apologize to me and tell me that she wanted to explore the mother–son relationship we never had a chance to have. I wanted her to look me in the eyes and tell me she loved me. It never happened.

Because of my mother's presence, I passed up the chance to have sex with Lilly. After the visit was over it felt as if my mother had never existed. I still felt the same void I had felt since I was eleven or twelve years old. I had this overwhelming need to know why I was dispensable to my own mother. I went to my room and cried. I lay there wondering what I had done that was so wrong that it had caused me to lose my mother. For one brief moment, as I lay there, I felt like getting under the bed to hide from the terror I imagined was awaiting me, just as I had done to escape beatings as a child.

My mother continued to come with Lilly on just about every visitation day. She never asked me about what had transpired in my life after she sent me to live with her drug-dealing stepson. Maybe it was because Lilly had told her everything already. Maybe it hurt her too much to think about or accept that she was responsible for how my life had turned out. Or maybe she had absolutely no clue or didn't care. I kept my desire for answers to myself; it was how I chose to deal with it. Life went on.

From the second visit on, Lilly and I had sex on every visitation day. My mother, or whoever else accompanied her, would wait at the table while we went and took care of business. Lilly would go into the men's or women's bathroom, whichever was available, and I would join her a few minutes later. She would go into an empty stall and ready herself for sex while she waited for me. Lilly made sure to wear dresses or skirts on visitation day so that the task of getting ready for sex would be an easy one. A couple of minutes after Lilly went into the bathroom, I would ask the designated guard if I could go to the bathroom. He would then escort me there and wait outside for my return. It was common knowledge to all inmates and their visitors what was going on, and they all played along. Failure to play along would probably have resulted in some form of repercussion, most likely to a family member on the outside.

Reconnecting with my mother as a prison inmate and not as a successful member of society bothered me, but for only a split second. In a way, I was happy that she found me there so that she could bear witness to what she had created. Unfortunately, I don't think she saw it that way. She didn't seem to be affected by the knowledge that her son was a convicted criminal. The fact that the mother I had not seen in years sat alone at a table inside a prison while I had sex in a bathroom stall told the story of our present and future relationship. I guess that, from my point of view, my mother had not earned enough of my respect to justify my choosing to sit with her over my sexual pleasure. I wondered which one of us would open the dialogue that would lead to at least a respectful relationship, if not a loving one. Apparently neither of us found it necessary.

Lilly mostly brought in drugs that were used for selling within Statesville. On several occasions, however, she brought in cocaine to pay off guards. In fact, because it was powdered, cocaine was the easiest drug to transport into Statesville, but she also brought heroin on several occasions. Lilly's method of transporting the drugs was to hide them in her vagina. At the entrance of the visitation room, guards routinely patted down visitors and searched their purses, but they never gave Lilly a strip or body cavity search. This method of transporting drugs, coupled with paying off the guards, made the exchanges easy. I passed the drugs in turn to the older Kings, who completed the transport. The guards being either members of the Latin Kings or an affiliated gang, or being paid off, made this seemingly risky task simply routine. As for Lilly, after the first time, she began to enjoy the sexual aspect of my retrieving the packages.

I was amazed and turned on by how much Lilly could fit inside her vagina. The process of retrieving the drugs from inside her made for some incredible sex afterward. In fact, the sex Lilly and I had at Statesville was the most passionate we had had without the assistance of being high. Lilly didn't mind being a mule. We actually started to make a little bit of money on our own on the outside by charging other inmates to bring in their drugs. Lilly would meet associates of inmates at a destination of her choice and would collect the money and drugs to be transported. The packages were always small, but we still charged fifty dollars for up to a dime of marijuana, a hundred dollars for up to an eighth of an ounce of cocaine, and two hundred dollars for up to an eighth of heroin. On the several occasions when she couldn't bring in everything herself, Lilly brought a friend, who would carry in the remainder. We justified our prices by playing on the risk factor.

It is common for women to do for their men in jail what Lilly did for me. For the most part, it gives them an adrenaline rush from living dangerously. For many, however, being a mule and daring to have sex with an inmate can be a career coup that earns them respect within gang society. In fact, women lucky enough to be involved with a leader could have more power on the street than any foot soldier and sometimes even street leaders. Lilly, on the other hand, had nothing to gain from transporting drugs for me other than knowing that I would be safer in prison because of her acts. Lilly, a veteran of the mule profession, knew that for every woman who didn't want to carry drugs for a known gang-banger, there were ten who did. Arranged sexual encounters were almost always reserved for these women. Lilly knew that, too.

My time at Statesville seemed like not doing jail time at all. It was easy to see why very few people feared incarceration. After about two and half months at the Statesville work camp, I was transferred to a work release center in Chicago.

9

Work Release

IN EARLY FALL I was taken by van to a work release center on Roosevelt and Ashland Avenues in Chicago. I wasn't handcuffed on the ride there, and I wore street clothes that Lilly had brought me for the occasion. At the work release center, I was far enough away from the neighborhood to feel safe, but close enough to where I felt like I was back in the 'hood. That, along with the cold weather beginning to set in, made the temptations of street life easy to ignore.

At the work release center, I was to start the process of integrating myself back into society as a law-abiding citizen. I wore street clothes all the time and was known by my name instead of by a prison number. I was trusted to go out in public on my own to seek employment and to attend Narcotics Anonymous (NA) meetings, which I was mandated to attend.

The NA meetings were held at St. Elizabeth Hospital, in what was once Spanish Lords' 'hood, and also where I had originally been introduced to gang involvement. The Lords and the Spanish Cobras violently shared the Tuley School area. The Spanish Lords could no longer hang out at Tuley as safely as they once had. From the work release center, I took a bus that headed north on Ashland Avenue. I got off on Chicago Avenue and took the bus there to Western Avenue. From there I would take the Western Avenue bus to Hirsch Street, where I got off and walked to the NA meeting. Although this route seemed long and complicated, it allowed for the least chance of running into any gangbangers. Once I got off the bus to walk to the hospital, I always felt nervous about the possibility of running into any members of the Cobras, or even the Lords, for that matter. Time and time again, I walked past the mouth of the alley where Afro had been gunned down when I was getting my first taste of gang life at age twelve. Afro was a sixteen-year-old member of the Spanish Lords, shot to death by the Spanish Cobras as he went to buy beer for some other kids and me. We waited for him sitting on the steps of a closed-in porch about fifty feet away from where the shooting took place. I could have avoided walking past there now, but for some reason I didn't. Each time, I looked down into the alley and saw the faded spray-painted "R.I.P. Afro" on the very spot where he had died. I saw myself staring down at Afro's bloodied body, feeling nothing. I saw myself running toward the end, trying to get home before the police showed up. I realized now that having to walk past there, where all the madness of my past had started, was by far more therapeutic than the NA meetings. I also began to realize how lucky I was to have avoided Afro's fate.

A FORMER LATIN King with indirect ties to my past conducted the NA meetings. Although he didn't remember ever meeting me, he told me he knew many Kings and Queens from the Kedzie and Armitage (KA) area, including Loco, then leader of the KA Latin Kings; Loca, the older woman who took me as a lover and whose son died in my arms; and even Morena, the murdered Latin

Queen who cared enough to show me how to survive on the streets, even if that meant being a ruthless gangbanger. Having him as my counselor allowed me to go to St. Elizabeth, have him sign my participation form, and then leave to go see Lilly without actually attending the meeting.

Lilly now lived on Damen and Division with a friend and her boyfriend. She had had a falling-out with Loca while I was in jail and had stopped working for her. Because of that, Lilly lost her apartment, so she sold everything except the bed and moved in with a friend. Lilly would often be waiting for me outside St. Elizabeth's when I arrived there. Lilly's roommates were watching television and getting high on just about every visit. To avoid the temptation of joining them, I locked myself in Lilly's bedroom and had sex with her. In essence, my visits to Lilly's were like conjugal visits. I would arrive, we'd go into her room and have sex, and then I would leave. We never said very much to each other.

DURING MY THIRD week at the work release center, one of the counselors gave me some information regarding temporary data entry positions at the University of Illinois at Chicago. He thought that my brief employment at the University of Chicago and the computer skills I had gained at Shawnee made me a prime candidate for the job. They would be accepting applications that upcoming Monday. The counselor had already taken the liberty of making arrangements for me to be there. "Call your people and tell them to bring you a shirt and tie and some good slacks," the counselor advised as he handed me his office phone. I called Lilly and told her what the counselor said. That weekend she showed up at the work release center with a black two-piece suit, a white shirt, and a tie with black and blue designs on it. She also brought me a pair of dress shoes and socks to go along with the clothes. The clothes and shoes fit perfectly; either it was a sign of good things to come, or Lilly knew me a lot more that I had imagined.

Monday I left the center dressed as I had never dressed before in my life. I felt uncomfortable, yet confident and mature. What I liked most about my attire were the looks of approval and respect I got from the passengers on the bus I took. I didn't see the customary looks of fear and nervousness. People just looked my way and smiled politely, some even said, "Good morning." As I approached an empty seat next to an older woman, she moved her bag away from the seat to make room for me instead of further occupying it, as I was used to people doing. I sat next to her and said thank you. "It's quite all right. Are you having a good morning?" the lady said. "Yes, I am," I responded. I didn't know what to make of all the politeness directed my way. I'm sure the lady would have wanted to have a brief conversation based on absolutely nothing to help kill time until she reached her destination, but I sat there quietly. I began to think about how she, and the rest of the passengers on that bus, would react if they found out that I was a convicted felon. I knew that the nice clean suit made all the difference in how they reacted. "Have a nice day," the lady said as I got up and started for the exit. "You, too. Thank you," I responded.

I will never forget that day. The reaction from the other passengers on that bus still makes me smile and helps me keep my priorities in order. Although I'm well aware that some of the world's biggest felons wear suits on a daily basis, I'm still satisfied with not projecting a fear of violence upon those around me.

I arrived at the University of Illinois at Chicago's employment office about twenty minutes before the appointed time. The receptionist gave me the application so I could fill it out while I waited. This would be the first time in my life that I actually completed a job application on my own. Loca's sister had filled out most of the application for the University of Chicago job I once had. I had never realized before how tough it was to write about myself, especially when I had very little information of positive substance to provide.

I became extremely nervous as I glanced down the application. When I got to the education portion, I began to doubt myself. Had it not been for the possibility of being taken out of the work release program and sent back to prison, I probably would have walked out without completing the application. The previous employment section further increased my self-doubt. Here I was, a man in perfect physical condition, in his twenties, and all the work experience I could account for was a year at the University of Chicago. It didn't help that the reason for leaving was "I quit." Then came the most embarrassing and anxiety-building question on the application. Have you ever been convicted of a felony? If yes, explain.

That question blew my mind. I slumped in my chair and just stared at it. Never in my wildest dreams did I think that I would have to share the fact that I was a convicted felon with the rest of the world. I stared at the "If yes, explain," and saw a clear reason why they would never hire me if I checked this. But I also knew that the address I provided as my place of residence was the work release center, and I would surely be caught in a lie if I chose to answer "no." As far as I was concerned, the consequence of choosing either was that I would not be considered for a job. Answering yes meant that the person reviewing the application would look at me and see a criminal instead of an applicant. The date of the conviction would alert them that I was on work release or on parole. Either way, they would know that I was the property of the Illinois correctional system. "You can go in now," said the receptionist, waking me up from my nervous daydream. I quickly checked the "No" box of the felony question, signed the application, and handed it to her.

I felt so humiliated looking at a work application and not having anything positive to put on it. I was incredibly embarrassed to be in my twenties and have no work experience or education other than a G.E.D. In fact, had I shared the life experiences that the application sought to discover, I would have painted the picture of a good-for-nothing bum. Up until then my only major accomplishment was straightening out my thought process via incarceration.

I have never forgotten the shame I felt that day, just as I'll never forget that at twenty-something I was elated to land a six-dollar-an-hour job. (Each and every time I fill out or see a job application I feel the same way I felt that day, especially when I read that question that still sends chills up my spine: "Have you ever been convicted of a felony?" I still check "no.")

The receptionist took the application and led me to a room that held about eight computers. She instructed me to sit wherever I wanted and wait for someone to come in and see me. In the next fifteen minutes, five other individuals joined me in that room. Then a woman came in, closed the door behind her, and announced herself as the test administrator. She explained that we would be taking several tests we needed to pass in order to be considered for the data entry position. We would be taking a reading and comprehension test, an alphanumeric code memory test, and a typing speed test. We had to score ninety percent or higher on the first two tests and had to accurately type at least twenty-five words per minute. The computer we were taking the tests on would tell us that we passed or failed at the end of each test. The woman advised us that, if we failed one, to continue and take the others, and that an opportunity to retake the test we had failed would be given at another date.

I passed all three tests and was surprised that I got a perfect score on the reading and comprehension portion. I stared at the computer screen, looking at my passing scores with a wicked grin on my face and a feeling of superiority. Even if I wasn't hired, I would definitely leave UIC feeling that I had accomplished something. Only two other applicants passed all three tests. The three that didn't pass were dismissed, and the rest of us were told to report to the admissions and records office the next day at eight in the morning. We were advised to arrive at least fifteen minutes early and to bring identification with us.

I left the UIC employment office feeling happier than I had ever felt in my life. The six dollars and twenty-five cents an hour this temporary position paid represented one of my greatest accomplishments. I walked toward the bus stop in a fantasy world built on the good things to come. At the center I immediately announced, "I got the job, I got the job," when I saw the counselor who had told me about the position. He shook my hand, congratulated me, and asked when I would start. I told him that I would start work the next day. As I spoke, it dawned on me; I had no means of identification.

"Oh, shit, man," I said as I sat on a chair in the office. A sudden feeling of doom engulfed me. I began to get the feeling that I had been put on this earth to suffer failure after failure, with only teasers for happiness. "What's wrong?" the counselor asked.

"They want me to show up with IDs tomorrow," I said, "and I don't have any." "Come on, let's go get you some IDs," the counselor said as he put some files away and got up from behind his desk. He pulled my file from a cabinet and off we went.

The counselor took me to get a State of Illinois picture ID and a social security card. That's all the identification I needed to present at UIC. On the ride to and from getting the IDs, the counselor explained the rules that came along with being an employed inmate at the work release center. He told me that I would have to sign over my check to the center every payday. They would provide transportation and lunch money until my first paycheck, and then I would have to pay my own way. He also told me that a small amount would be taken from my paycheck as payment for room and board. Also, an allowance would be granted to me for clothes and other personal items. The remainder of my pay would be put into a savings account that would be given to me in full upon my successful completion of the work release program. This procedure was set up to teach me the responsibility of taking care of my finances and myself. I had no problem with the rules; I was just eager to start a new life.

On Monday, I showed up at UIC confident that I would do a good job. I showed up at seven-thirty in the morning and waited for the woman who would be my new supervisor to arrive. While I waited, I filled out a W-4 and had copies of my IDs made. When the supervisor arrived, I was all ready to go. While the other two applicants waited for their paperwork, I had already started training for the job at hand.

My job was to key student grades into the university database. It was a simple procedure. All I had to do was call up the student record by ID number, fill in the blanks with a letter grade for the respective class, and hit the enter key to update the record. I caught on quickly and did a good, efficient job. Overtime was available, so I worked ten hours a day for the first two weeks. I loved my job at UIC and did not look forward to the end of this temporary assignment.

AT THE CENTER, the distractions were minimized to the point where they became nonexistent to me. While others planned on how to get high, or get laid, I planned out my next day of work. I got to the center from work, showered, ate, and prepared myself for the next day. When I didn't work overtime, I would go to NA meetings in order to see Lilly for my sexual fix.

I wasn't doing any drugs, and I really didn't want to. I saw several guys sent back to the penitentiary because they couldn't fight that temptation. They got caught in a crack house just days after they arrived at the center. They were supposed to be out looking for work. That the crack house was just several blocks away from the center, and that it was raided on the day these guys had decided to go there, was a sign of destiny to me. It made me think hard about the actions I took when I was allowed to roam the streets. I considered that it was a privilege that could be taken away from me at any moment, and I treated it as such. My only vulnerability was my desire for sex. I had no second thoughts about going to be with Lilly when I should have been at the NA meetings.

A few guys at the center came in from the streets noticeably intoxicated and were tested right away. When the results came back positive, Chicago police officers escorted these men to Cook County Jail, where they then waited to be sent back to the penitentiary. I was also tested on several occasions—a standard procedure—and the test always came back negative. Although I knew the results could not be anything other than negative, I was always nervous. Seemed like all the years I spent involved in criminal activity now made me feel guilty even when I was innocent.

Some people thought of me as sort of a goody-two-shoes Latin King around the center, which was just fine by me. Although the jokes flew freely in the presence of many, on a one-on-one basis, many talked to me with respect and asked for advice. I was also asked by one guy to sell him my urine so he could pass a drug test. He had apparently found a way to cheat the system but still required a clean urine specimen. I refused to cooperate with him. I didn't want to do anything that would risk my losing the new freedoms I had gained. I could smell total freedom just ahead in my life, and I lived every day with the intention of gaining it and keeping it. (The guy did pass the test. I guess he found somebody to sell him some urine.)

I had many reasons to keep to myself while I lived at the center. The only casual conversations I routinely pursued were with a man named Kalil. Kalil had been born in Jamaica and raised on the south side of Chicago. He was about ten years my senior, a Muslim, and a member of the El Rukn street gang. The El Rukns were best known for plotting to commit acts of terrorism in the United States for Gadhafi's Libyan government. The FBI raided them and dismantled the alleged plot before any terrorist act had actually taken place. The El Rukns exemplified the power and connections street gangs had been able to acquire.

I enjoyed my conversations with Kalil mainly because of the spiritual terms with which he connected everything. I told him about how I had ended up in prison, and he said it was the hands of Allah that took a hoodlum headed for a certain tragic end and led him to see the truth. Kalil tried to make me understand that everything that had happened was Allah's way of teaching me and opening my eyes to the ways of the world I had been living in. "Think about it, my Latino brother," Kalil said. "Can you deny that the time you spent in jail served as a salvation for your life? Not many brothers can say that, nor can they even begin to think it. Allah works his miracles for those who seek them faithfully." "But I don't believe in or even recognize Allah," I responded. "Call him what you will," Kalil answered. "It's faith that will lead us all to the promised land. As I sit here talking to you, all my questions regarding the path my life suddenly took are being answered. Your journey has just begun, young brother. Just be faithful, even when faith seems not to exist." Of all the conversations I had with people who tried to give me advice on where and how my life should go, Kalil's words were the ones that stuck with me the most.

My nights at the center became restless as I slowly became an everyday working citizen, and continued talking with Kalil. I became obsessed with the idea that the possibility of a fruitful, successful life could be ripped away from me without my realizing it. This idea began to control all my thoughts. I regretted not finishing school. I regretted not staying away from drugs. I regretted joining the Latin Kings. I began to consider hard work and intelligence the only reasons for deserving respect. I no longer bought into the theory that, to be a man, one must be violent and uncaring. I would twist and turn all night, trying to find the reasons why I had fallen into the path I had. I could only fall asleep when I lost myself in the fantasy of a woman there at my side, holding me and understanding me. I got into the habit of conjuring up imaginary relationships with women whose sole reason for existence was to worship me. I have no doubt that every man has done this at least once in his lifetime, but for me, it became something I could not function without.

I CONTINUED TO experiment with the talents I had discovered within myself to put words together and create poetry. Unfortunately, no one understood their meaning except me, so I kept them to myself. I also believed my art should have a clear meaning to all who looked, but I found that not to be true either, so I kept my drawings to myself as well. The more I wrote and drew, the more I realized that my inspiration came from the feelings of anger and desire for love I harbored for my mother. I realized that I could not just sit down and write a poem or draw images without some kind of turmoil running through my head. When I did work without turmoil, it was usually on something I did for someone else, something that was not for my own self-expression. My frustration with no one understanding my work intensified when I showed the art and read the poems to my mother and she just stared into midair, clueless. I though that if anyone would get my meaning, she would.

My mother visited me every week with Lilly, and I hoped the art and poetry would open a dialogue that would allow me to express to her how I felt. I was wrong. I could never find a way to just come out and say the things I wanted to say. I waited eagerly for her to come to me, hold me, caress me, and tell me how much she loved me. I waited with my heart exposed to the elements for her to tell me she was sorry for having neglected me. But as the days came and went, it became obvious that I would never hear those words come out of her mouth. I distanced myself from her emotionally to the point where she didn't exist as a person who radiated love. She became only my mother, the person who gave birth to me, and nothing more.

For some reason, I came to the same conclusions regarding my sisters. Maybe it was because they visited so few times. We had very little to say to each other. One would think that after so many years of separation we would have a lot to say to catch up on one another's lives, but not us. We talked briefly about the circumstances that put me in jail, but only back to the point when I met Lilly. They seemed to have this unspoken feeling that if I had taken better care of myself, if I had been a better person, a real man, then I wouldn't be where I found myself. The unspoken words seemed to express that I had betrayed my own manhood and let the family down. Had I not been at the work release center, I probably would have gone out, gotten drunk, and committed an act of violence against someone in the name of my family. Instead, I secluded myself in my room and wrote this poem:

Unearth the darkness of shadows long past,
of screams and blood and sorrows.
Unveil the nightmares and the fear of sleep.
There you'll find a soul crying to be talked to
and understood, not laughed at and dismissed.
God protects the soul that has faith and knows its
boundaries, but man sets boundaries in the name
of God and distorts the direction of the faithful.
And therefore the faithless, flesh-loving creatures inflict
torture on the already wounded spirit.
As they rejoice at their position in life.
The pain. The agony.
Time stands still and awaits mercy,

but the feeling is forsaken, overlooked, ignored.
The so-called family, friends, all the same,
distant, oblivious, blind.

This was the last poem I would write for a long time. In many ways it still applies to the relationships I have with certain members of my family today.

AFTER SIX MONTHS at the work release center, I was released on parole. The conditions of my parole were simple: stay off drugs, don't commit any crimes, and continue the exemplary behavior I had shown as an inmate. The time I spent at the work release center really helped me get myself together. There, I saw how little freedom meant to so many, and how they wanted it so very much, but for all the wrong reasons. I discovered how easy it was to lose freedom and how much easier it was to keep it. Mostly, I learned that I would never be able to have the meaningful conversations with my mother that I wanted to have. I learned how to block out my desire for her acceptance and think only about me.

The real test of who I was had begun. I would be on my own with no rules or on-the-spot testing to keep me in line. No doubt temptations would come at me from all directions. It was time to really find out what the future had in store for me, and to take the measure of my own strength.

10

New Beginning

I WAS RELEASED from the center on a Friday, at my own request. That gave me a whole weekend to get settled into my new living quarters before going back to work at UIC on Monday. With all the overtime I worked while I was at the center, I had managed to save almost four thousand dollars. I used the money to rent an apartment for Lilly and me, and for a used car to get myself to work and back. I had been promoted to a full-time clerk's position at the Admissions and Records Office and had gotten a raise to seven dollars and fifty-five cents an hour. It certainly wasn't the kind of money I had once made in the cocaine business, but it was mine and the legal system could not take it from me. As far as I was concerned, I was making more money than I had ever made in my life.

That weekend—my first weekend of freedom in two years— I did nothing but stay in the apartment and enjoy the littlest of freedoms that I had once taken for granted. I could watch television any time I wanted, and any channel I wanted. I took a shower, knowing that there would be no naked male bodies there other than mine. I looked out the window, knowing that I could walk the streets whenever I wanted, but I chose to stay in and rejoice in the peacefulness of my freedom.

Monday after work I had to go check in with my parole officer, who told me that I no longer had to attend the NA meetings, but that I could be tested for drugs at any moment without notice. He also told me that my exemplary prison and work release records put me on an honor system with him. We agreed that he wouldn't show up at my work or home if I would show up to my monthly visits with him, and on time, and kept myself clean. He did, however, make it clear to me that if he suspected any wrongdoing on my part, he could, and would, show up at places I wouldn't want him to, and could revoke my parole if he felt it was necessary. I readily agreed with him. I shook his hand firmly and told him that I would be the easiest case he had ever had. I left his office confident that I would see him only once a month, when I went to his office. The rules he had laid out were no-brainers for me—someone set on keeping himself out of trouble and out of jail.

Living with Lilly provided every single temptation I worried about. She still smoked weed laced with cocaine whenever she could. When cocaine was not available, she would smoke plain marijuana. Although I worried that her habit would get me in trouble, the sex we had when she was high was so incredible that I learned to live with the risk.

Lilly had a couple of friends who would come over and get high with her. One of them was a girl named Lisette. Lisette dressed very provocatively. Whether she knew it or not, she was invoking sexual thoughts in the men around her, including myself. Lisette was indeed an attractive girl and seemed to be sort of a tease, but she was also very intelligent and quick-witted. My comments on the way she dressed led us to become very comfortable talking to each other and joking with each other in a sexual way. Lilly realized it was all in good fun so she went right along with it. Lisette and I also had discussions about topics that Lilly and I never even mentioned, much less had conversations about. We discussed the idiotic nature of gangs, and the hypocrisy of people who lived in gang-infested neighborhoods. We shared our thoughts about the need for education and the lack of interest Latinos showed in getting it.

Unbeknownst to Lilly, I looked forward to Lisette's visits. I found myself thinking about Lisette while I had sex with Lilly. I didn't, however, come on to her in any sexual way. It was her conversation I appreciated more than her sexual presence, and I didn't want to ruin that. Lisette satisfed me in a new way—she fed my mind.

On one occasion, when Lilly, Lisette, and I sat in the living room talking, it became apparent that Lilly had told Lisette about our bathroom escapades while I was in jail. I found it surprising yet fascinating that Lisette wished she had had that experience. I tried to get her to comment further about her desire, but she would say no more. I became overwhelmed with sexual desire for Lisette and fantasized about having sex with her as I sat there trying to provoke a sexual conversation.

I persisted and even decided to join them in smoking a joint in order to keep the subject alive. Lisette didn't elaborate any further, but I continued smoking weed. That night led me to rekindle my relationship with marijuana. I shrugged off cocaine and even cocaine-laced joints, but from that night on smoking weed again became a daily thing. The thought of being drug-tested on one of my visits to my parole officer never crossed my mind. I didn't think it would be too hard to get my parole officer to believe I was clean. In fact, even though I was smoking weed I was convinced that I wasn't breaking any rules or deceiving anyone. Not even myself.

My work at UIC continued to excel. I was given more and more responsibilities and was trusted with deadlines and critical duties. I relished the idea that I was an important part of the day-to-day functions of the Admissions and Records Office at UIC. With these new responsibilities came more interactions with highly educated people, and with those on their way to being highly educated. My lack of vocabulary skills made me feel inadequate around them. I usually resorted to joking around and making people laugh in order to mask my lack of education. I also began to seek information about attending classes at UIC, which I could take at no charge because I was a full-time employee.

Lilly worked as a cashier at Woolworth's. She always complained about being underpaid and not having enough money to buy the things she liked. Her solution to that dilemma was to start selling small amounts of cocaine. At first I was indifferent about it, but when I next went to see my parole officer, I left his office with a very uneasy feeling. The fact that I was smoking marijuana daily didn't bother me the way Lilly's cocaine business did. I only smoked marijuana when I was at home. I never smoked before or during work or out in public. In fact, the only people I smoked marijuana with were Lilly and Lisette, and a few others related to them in some way. Lilly's cocaine selling was different in that it attracted strangers who more than likely had some sort of criminal background. My fear of violating parole led me finally to protest Lilly's actions.

Lilly had built a small customer base she felt was safe to do business with. She said we needed the extra money and that she was taking the necessary precautions to make sure she didn't get caught. She did not acknowledge my argument that people were coming to our apartment to get cocaine. Lilly simply dismissed it by saying that the people who came there for cocaine already knew where she lived and would not bring people she didn't know with them.

"Listen, Lilly," I told her, "I'm afraid to go back to jail, and what you are doing can make that happen." "Don't worry, *papi* (daddy)," she responded. "I love you and would never do anything that would take you away from me."

I told Lilly that I had gone through the admissions process at UIC and had been accepted as a student. I told her that I had planned to surprise her with the news over dinner once I actually registered for my first class. I tried to make her understand that I would most likely need all the help I could get to get through college, and that meant having students come over to help me study. "I don't want this shit in our lives, Lilly. Please leave it alone," I begged her. "Oh, so you're going to be a college boy, huh?" Lilly responded. "*Pendejo* (idiot), you're a fuckin' con. Don't think you'll ever be anything else."

Lilly's words shot through me like steel blades that repeatedly stabbed my heart. I retreated to the bedroom and sat at the end of the bed with my head in my hands. For a moment I felt that I was in the loneliest, darkest cell I had ever been in. I imagined the steel bars and the sounds of inmates begging for freedom while blaring, dissonant music drowned out their pleas. I was awakened only by the sound of Lilly's voice in the distance, saying, "He wants to be a college boy—*que pendejo* (what an idiot)." I began to question my decision to attend college. Lilly was right, I would always be nothing more than a convict in the eyes of the world. The only change I could look forward to was being an ex-convict.

I lay back on the bed and stared at the ceiling, half expecting Lilly to come into the room and apologize for what she had said. I guess she didn't feel an apology was in order, because she came in the room only to offer me a hit from her cocaine-laced joint. When I turned it down, she left the room and returned with a regular joint, which she laid on my chest with a cigarette lighter, then left. I lit up the joint and smoked it in the dark, throwing the ashes on the floor. I stared into nowhere and saw prison bars surrounding me every time I blinked my eyes.

When I finished the joint, I went to take a shower. I had a sudden craving for some Puerto Rican food from one of the portable food shacks in Humboldt Park. While I showered, Lilly came in and joined me. She immediately tried to kiss me and began kissing my neck and chest when I rejected her kiss. Lilly worked her way down until she was performing oral sex on me. I watched her. I had always enjoyed every aspect of Lilly's sexual ways, but for the first time since I had met her, this sex wasn't enjoyable. I watched with no feeling of pleasure whatsoever and placed her with all the rest of the women in my life. She was Rosie, the girl who became my lover only to set me up to be killed; she was Maria, the thirty-five-year-old who fucked me when I was thirteen and ruined me sexually forever; she was Blanca, my girlfriend who became pregnant by an prison inmate; and she was my mother.

The sight of Lilly performing oral sex on me as if it were going to make everything better sickened me. I grabbed her violently by her hair and thrust my penis deep in her mouth. Lilly gagged and fell backward, hitting her head on the shower wall. I walked out as she lay on the shower floor holding her head and gagging. By the time she recovered enough to come out of the bathroom, I was gone.

Lilly and I had never had any type of meaningful communication in our relationship. It was based solely on our sexual desires and drug use. As long as we were high, the sex was good; we were OK. After that day, the one thing that had kept us together ceased to exist. I no longer felt any urge to be with her sexually, and really didn't even want to see her face anymore. I began to threaten her with calling the cops if she didn't stop dealing cocaine, and I lost all interest in her sexual needs. When we did have sex, which wasn't often anymore, I fulfilled my own pleasures and left her sometimes literally begging for more attention. Lilly became very upset at my sudden change in attitude, and blamed my desire to go to college. She threatened to leave me if I didn't change and see things her way. When I told her to please go ahead, she took it as sarcasm—that I would be sorry for if I didn't stop. What she didn't realize was that I really *did* want her out of my life. And I wanted her to leave because I was the one paying the rent. It was my security deposit being held.

While my relationship with Lilly deteriorated, my work life blossomed. I treasured and valued the respect and acceptance I received from my colleagues at UIC. After six months of parole, I was given early release. An early termination of parole time was reserved for those individuals who completely rehabilitated themselves, and I was one of them. I had done a good job of keeping my relationship with marijuana hidden. As far as I was concerned, I was rehabilitated. "You proved me wrong," my parole officer said the day he announced that he was terminating my parole. "You're a Latin King. Seems like the only thing they know how to do is to be Latin Kings. Latin Kings have it easy in jail and don't mind going there over and over."

"That's where you are mistaken," I retorted. "I'm not a Latin King; I was never a King." My definition of being a King had changed since the days when I was simply an animal, destroying my own people. If I had truly been a King, I would have stood up against all the drug dealing, gun trafficking, and destruction of our neighborhoods. But that's not what the Latin Kings stood for anymore, and that's why I was never a King.

My parole officer explained that he had put in a request to terminate my parole early after my fourth visit with him. He said that the change in my attire, the way I walked, and the way I expressed myself impressed him so much that he felt he was wasting his time and mine. "Rey, you looked like a punk gangbanger when you first walked into my office six months ago. Now look at you, neatly dressed, walking with your head up, not with a lazy slouch, and you act like you care," he told me as he handed me the parole termination papers to sign. "I got a lot to make up to God," I told him as I signed the papers and handed them back to him. "Oh, so that's it," he responded. "You found religion." "No, not quite," I told him, "I just decided to deal with my God and let everyone else deal with theirs. My God has been waiting for a long time for me to start dealing with him as he has been dealing with me." The parole officer got up and extended his hand to me. "Good luck, Rey. I see good things coming your way," he said. "You have my card. Call me if you need anything." I thanked him as I walked out of his office.

I left feeling the same way I came in. I didn't feel a sudden relief or any burden lifted off my shoulders. To me, being on parole wasn't a burden at all. I thought of it as a mere formality, but a formality I didn't want anyone to know about. Being an ex-con, however, presented me with a burden I would have to carry around for the rest of my life, one that deeply embarrassed me. In the back of my mind lay the fear that if anyone ever found out, then I would certainly end up back where I had started.

THE HOME SITUATION with Lilly got worse by the day. She began to question my sexuality and at one point called me a coward for not standing up to the Kings when they were after me. I stopped sleeping with her altogether and repeatedly asked her to leave. I was still stubborn enough not to pack up and leave myself. In an act of desperation, Lilly got my mother and sisters involved in our personal problems. They began stopping by my apartment to offer advice to Lilly, someone they barely knew. It upset me that, before our problems began, my sisters rarely came by, and now when they did visit, it was to see Lilly, not me. Their lack of concern for my feelings or my opinions pissed me off. After all, they were supposed to be my family, not hers. Their presence made me despise Lilly even more than I had before.

I started working later hours and hanging out with coworkers after work to avoid being around Lilly. I learned how to play racquetball and played almost nightly at the university's courts. During that time my coworkers had no clue about the problems I had at home. I was living two different lives, and I preferred the one I had separate and apart from Lilly.

One Thursday night, Lilly sat in the living room with my sisters and Lisette. When I arrived, she immediately gave me an ultimatum. "This is it, Rey," Lilly said. "If you are not here by seven tomorrow night, you are not going to find anything here except your clothes when you do get here." Looking at Lisette, I asked, "You will still come by and visit, won't you?" Lisette hesitated, then replied, "You're my friend, of course I will." With that I retreated into the bathroom, took a shower, and went straight to bed.

The next day, Friday, I went out with several coworkers for happy hour. I ended up staying out on purpose until just after midnight. All my coworkers had left the bar to go home about nine that evening. I stayed and talked baseball with a couple of guys at the bar and had something to eat while I was there. When I got home I found that Lilly had finally made good on her threat to leave. She moved out and left nothing behind except my clothes. As I walked around the empty apartment, I couldn't help but laugh out loud at the whole predicament. Then a sudden feeling of peace came over me. I felt as if I had been released from prison all over again, only this time it was true freedom.

I left the empty apartment to go look for a department store open all night, where I could possibly buy something comfortable enough to sleep on. As I left the neighborhood, I realized that I had no clue which direction I should drive in order to find a store open that late. I ended up at a pay phone calling Lisette. Lisette acted surprised that I was calling her. When I told her Lilly had left, she told me she didn't know anything about it, but the tone of her voice said something different. Lisette assured me that Lilly wasn't with her—she lived with her mother. I asked if she knew of a store where I could go shopping at that hour of the night and she said no. "I don't care that she left," I told Lisette, "but I would certainly like to find something to place on that floor to sleep on." Lilly paused, then said, "Go home and wait for me. I'll be right over." "It's OK, you don't have to," I responded. I said good night and hung up the phone.

I drove around for about half an hour with no sense of direction, and finally headed home. When I got there, Lisette was parked in front of my building. "Didn't I tell you to come home and wait for me?" she asked as I walked toward her car. She pulled two comforters, a sheet, and a pillow from the back seat and handed them to me. "I've got a couple of joints upstairs. Come on up and smoke one with me," I offered Lisette. She locked her car and followed me up to my apartment.

We lay the comforters on the floor and sat down and smoked a joint. Lisette said she felt guilty for helping me out. She felt that she was betraying one friend, but at the same time she couldn't find the heart not to help another friend. I had no desire to talk about Lilly. That chapter in my life was over. I didn't want to even think about her. I changed the topic of conversation to my desire to attend college. Lisette seemed happy about my decision to do that, and told me that she planned on going to college herself. We lay back on the comforters talking and staring up at the ceiling. Next thing I knew Lisette was fast asleep. I turned off the light and went to sleep myself.

In the morning, Lisette had mixed emotions about having spent the night there with me. One moment she was joking about how people would say that she was the replacement girlfriend, the next she was down about people thinking she was a bitch for being with her friend's ex. She finally concluded that, as long as she knew the truth, it didn't matter who said what. I tried to take

Lisette's mind off her worries by joking that I'd never seen her in a T-shirt and sweatpants and without makeup until that day. I teased her about the torture she was putting my eyes through, and that got her laughing and throwing friendly insults my way as well. We ended up deciding to go shopping for furniture after she went home and changed into the "real" Lisette. After she left, I again walked around the empty apartment, looking for any feeling of regret. I found nothing. I took a shower, got dressed, and waited for Lisette to return.

Lisette took me to a furniture store owned by a friend of her mother's. She told me that, with her there, I would get a hell of a good deal. When we got to the store, I realized as I walked through the door that there was nothing there I could afford. Lisette talked to the saleswoman, who had greeted her by name, and was able to get me approved for credit on a bed and a living room set. Lisette would have to co-sign in order to complete the deal, which she did without hesitation. I was very thankful. I picked out relatively inexpensive bedroom and living room sets and charged them, and then used the cash I had planned to use to take Lisette out to dinner. We waited for the furniture to arrive and then went out. That night Lisette spent the night with me again, only this time we lay on the new bed and did very little sleeping.

My landlord had heard about Lilly's departure, and, during the following week, came by to make sure that everything in the apartment was OK. I told him that I would be living there by myself and that he shouldn't worry about the rent being paid. He surprised me by offering to let me use a stove and refrigerator he had stored in the basement with the agreement that I find a way to bring them up to my apartment, and that I would take good care of them. That weekend a couple of guys from work came by and helped me move the stove and refrigerator upstairs. I thought it was a miracle that, within a week of Lilly's leaving me, I had refurnished the apartment without spending a cent.

Although Lilly made no attempt to contact me, she was in the constant company of my mother and sisters. They would come over and plead with me to go and beg Lilly to come back to me. They told me where I could find her and berated me with the notion that I would never find a woman as good as Lilly. As far as they were concerned, the breakup was my fault and I should therefore find a way to do right by Lilly so she could take me back. Their words only distanced me further from Lilly and the idea of ever taking her back. I grew to hate Lilly.

Three weeks after she left me, Lilly showed up at my door. Lisette and I were watching a movie when there was a knock on the door. Lisette thought it was a friend of hers who was supposed to come by and drop off some weed for us, so she went with me to answer the door. I opened the door looking back at the television and without asking who it was. When I turned toward the door, I saw Lilly standing there, staring right past me and into Lisette's eyes. Without saying a word she lunged past me and scratched Lisette's face. I picked her up and carried her out on my shoulders. "You left, so stay gone," I yelled as I put her down on the sidewalk in front of the building. Lilly was so upset that she lost her balance when I put her down and fell. "I don't want you anymore, Lilly," I said as I turned and walked back to my apartment. Before I got there, my neighbor came up to tell me that Lilly was outside, scratching my car with her keys. I ran back out only to have Lilly attack me. Somebody called the police. They found me holding Lilly face down over the hood of my car so that she couldn't hit me. The police officers put me in handcuffs until they found out what was going on. Lisette came out and told the officers what had happened and my neighbor told them what she had witnessed. After the police were satisfied that Lilly was the aggressor, they took the handcuffs off me and asked Lisette and me if we wanted to press charges. Neither of us wanted to see Lilly go to jail; we just wanted to be left alone. The police instructed Lilly to leave and warned her that she would be arrested if she returned. Lisette and I went back to my apartment where I nursed the scratch on her face and apologized for what had happened. I would see Lilly again only once. We ran into each other at a dance club about a year later, and she slapped me.

The events of that night ruined what had seemed to be a solid, growing relationship between Lisette and me. Lisette was not able to get past Lilly's anger, and we slowly grew apart. A month and a half after the incident, we officially stopped seeing each other. We never talked to each other again.

For the first time in my life, I went through the routine of going to work and then back home to be alone. I paid my own bills, and cared for my own sanity. I had no woman in my life, and I didn't desire one. My goal became to establish a relationship with myself before I tried to share myself with others. I started taking classes at UIC and spent most of my nights studying. Every so often I would visit my mother, but I never felt that I belonged with her. I always had this odd feeling at her place that I was a burden to her. There was this tension in the air, like something needed to be said, but no one was able to take that step to say it. My sisters had all become romantically involved with gang members, so I rarely saw them, by choice. We never got around to talking about the dysfunctionality within our family, to this day. I think we all purposely avoided the subject so as not to deal with issues we might not be able to understand or cope with. This has always made me feel that we are strangers.

The time I spent by myself helped me to slowly deal with the demons in my mind. I began to have the nightmares again. They haunted my sleep. I sometimes went days at a time without sleeping because of the horrors that awaited me when I closed my eyes.

I also still had problems dealing with women. Although I was learning that not all women were out to hurt me, I was still unable to have a relationship with a woman that wasn't sexual.

Beyond that, I still had to watch out for the idiots who didn't know how to leave gang life behind, who therefore concluded that everyone was like them. Trying to get completely out of gang life is like trying to quit an addiction. Just when you think you've got it beat, it seems like temptation comes up everywhere in your life. The fact was that I could still easily have acquired a weapon to carry for "protection." I could still have visited a Latin King in the penitentiary and gotten brothers on the street to back me up if I ever wanted. I did neither. What I did was acknowledge the cowardice of those who felt they needed to prove their manhood through mass violence without provocation, and I moved on. I accepted that the ignorance of gang life was once my way of life, and I refused to ever be so stupid again. But I knew that sooner or later I was bound to be backed into a corner where that addiction that is gang life would again get hold of me, and I knew it could destroy everything I was working so hard to accomplish. I just hoped I would be able to resist that temptation.

I was tested the first time I tried dating a woman who wasn't in some way connected to the 'hood. Her name was Michele, a petite Caucasian girl who had grown up in the Chicago suburb of Addison. Michele and I met in a creative writing class I was taking at UIC; she was drawn to me by what she thought were "very descriptive" stories I wrote for my assignments. We started going out for coffee after class and helping each other out with assignments. We went out to the movies a couple of times and had several lunch dates. Then one night after class we decided to go get some pizza. I took her to my favorite pizza place in Chicago, Bella's Pizzeria on Damen and Chicago Avenue. Bella's had been located on that corner for as long as I could remember. In my opinion they had the best deep-dish pizza in town.

We got to Bella's at about eight P.M. We sat across from each other in a booth and ordered a couple of beers and a deep-dish pepperoni and sausage pizza. We made small talk and sipped our beers while we waited for the pizza. About ten minutes after we arrived, a group of Puerto Ricans walked in and sat two booths up from us on the opposite side of the restaurant. I noticed them immediately and knew that they were gang-bangers, but paid them no mind. They didn't seem to be paying any attention to me, either. Our pizza came. We began to eat as we continued to talk, mostly about Michele's family. At that moment, one of the Puerto Ricans got up, looked my way, and started staring at me as if he knew me. Then he walked toward the back of the restaurant.

I became nervous and oblivious to what Michele was saying. I pictured his face in my mind and tried to remember if I knew him or not and where he might know me from. I finally figured he was just giving me the "I'm tougher than you" stare that all gang members seemed to give strangers and tried to put it out of my mind. The guy came back to his booth and again stared my way. This time I stared back, not so much to stare him down but to try and figure out who the hell he was. He sat down and apparently told the others at his booth about me because all of a sudden everyone with him was trying to take a look at me.

I sensed that something bad was about to happen but I didn't know how to react. I feared more for Michele's life than for mine. Michele had heard many stories about the Chicago gang crime problem but had never experienced it firsthand. She had no clue how real and dangerous gangs could be. She also had no clue that I was once a Latin King.

I glanced toward the booth several times, and each time I found myself being stared at in a manner that wasn't at all friendly. I thought about going over there and asking what the problem was, but I didn't want to be fingered as the one who started a fight. I thought about asking Michele to leave with me but realized that we were probably safer staying inside the restaurant. If we went outside, we could be followed and murdered right there on the street. I sat there and tried to remain calm and ignored the occupants in the booth the best I could, but at the same time I kept my eye on them so that I could see what was coming my way.

The group of Puerto Ricans suddenly began to make it clear why they were looking my way. They had apparently recognized me from my days as a King and began making gang hand signs at me. Every time I looked their way they would flash the King sign going down while putting the Disciples hand sign up. I hoped that not reacting to their signs would make them realize that I wasn't a gang member anymore or at least give them the pleasure of having punked me out. In the meantime I decided to come clean with Michele and let her know what was going on.

I leaned toward Michele to talk to her and noticed one of the guys at the booth get up and walk our way. I leaned back and got ready to jump out of the booth at him. The guy stopped right at our booth and looked at me. He was young, about sixteen or seventeen years old, with his hair cut really short with six earrings in his right ear. Michele just looked his way and smiled, not knowing what he was there for. I looked him in the eyes and prepared to grab his hand in case he went for a gun.

"Are you Lil Loco from the Latin Kings?" he asked me. "No, I'm not in a gang," I answered. "My Folks recognized you as Lil Loco. You're a pussy denying it," he said. The others at his booth were now getting up to stand behind him. One of the waiters noticed what was going on and told the manager of the restaurant. "Get the hell out of here before we call the police," someone yelled from the back of the restaurant. "Get out of here now!" the voice came closer and louder. "King Killer, motherfucker, Disciple love," the guy standing in front of our booth said to me. Michele didn't say a word but I imagined she must have been scared out of her mind. "I'm not in a gang," I said one more time. "Fuck you, punk. You won't live long," one of the other guys said as they began to walk out. "You lucked out tonight, pussy," the last guy to walk by us said as he lifted his sweatshirt to brandish the head of a semiautomatic pistol. "Oh, my god," Michele gasped. She began to cry.

"Don't worry. I'm going to tell the waiter to call the cops," I told Michele. "Leave me alone, just leave me alone," she responded. The manager of the restaurant asked if I knew the guys. I told him I didn't. Everyone in the restaurant was now staring at me as if I was some kind of freak. I knew what must have been going through their minds. They were thinking that I was one of those "damn gangbanging Puerto Ricans" ruining the city for everyone else. I felt like crawling under a rock. The fact that Michele was crying, asking me to get away from her, and asking the restaurant manager to call her a cab didn't help the situation.

I sat back down and began to plead with Michele, but I didn't get very far. "Please leave me alone. Go away! I'll take a cab," she yelled. I got up, gave the manager enough money to cover the food and tip, and headed for the door. "Wait in here until the cops come," he said. "I'll be alright. They know you called the cops and are gone," I said with certainty. I walked out, got in my car, and drove away unharmed.

At my next creative writing class, I couldn't look Michele's way and she avoided me completely. I don't know if she ever mentioned the incident to anyone in the class, but nobody ever said anything, so it was easy to put the incident behind me. I was embarrassed to be a Puerto Rican. I didn't, however, let any of this keep me from continuing on my quest for a new way of life.

11

A Different Kind of Girl

THE INCIDENT WITH Michele made me realize that to many people I would always be just a gangbanger. Even if I succeeded in making a positive contribution to American society in the streets of Chicago, I would always be Lil Loco to some folks. I finally realized the true meaning of "once a King, always a King." I began to understand why so many claimed that once you become a member of a gang, you could never leave.

My fear that the Michele incident would repeat itself over and over again turned me into a loner. Although I still went to an occasional happy hour with my coworkers, I stopped trying to pursue any lasting friendships. I spent most of my days locked up in my apartment, alone, but in peace. Every so often I would talk myself into going out to a dance club, but I would always see faces I didn't want to see. I was satisfied with my life, going through a daily routine with minimal human contact. Even at work I tried my best to avoid any conversation that didn't have to do with work. The few extremely nice people who tried to enter the shell that had become my life soon left, most likely feeling that I was some kind of antisocial being. I can't say that I did any deep thinking or that my loneliness led to enlightened thoughts. No, what I felt was lonely, incredibly lonely. This was my life for several months. The only thing I had to think about was the nightmares that unexpectedly haunted me from time to time. At least they didn't haunt me as often as before. I lived with the feeling that everyone was better off without me around. I didn't see how I could contribute anything positive to anyone's life. I did, however, observe how my presence caused pain and suffering to many. (That thought process has become part of my personality and has led to a life where no long-lasting friendships can exist.) It did, however, help me prepare for the arrival of the most significant person who ever came into my post-gang-member life—Marilyn Garcia.

On a cold February morning a couple of days after Valentine's Day, I got a call at UIC from a woman looking to see if her diploma had arrived. I asked for the necessary information to do a search for any record of the diploma. She was seeking the whereabouts of her master's degree. While I scanned the paperwork of ordered and received diplomas I made small talk with Marilyn. "Garcia?" I said, "Are you Puerto Rican?" "Yes, I am," she responded. "I'm Puerto Rican also," I said. "My name is Reymundo Sanchez. It's nice to see someone from my own *raza* (race) graduating from college; not many of us do." Marilyn didn't respond to my comment; she seemed to just want to get her information and get off the phone.

"OK, here you are," I finally said, breaking the silence that had developed. "I see that we made a mistake on the first diploma. It should have read Master's Degree with Honors." "Yes, you guys messed up," Marilyn replied, with soft, almost apologetic laughter in her voice. I looked through a box of newly arrived diplomas while I listened to Marilyn, in awe of her accomplishment. I found the diploma and decided to search for her records on my computer to find out a little more about her. When her records came up, I looked at the screen and saw everything that my dreams were made of. Marilyn was just twenty-four years old and had already earned a master's degree in education. I felt as envious as I was astonished. I just sat there looking at the screen.

"Did you find it?" Marilyn asked, breaking me out of a deep daydream. "Yes," I said, "I have it here in my hands, a master's degree with honors. Congratulations." "Thank you," Marilyn responded. "So they got it right this time, huh?" There was sarcasm in her tone. "Yes, they did," I told her. "What would you like me to do with it?" "Can you please mail it to me?" Marilyn requested. I read out the address from the university records. Marilyn said she didn't live at that address anymore and began to give me her new address. I expected her to give me a far suburban location. To my surprise, Marilyn lived near the Humboldt Park neighborhood.

Without giving it much thought, I told Marilyn that I knew the area where she lived and I could drop off the diploma to her on my way home. Marilyn hesitated at first, saying it would be too much trouble for me, but then she agreed. "That would be very nice of you to do that," Marilyn said. "I didn't know the university allowed that kind of thing." Until then UIC policy had not crossed my mind. I convinced myself that I would find a way to deliver the diploma and told Marilyn not to worry, that it would be OK. "I will see you this evening then," Marilyn said. "Yes, you will," I responded. "Have a nice day, Reymundo," Marilyn told me. "You, too, Marilyn," I said. "I'll see you later," and then I hung up the phone.

I began to think about how I was going to deliver the diploma. I concluded that walking out of the office with it was too risky, so I began to think up a lie that I could tell my supervisor. I told my supervisor that a friend of the family had asked me if I could take the diploma to her mother because she would be out of town for at least two months. I explained that we had grown up together and that she had asked for the favor through my mother. I added that if it wasn't possible that it would be OK, and asked if my friend's mother could pick up the diploma for her. My well-thought-out lie did not go to waste. My supervisor said that he didn't see a problem with it and reminded me to sign it out.

I couldn't wait for the day to end so that I could meet Marilyn. I wasn't thinking sexual thoughts about her, as I normally did when I was about to meet a woman. I was fascinated by the fact that she was a Puerto Rican who lived in the 'hood and had already earned a master's degree. I continued to look over her grades in envy. Marilyn had earned an A in every class as an undergraduate except for one B. Her master's coursework was unblemished with straight As. I had never heard of any Puerto Rican with such good grades. In fact, Marilyn was the only Puerto Rican I had heard of who had any kind of college degree. That in itself signaled to me the waste of life that the streets of Humboldt Park offered.

I was envious of what Marilyn had accomplished, and it saddened me to look back at how I had wasted my life. Marilyn's records depressed me as much as they excited me. I was happy for her and at the same time knew that I had no excuse for my own lack of education. My self-criticism was compounded by feeling that I could no longer stand being a lost soul in Humboldt Park. I had nothing positive to say about myself.

I left the office around 6:30 that evening. It was already dark outside. A typical cold Chicago February evening awaited me. It had snowed two days in a row, so traffic was denser and slower than usual. It normally took me about an hour to get home with good road conditions. I expected to be stuck in traffic for at least an hour and a half just to get to Marilyn's.

As traffic crawled, I tried to picture what Marilyn would look like but could not come up with an image. All the Puerto Rican women I had ever known were from the streets. I couldn't picture a woman with a master's degree in a microminiskirt, or in skin-tight Lycra pants. I couldn't imagine her cursing, threatening to beat people up, or carrying a weapon with the intention to kill. As I sat there in traffic running my hands over Marilyn's diploma, I realized how negative the feelings were that I had developed toward my own people, especially women. I looked out the car window at the graffiti-covered walls that symbolized Puerto Rican youth. The gang signs showed the contempt that Puerto Ricans had for one another. Then I saw a Latin Kings insignia, and I suddenly remembered how I had played a role in building the reputation that Puerto Ricans carried in inner-city Chicago. My life had never seemed as worthless as it did in that moment. The contrast of what I helped create splattered all over the city's walls and Marilyn's contribution to the Puerto Rican reputation that lay under my hand made my eyes swell with tears of shame.

I arrived at Marilyn's feeling serious second thoughts about my decision to deliver her diploma. I felt embarrassed and not worthy to be in her presence. I parked and held her diploma in my hands for several minutes. I went over what I would say, trying to make sure not to speak in slang. Finally I got out of the car and headed for her door.

The snow was deep along the sidewalk except in front of a handful of houses where the residents had taken the time to shovel. This was customary on the side streets of Chicago. Marilyn's was one of those houses where the snow had been cleared. It was a fenced-in two-story house toward the middle of the block on Monticello Street. I let myself in through the front gate, walked up the stairs, and rang the doorbell marked Garcia. Apparently the house was divided into two apartments, because there was another doorbell with a different last name next to it.

I stepped back and waited for someone to answer. I hoped that someone other than Marilyn would answer, saving me from embarrassing myself. The light behind the door that led to the upstairs apartment lit up and I heard someone coming down the stairs. I could see through the sheer curtains that it was a woman, but I couldn't make out any of her features. I held my breath as the woman on the other side of that door opened it.

"Hi, are you Rey?" she asked. "Yes, and you are Marilyn?" I asked. "Yes, I am," she said. Marilyn was fair-skinned with curly, almost kinky hair, and the biggest, darkest eyes I had ever seen. She seemed shy, even though she was wearing a T-shirt that led me to believe otherwise. It was white and printed with talking penises. "It's so hard to be a dick," the caption said. "I have a head I can't think with, an eye I can't see out of, I hang around with a couple of nuts, my neighbor is an asshole, and my best friend is a pussy." "Nice T-shirt," I commented. "Here is your diploma." I handed it to her. "Thank you. It was nice of you to bring it by." Marilyn took the diploma from my hand and ignored my comment about her T-shirt. "It's OK," I responded. "I don't live that far from here." There was a moment of silence. We just looked at each other with smiles on our faces. Finally, I told her that it had been nice meeting her and said good-bye. "Bye, thank you very much," Marilyn said as I headed down the steps toward my car. "You have a good night," I said as I reached the bottom of the steps. Marilyn closed the door. I got into my car and hit the ice- and slush-covered Chicago streets one more time.

Now that I had finally met her, I began comparing Marilyn to what I thought a woman with a master's degree should look like. She certainly didn't fit my image of the stereotype of a highly educated person—no nerdy look or thick glasses. She didn't resemble any other Puerto Rican woman I had ever known, either. Finally, I dismissed her from my mind as a Puerto Rican woman whose success I would always envy but who I would never see again. I reached into the inside pocket of the leather jacket I was wearing, pulled out a joint, and smoked it on the way home. This was the first time since I had started smoking marijuana again that I lit up in public. It felt natural to me, and I would continue doing it, but not with the total disregard for others I once had.

TWO WEEKS PASSED. I had pretty much forgotten about meeting Marilyn. Then, one day one of the clerks at the front desk at UIC came back to tell me that a woman was asking for me. I didn't think anything of it. Many people asked for me at the front desk. Normally it was about an incorrect transcript they had received or something regarding university business. This time, however, I went to the front desk and found Marilyn sitting in the waiting area, waiting for me.

"Hi," she said when she saw me. She had a big smile on her face that made me feel warm. "I came by to thank you and to give you this. I tried to just drop it off but that guy asked me to wait while he went to get you." Marilyn handed me an envelope and motioned toward one of my coworkers. I opened the envelope in front of her and took out a thank-you card. I smiled, thanked her, and told her that she shouldn't have gone to the trouble. "It was a nice thing you did," Marilyn said. "I wanted you to know that."

I didn't know what to say. I was so taken aback by the thank-you card that I just stood there, staring at Marilyn, speechless. Marilyn broke the silence to say that she had to get going, and that I better get back to work. Without thinking I asked Marilyn to have lunch with me. At first she said she couldn't, but I insisted until she agreed. I went to my desk, got my jacket, and told my supervisor that I was going to lunch.

Marilyn and I walked to an Italian restaurant half a block away, around the corner from where I worked. On the way there I expressed my surprise that she had come to see me. Marilyn didn't say much, but she didn't seem uncomfortable with the idea of having lunch with me. She had a big smile on her face, and once inside the restaurant she took it upon herself to order—a cheese pizza for us to share.

After we sat down and got comfortable, I found to my surprise that Marilyn was somewhat talkative. She began telling me about the problems she had had getting her diploma and the experiences she had with the university that had led to our meeting. First, due to her teacher not turning in grades on time, there was no record of her having completed her coursework. Then, when the grades were finally received, many of them were wrong, including hers. And finally, there had been the little problem with the initial diploma not giving her credit for having completed her degree with honors.

I sat there, watching her, paying more attention to how Marilyn expressed herself than to what she said. She made very little eye contact with me; instead, she positioned her silverware many different ways as she talked. Marilyn didn't seem at all irritated by the ordeal with the university; in fact, she explained it as a comical experience. When I tried to apologize for the university, she dismissed it as not important enough to apologize for. I figured she was just going on about it to make enough conversation to make it through lunch. Then out of nowhere came an unexpected request. "Tell me more about you," Marilyn said.

That request put me in a tight spot. I didn't know how much to tell her about myself, or how truthful I should be. A vision of Marilyn suddenly losing interest in our conversation and excusing herself to get away from me filled my mind. Why would a woman with a master's degree want to associate with an ex-con if she didn't have to? I started telling her about where in Puerto Rico I was born and where in Chicago I was raised. I studied her as I spoke. She was attractive but not in a manner I was accustomed to. Marilyn did not have a face accentuated by makeup, and her hair did not reflect that fresh-from-the-salon look. Her clothing was far different from the overly sexy, overly revealing attire that the women I had known mostly wore. Yet the way she dressed reflected a sort of charm that did not need to expose skin to be sexy. I found Marilyn attractive but not solely because of her looks. I wasn't preoccupied with the vivid sexual thoughts that I usually had in the presence of a woman. I was intrigued by her thoughts and what she had to say. I wanted to know what made her so extremely intelligent. Because of that I decided to let Marilyn know everything about me, and let her draw her own conclusions.

"I used to be in a gang," I started. That comment alone got her attention. She stopped playing with the silverware and gave me her full attention. "I was a member of the Latin Kings," I continued. Then there was a pause to allow the waiter to serve the pizza she had ordered. I put a slice of pizza on a plate and took a bite before I went on. "I don't have a college degree," I told her. "I didn't even finish high school. I only have a G.E.D." Then I stopped talking and turned my attention to the slice of pizza. I waited for Marilyn's reaction.

She gave no indication that she was bothered by what I said. She slowly and calmly ate her pizza, not making much eye contact except for brief glances that indicated she was waiting for me to continue. When I didn't speak, Marilyn finally asked why I had joined a gang.

She caught me by surprise. It was the first time anybody, ever, had asked me that question. I really didn't know the answer. I remembered that I had been angry at my mother, and I remembered that I had been in a situation where only my ruthlessness could keep me alive, but I didn't remember *why*. I told Marilyn about the events that had led me to the streets. Even with the embarrassment I felt, for some reason I felt I had to be totally honest with her.

I told Marilyn about my mother and her lousy choices in men. I told her about the physical abuse and the illegal activities in my everyday home life. Then I gave her a brief description of my life as a Latin King. Marilyn asked me if I had ever been in jail. Without hesitation I told her that I had been but that I was not at all proud of that fact. After that I sat silently questioning myself about why I was revealing so much to someone I had just met and would probably never see again. Maybe the incident with

Michele had left me feeling obligated to tell everyone who stepped into my life who they were getting involved with. Maybe I was just waiting for a willing ear so that I could speak my piece without fear of judgment. Whatever the reason, I felt at ease and didn't regret opening up to Marilyn. Her reaction reinforced my feelings.

"You really ought to be proud of yourself," Marilyn said. "I don't think many people who went through what you have would be able to change their lives." I couldn't respond; I didn't know how to react. I just sat there, looking at her, waiting for her to make eye contact with me. She finally looked up at me and asked if I had ever talked to my mother about how I felt. "No, I haven't," I responded, and didn't say anything more. Marilyn must have noticed my discomfort, because she changed the subject by saying, "I think we better pay for this so you can get back to work."

She offered to help me pay for lunch but I insisted on paying. As we made our way back to the university, I asked about her phenomenal grades. She brushed that off as if fantastic grades were no big deal. "I just did all the studying I was supposed to do, that's all," Marilyn said. When we got back to the university, I thanked her for having lunch with me. She smiled and thanked me. I took the opportunity to ask her if we could do it again. Marilyn said that she would like that and offered to give me her phone number. We exchanged phone numbers, shook hands, and said our good-byes. "Maybe I'll call you tonight," I said as Marilyn began to walk away. "Just don't call too late," Marilyn responded. We both smiled at each other and went about our business.

For the next couple of weeks Marilyn and I spent hours upon hours on the phone. We didn't see each other at all, but we did get to know each other through those conversations. Marilyn had a warped sense of humor like I had never known. She was funny, outspoken, and full of ideas about what a perfect world would be like. We touched upon my gang life briefly, but never enough to carry on a long conversation about it. We mostly talked about the world and everything in it. I also got to know a little about Marilyn's life.

Marilyn was born in the Bronx in New York. She was the second youngest of four sisters. When she was seven, her father moved the family to Miami, Florida. In Miami her father met another woman and left her mother, her sisters, and her behind. Marilyn's mother had family in Chicago, so she moved her daughters there. Marilyn's uncle owned the house she lived in. Marilyn's uncle and his family occupied the first floor, and Marilyn, her mother, and her youngest sister occupied the second floor. That was all I knew about Marilyn's personal life.

Two weeks into our telephone friendship, Marilyn showed up at the university office along with a friend, an African American woman named Tish. She was at least six feet tall and heavyset. They arrived at about four o'clock on a day when we were doing preregistration. Because of that, I was working up in front of the office instead of at my normal position in the back. Marilyn and Tish waited in the lobby until five, when I got off work. From the university we went downtown to hang out.

Marilyn's sudden appearance surprised me, but what really got my attention was how much she had told her friend about me. Apparently Marilyn had told Tish so many good things about me that Tish referred to me as Marilyn's "love interest" on several occasions. Up to this point I couldn't see Marilyn being attracted to someone with a past like mine. I had not wandered into my usual sexual fantasies with Marilyn in my mind. I had only thought about the educational advantages of having Marilyn as a friend, and I had convinced myself that I was nothing but a charity case to her.

Tish's remarks, however, awakened a sexual desire for Marilyn within me. All of a sudden I started to notice how sexy her eyes were, how luscious her lips were, and for the first time I noticed that, underneath her conservative clothing, Marilyn seemed to have a gorgeous body.

It was a Friday so traffic toward downtown was exceptionally heavy. On the slow drive, I listened to Marilyn and Tish talk about their jobs. Marilyn and Tish weren't just friends, they also worked together at the Art Institute of Chicago, where Tish was also a student. In all the years I had lived in Chicago I had never visited the Art Institute. In fact, I didn't even know where it was. It was just one of the many great things in Chicago that I had never gotten to enjoy because of the possession the 'hood had had over me.

Now knowing where they worked, I decided to share my interest in art. Marilyn seemed to be pleased knowing that I was involved with art. In our phone conversations I had shared with her about how I wrote poetry but had never mentioned that I also liked to draw. Then again, Marilyn had never told me that she worked at the Art Institute. Marilyn asked me if I wanted to visit the Art Institute, and I eagerly agreed.

When we got to the Art Institute we went into its gift shop, where Marilyn and Tish worked. I thought Marilyn worked there in some kind of administrative position—I assumed that Marilyn, with her credentials, would have some kind of high-profile job—but that was not the case. She just worked in the gift shop. Tish went to the back of the store and came out to tell us that she would be there for a little while, so Marilyn took me on a tour of the Institute's art galleries. The Art Institute of Chicago exhibits works by some of the world's greatest artists, and at that particular time it was exhibiting art by Mexican artist Frida Kahlo. I was mesmerized by Kahlo's work. It was filled with so much realism and passion. Kahlo's paintings told stories that left very little doubt what she was feeling at the time. Viewing that exhibit got me itchy to express myself through painting again. This visit also influenced the way that I would paint in the future.

We walked out of the exhibit floor and noticed that Tish was outside waiting for us. From the Art Institute, the three of us walked about four blocks to a McDonald's to get something to eat. We got our food, sat down, and then I watched and listened in amazement to Tish and Marilyn's conversation.

"This is the only McDonald's I know where there are no blacks eating or working," Tish said as she drowned her fries in ketchup. Tish's words were loud. She intended for everyone in the restaurant to hear her, and she succeeded. We now had the attention of everyone there. "And I bet it's the only one in town where the pay is much more than minimum wage," Tish continued. "How else can they attract top burger-making talent?" Marilyn followed. "Well, the fry guy needs to be demoted, because these fries are not up to the McDonald's soggy, cold standard I'm used to," Tish said. As I glanced around the restaurant, I could see that many of the customers were becoming uncomfortable with Marilyn and Tish's exchange. It would get worse.

About fifteen minutes later, a young interracial couple entered the restaurant. He was a good-looking, tall African American, and she was a beautiful, blue-eyed white woman. Their presence seemed to bother Tish to no end. As they walked past our table on their way to the counter, Tish looked at Marilyn and said, "She got jungle fever." "He got jungle fever," Marilyn responded, without taking her eyes off her food. "They got jungle fever," they said simultaneously. The couple passed by, either not hearing the comments or ignoring them. That seemed to aggravate Tish even more.

Marilyn saw the puzzled look on my face and began to explain what the "jungle fever" comments meant. She told me that *Jungle Fever* was a movie about the relationship between a black man and a white woman. "I don't think it's such a big deal," I said. "It's not," Tish said, "except that the white girls only take the black men that got a life, money, or both." Tish's comment echoed throughout the restaurant. There was no doubt in my mind that the interracial couple had heard Tish, yet they continued to ignore her.

Marilyn continued to tell me about the movie while Tish rambled loudly about the interracial issue. "I don't ever see white girls going after homies, unless they are white trash, and who needs them?" Tish said. "What I thought was stupid about the movie," Marilyn said, "was that they gave so much importance to a black stud screwing a white girl and not to the fact that he was a married man." "A white girl is a sign of success for a black man," Tish continued, "and it pisses me off that when they are broke they come back wanting to expand their African roots." "It sucks to know that in our society who's screwing who is more important than marriage vows," Marilyn finished. Then finally there was a moment of silence.

Marilyn and I stared at each other, Tish contemplated her food, and the McDonald's dining room became silent. Many people had either left or moved as far away from us as possible. Although I had spent most of my life making people uncomfortable with my presence, I was surprised at the events of that day. After all, I was in the company of a person who had earned a master's degree, whose opinion I never expected would be expressed in such a manner.

We made our way back to my car and then I drove Tish to her place on the south side of Chicago. From there, I headed toward Marilyn's house to drop her off, but that didn't happen. We arrived at Marilyn's and parked about a block away so we could talk for a little while. The next thing we knew it was six in the morning.

That night I got to know Marilyn a little more. I learned about her feelings regarding race issues and also learned more about her past. Marilyn told me that the woman her father had left her mother for was a white woman. Soon afterward, the woman didn't like him visiting his kids, so he stopped all contact. I tried to dig more into how she felt about the situation, but that's all Marilyn would say on the subject. I insinuated that maybe her father's actions were why she harbored such animosity toward white people. Marilyn denied that any animosity existed and went on explaining her feelings about race.

Marilyn started by telling me that most of the bad experiences she'd had as a child were with blacks and not whites. There were never any whites around her to give her bad experiences. She told me that in Miami, there was one black girl who constantly picked on her and her sisters, and then other blacks followed suit. When they finally stood up to her, they became friends, and all the harassment stopped. In Chicago, where she went to high school, it had been more of the same. This time, she said, she just ignored them, feeling sorry for them because most of them were failing out of school, were already mothers, or both. Marilyn said that she realized that these girls saw that she was at the top of her class and did not waste her time chasing guys. They saw her as someone they should have been more like, and were trying to draw her into the same failures they were victims of. Marilyn felt pity for them because she sensed that their tough attitude and ignorance were their only tools for survival.

She told me about an incident she experienced while she was still an undergrad that helped shape her feelings toward whites and how she felt whites felt about her. One day, as she and an Asian friend walked toward her friend's Uptown apartment, they approached a nightclub where several white men stood outside. As they crossed the street toward the nightclub, she saw very scantily dressed white women walking past the club and several entering it. The white men didn't do anything but stare at those women. When Marilyn and her friend walked by them, however, the white men bombarded them with obscene remarks—extremely sexually and racially degrading remarks. Marilyn could not understand why two decently dressed women minding their own business were harassed while half naked, flirtatious women were left alone.

Marilyn was obviously bothered by what she saw as whites' racial opinions of others. I told her that maybe these guys knew that they would never have a chance with her or her friend and therefore didn't care. The white women, however, were right there in the club, and the possibility of meeting and maybe dating them was higher. The men didn't make any degrading remarks to them because they didn't want to ruin any chances of being with them. Marilyn without even thinking about it rebutted my statement.

She felt that even if that were true, it didn't justify the racial remarks. Marilyn felt that whites throughout history had fabricated many stereotypes about other races in order to justify their claim as the supreme race. Even now when those stereotypes had been disproved, whites held onto them for no other purpose than to spread hatred. Marilyn was certain that if she had turned around and confronted the harassers that night, she would have ended up in jail while the white guys got a slap on the wrist. I certainly agreed with that.

After our all night talk-a-thon, Marilyn and I didn't see much of each other for several days, but we talked on the phone, and met for lunch during the week.

My friendship with Marilyn introduced meaningful conversations into my life. Never before had I been in the company of someone who wanted to hear my opinion on issues that actually mattered. Marilyn's friendship also highlighted to me how empty my life had been until then. To me, Marilyn was evidence that a person put into a bad life situation could find a way out through a dedication to education.

Lack of education seemed to be one thing the majority of residents in the Humboldt Park area had in common. Marilyn proved that this problem had nothing to do with being Puerto Rican. The problem seemed to me to be more about fear of being challenged in an arena where fists were not a bargaining option.

12

There Is Such a Thing as Friendship

MY FASCINATION WITH Marilyn continued to grow. Although I was becoming more and more sexually attracted to her every day, it was the things she said that I looked forward to. Marilyn was the first woman I had ever encountered where I found myself listening to her instead of demanding she listen to me. She was the only woman I had met who had very strong feelings against smoking, drinking, and doing drugs. I still did all of those things, but I was doing them less and less now that I knew Marilyn. She seemed drawn to me, too, but I doubted that her feelings toward me were romantic. I decided to test that theory on our next meeting.

We met on a Thursday outside the UIC admissions and records office. We headed to a Greek restaurant located about a block and a half off campus. During lunch Marilyn and I did nothing but make jokes about the people who were walking down the street past the restaurant where we sat. The laughter we shared made me feel comfortable enough to pursue my romantic interest but skeptical enough about ruining the moment. I decided to wait.

We left the restaurant walking slowly and very near each other like a boyfriend and girlfriend would. We planned on meeting later on that night. Marilyn didn't want to commit to going out on the weekend because of some problems Tish was experiencing, but she promised to do all she could to try and be free on the weekend.

When we got to the front door of my office, we stood there making small talk as if neither one of us wanted to say good-bye. It was only when I realized that I was already half an hour late that we decided to part. I watched as Marilyn walked away and called out to her. I walked fast toward her as she waited to see what I wanted. When I got to her I kissed her. Marilyn kissed me back. After the kiss we looked into each other's eyes and parted without saying a word.

For the rest of the day I wondered if I had made a big mistake by kissing Marilyn. I wondered if she'd kissed me back in order to not embarrass me or if she really meant it. I didn't think her walking away silently was a good thing. I concluded that the best thing for me to do was to rush home and call her before I went to see her. I was going to apologize for my actions and tell her that her friendship meant much more to me than the possibility of having her as a girlfriend and I wanted to make sure she knew that.

That night I rushed home and called, and she wasn't home. Her sister answered the phone and told me that Marilyn had gone to Tish's and would call me the next day. As I hung up the phone my heart sank. I just knew that Marilyn was using Tish as an excuse not to see me. I was certain that kissing her had caused her to not want to see me or talk to me again.

The next day, Friday, I daydreamed all day. I began to question my ability to maintain any lasting friendship and saw myself for what I was—a loner. But I couldn't dismiss Marilyn the way I had dismissed every other person who'd come into my life. I saw her as not just a piece of pussy I wanted to get some of, the way I had always looked at women previously. I worried so much that I had jeopardized our relationship that at lunchtime I went to my car and smoked a joint. It was the first time I had gotten high during work hours. I spent the rest of the day in my own little world. I was surprised that my nonproductivity was not questioned that day. On my way home I smoked another joint and decided that I would get home, change my clothes, and go hang out with people from my old ways—I'd return to where I felt I belonged.

At my apartment I jumped into the shower right away and changed into my go to a club and pick up a chick clothes. But before I walked out the door, I decided to call Marilyn to see whether she would take my call or if I would get the "she's counseling Tish" excuse again. To my surprise her sister answered the phone and handed it right to Marilyn. Marilyn said she was happy to hear from me and that we could go out that night. I felt so relieved to hear her words. I agreed to go pick her up as soon as possible as she was looking forward to seeing me.

Only half an hour after we hung up the phone, I arrived at her door. I rang the doorbell and she came right down, ready to go. Marilyn hugged me when she saw me, which made me realize that I had worried myself out of my mind for no good reason. We got in the car and headed for what I thought would be a night of dancing. It didn't work out that way, though.

As we headed toward the dance club, we talked about the Chicago night life. It was then that she expressed her distaste for the club scene. She loved the music but she hated the smoke-filled air, the excessive drinking, and the meat market atmosphere. She told me how her older sister frequented dance clubs and was always complaining about meeting phony guys there. Her sister, however, apparently didn't know any other way to meet guys.

Now that I knew that Marilyn wouldn't be caught dead in a dance club, I had no clue where to take her. My knowledge of things to do and places to go in the Chicago area was very limited due to my many years of refuge in the 'hood. I was embarrassed that I had no clue where we should go. Finally I just admitted to Marilyn that my plans had been to go dancing. Marilyn said she was sorry to have ruined my plans and offered to let me go by myself. I disagreed with that idea right away. We decided to go have a bite to eat in Uptown and then just walk around for a little while.

We had been driving for about half an hour already and Marilyn suddenly needed to use the bathroom, so we stopped at a bar/restaurant. I was filled with anxiety while so many ideas ran through my mind about our date. Instinctively I walked up to the bar and ordered a beer. I took the beer and sat at a bar stool near a window. I looked out as cars maneuvered up and down the snow- and ice-covered city streets, wondering where my relationship with Marilyn would lead. I wondered if I should take her up on her offer and go dancing by myself. I was certain to meet a friendly girl who wouldn't give me the anxiety I was feeling over trying to be an intellectual.

I turned around just as Marilyn was walking my way. I watched her walk straight toward me as I prepared to take a drink from my beer. She reached out and grabbed the beer from my hand and put it back on the bar. "You don't need that," she said as she quickly glanced at me and headed toward the door. I looked back long enough to see the bartender watching us with a "boy, you have your hands full" look on his face. I followed Marilyn onto the cold Chicago streets and got into the car.

Marilyn's actions surprised me and left me intrigued. I desired to learn more about her and the way her mind worked. Not a word was said about what had happened in the bar. She didn't bother explaining why she did it, and I didn't ask. It was like one of those unspoken rules where no words are required as everything is understood. I did, however, wonder how Marilyn would react if she found out that I also smoked cigarettes and marijuana. I was going to make sure she never did find out.

Marilyn and I drove around, directionless, just talking, mostly about Tish. Tish had a boyfriend who she thought just wanted her for physical pleasure. She also had parents who kept pressuring her to leave home because they thought she was a lesbian. Tish was actually bisexual.

Her boyfriend was apparently trying to pressure her into setting up a threesome. He was trying to convince her that he only wanted to share something that already existed within her and that it had nothing to do with him or his fantasies. When she refused, he began to throw angry fits and questioned her devotion to him. Marilyn said that what bothered her most about Tish was that, regardless of what the guy did or said, she continued to see him. It also bothered her that Tish's only solution to the problem with her parents was to get an apartment with Marilyn. Tish would not leave her parents' home unless Marilyn became her roommate.

At this point, we had been driving around for about three hours, so we decided to go have a cup of coffee. We started toward Uptown but ended up at a Dunkin' Donuts on the Near North side of the city.

The Dunkin' Donuts was empty except for one old bum and a couple of cops. The bum sat in a booth, the cops sat at the counter near the door, and we situated ourselves at the far end of the counter. We ordered a couple of cups of coffee and four donuts. Marilyn took two of the donuts and walked over and gave them to the bum. It made my curiosity about Marilyn grow even more.

When she got back to the counter, I asked her what she thought were the circumstances that had led that bum to where he was in his life. Marilyn said she couldn't even begin to imagine the circumstances. "There are just so many ways to end up homeless, and most have nothing to do with drugs, alcohol, or crime," Marilyn said. "There are many people who have mental defects that their families don't want to deal with. They prefer to let them fend for themselves on the streets instead of taking care of them." Marilyn didn't make eye contact with me as she said these things. I recognized that it was Marilyn's way of expressing herself. I also noticed that when she got into that part of her personality, words flowed so clearly, intelligently, and with conviction. Her point came through loud and clear, and in some ways it made listeners realize they had been looking for answers in all the wrong places. Marilyn continued to express her point of view.

"That man may have been rich, educated, and living the American dream," she said. "People don't think about how it could feel to lose that dream until they lose it, and then that's when you really find out what friends are, and what family is.

There are so many people whose sole purpose in life is to destroy the lives of others. They live by the rule that, in order to have more, everyone else has to have less." I had never seen the world in the light Marilyn was presenting it in. For the most part, I believed that as long as one worked hard and went to school, all would be well. Then Marilyn laid a comment on me that really sent me into a spin. "That's why I admire you so much," she said. "So many people worked so hard to destroy you and you still found a way to survive."

For the first time in my life, someone who wasn't in the business of saying self-serving positive things was saying something good about me. Granted, I had no clue how she came to her conclusion. Still, I took a moment to bask in my glory.

I watched Marilyn as she took her spoon, my spoon, the sugar container, the cream container, and the napkin holder and slowly positioned them in many different ways on the counter. She seemed hypnotized by the countless positions that these objects could be arranged in, but I knew that she was just waiting for me to respond to her remark. I just didn't know how, and maybe I didn't want to just yet. Finally I broke the silence, which had lasted several minutes.

"I see you're into modern art," I joked. "Yeah, the meanings are endless," Marilyn responded in laughter. "So what meaning does your present work of art have?" I asked. "Well, the cup represents how deep life is and the coffee shows how dark life can be," Marilyn started. "The spoons represent the manner in which we dip into things we're not supposed to, and the cream shows that we try to artificially lighten what should remain dark. Of course we end up making a big mess." Marilyn pointed at the coffee trickling down the side of the cup and onto the saucer.

"And then we try to cover it all up, knowing that messes always soak through." She covered the coffee on the saucer with a napkin and watched it soak right through.

It was at that moment that we realized that we had drawn the attention of the cops and the gentleman behind the counter. "You got all that from a cup of coffee?" one of the cops asked. "The meaning of life is implanted in everything around us," Marilyn responded without looking their way. "Or you can do what I do and make it all up as you go along." She finally looked up at the cops and let out a slight laugh.

The cops and the guy behind the counter laughed. "That's more like it," one of the cops said. "For a minute there I thought I had gone through life missing something."

Marilyn went back to her objects, arranging them and encouraging me to help. We sat there giving ridiculous interpretations to the placement of the objects. The cops left, and we were all alone except for the attendant, who went about his business of wiping tables. By the time we realized it, it was two-thirty in the morning.

We left Dunkin' Donuts feeling intoxicated from all the laughter and headed toward Marilyn's home. We seemed to arrive there much too quickly. Neither of us was ready for the night to end. We again parked nearby and talked all night. Only this time, deep, passionate kissing interrupted our conversations. It was one of the very few times in my life when I didn't feel that I was initiating all the action. In fact, I consciously made sure not to get carried away and ruin what was becoming something wonderful.

From that point on, Marilyn and I became almost inseparable. We saw each other almost every weekday and spent all of our weekends together. She finally began to open up to me completely. That in turn gave me the confidence to open up and talk about things I had never been able to talk about before.

Marilyn told me about her ex-boyfriend and how deeply he had hurt her. Their relationship had lasted for a little over two years. From the moment he met her, she told me, he complimented her looks. She was the most beautiful woman he had laid eyes on, he told her. That guy was Marilyn's very first boyfriend, and therefore she had never heard such sweet words coming from someone she was physically attracted to. Eventually they became sexual, and according to Marilyn that's when everything between them began to change.

For whatever reason, Marilyn wasn't able to give her boyfriend the sexual pleasure he expected from her, and, because she was new to sex, she didn't know how to stroke his ego by faking it. Instead of talking to Marilyn about how he felt, what he liked, and so on, he barraged her with insults. Because Marilyn was in love with this guy, and he had been her first, she concluded that there must be something wrong with her. As time passed they saw each other less and less. For reasons Marilyn couldn't comprehend, when he did come around, it was only for sex. This was the same guy who had said he didn't find her sexually satisfactory. After the sex, he would insult her in one way or another and then leave. Marilyn grew tired of this routine and finally put a stop to it. He responded by yelling obscenities at her and insulting her sexual ability in broad daylight in front of a lot of people. This incident left Marilyn emotionally and sexually traumatized. She questioned her womanhood and became afraid to have relationships with the opposite sex. She told me that she didn't know why she was opening herself up again with me, only that she felt we were soul mates.

I reached over and kissed Marilyn and held her for a while. I told her that many men base their sense of macho superiority on being able to please a woman sexually. I explained that men like that usually feel that, as long as they please a woman sexually, they have created a miracle and therefore should be worshipped. These men usually run around with many women who for the most part buy into the macho superiority with the sexual pleasure theory. Nothing more than sex can be expected from men who think this way, and not worshipping their sexual manner is the ultimate insult to them. I assured her that there was nothing wrong with her. I tried to make her understand that she just needed a lot more than the physical pleasure he was offering to be whole, and he couldn't provide that and would probably never understand that. While I spoke, I wondered to myself if I was that same type of guy.

Marilyn sat quietly as I spoke. When I was finished talking, she reached out to me and said, "you truly are my soul mate," before she kissed me. This time her kiss felt much more passionate than it had before. It was as if Marilyn had been holding back the best of herself until she found out certain things about me. I in turn wondered whether or not she would still consider me her soul mate when she got to know more about me.

"What about you?" Marilyn asked. "What kind of man are you when it comes to sex?" The question took me by surprise and left me speechless. There were so many ways I could answer this question. I could plead ignorance, giving the impression that I was as inexperienced as she was, or I could pound my chest like Tarzan and stake my claim as a sexual dynamo. The more I thought about it the more I realized that I didn't know what type of man I was, sexually or otherwise. What I did was take that opportunity to let Marilyn know about the sexual traumas of my life. I told her about the thirty-five-year-old woman who thought she was doing me a favor my having sex with me at age thirteen while she told me and showed me what I should do to please a woman. I told her how I had had sex with prostitutes and how I had forced a Latin Queen to have sex with me. I decided, however, not to tell her about being raped by my cousin. I still wasn't ready to share that with anyone. After I told her about my traumatic sexual past, I finally tried to answer her question.

"My answer is I don't know. All I can tell you is that you are the only woman I have ever met who I respected as a person before I became sexually attracted to you. I have a problem with seeing women as anything more than an instrument of sexual pleasure. With you it is different," I told her. I suddenly realized that what I was saying could be construed as not finding her attractive and made sure to clarify what I meant. "Don't get me wrong. I find you very attractive and thought you were gorgeous from the beginning, but it just never crossed my mind that you could go for someone like me. I respect you so much for what you have accomplished in your life, in the same period of time that I have done nothing. And now, well, now not only do I respect you but also I feel so good when I'm with you. I don't think I can say that about any other woman who has come into my life," I concluded.

"Why?" Marilyn asked. "Because you have a master's degree, Marilyn, that's why," I responded. "Me? I'm just an ex-con!" I stared out the windshield into nowhere. "Silly goose, that's not what I meant," Marilyn said, "and besides a master's degree is only a piece of paper that has no value in determining how a person is inside." I was prepared to tell Marilyn how I felt about the importance of having a degree, but she was more interested in finding out my thoughts and what shaped them.

"Why do you feel confused about who you are sexually?" she asked. "The first woman I had sex with," I began, "or actually, who had sex with me was thirty-five years old and I was only thirteen. I was like the hero of the neighborhood, a stud. But then it freaked me out to find out that girls my age were not interested in the things I had learned from a thirty-five-year-old." I told her about the night that Maria had taken it upon herself to take my virginity and teach me how to please a woman. I told her about how sexually hungry I became from that day forward. I told her how I would shoot drugs into a prostitute named Gina's veins in exchange for sexual pleasure, and I told her about how I had used Jenny, my first girlfriend and high-school sweetheart, as a sex toy and became upset when she became just that. I then paused and waited for Marilyn's reaction. I thought for sure I had lost her.

"Maria molested you," Marilyn said. "She took advantage of your ignorance and childhood curiosity and molested you." This was the first time that anyone who knew what had happened between Maria and me had come to that conclusion. For the most part I had always been told how lucky I was, whether it was a man or woman hearing the story. Now here was someone I respected telling me that it was not normal, and that I had indeed been molested. I felt as if such a big burden had been lifted from me. It was as if I finally understood all my romantic failures. I suddenly understood why I felt about women the way I did. Marilyn now got that serious look where she talked without making eye contact. She continued to dig into my past.

"You were thirteen and doing drugs—where was your mother?" she asked. My silence and blank expression must have alerted Marilyn that clearly she had hit a major artery as she had done once before. She didn't pursue the topic as she normally would have. In fact, she brought our night of discovery to a conclusion by calling to my attention that it was six in the morning and that we should go home. I drove to the front of her house, walked her to the door, and gave her a deep, lasting kiss. "I'll see you tonight," Marilyn said as she opened the door. With that we both made our way home.

My head was spinning from the night's events. Had I not been so tired after being up all night I would have twisted and turned in bed with many thoughts running through my mind. I thought about Marilyn's reaction to all of what I had said. I wondered if her words were sincere or just words that she thought would get her safely through the night. I wondered if she would continue to be that special woman in my life or if she would be yet another unsympathetic bitch who came into and out of my life. As soon as I woke up I called her. She was up and around and eager for me to go pick her up. I showered, got dressed, and headed her way.

Marilyn was apparently looking out the window to see when I arrived, because she walked out to meet me before I got a chance to park my car. She got in and we drove off. We decided to go have dinner and then walk around Uptown.

During dinner we talked about our jobs and during our walk we talked about the different things we saw in the shop windows lining the street. Finally we decided to go somewhere where we could sit and talk. We ended up parked by the lakefront and talking the night away again. On this night the topic was mostly our families.

Marilyn was upset because, from the time she awoke, her mother had been bitching at her about her staying out all night. What upset her the most was that her mother seemed to be angry more about what her brother would say or think about such behavior than about Marilyn's well-being. She told me that her mother routinely overlooked the fact that she was an adult and was paying most of the rent and household bills and, in fact, the only reason why Marilyn wasn't living on her own was because her mother needed her financial assistance.

Marilyn told me that her mother and father had been married in Puerto Rico and relocated to New York before they had children. She said her father had never been the romantic gentleman type. He had, however, always provided for the family even though he had a knack for getting drunk. She told me that on the first day of her parents' honeymoon, her father got so drunk that he broke down the bathroom door to bring his new wife to bed for sex. Her mother was having her period at the time and was embarrassed to make love to her new husband under those circumstances. Marilyn's father didn't care and probably never even noticed.

All four girls had been born in New York. Marilyn's fondest memories of her youth were running around the streets of the Bronx. Her father moved the family to Miami due to a job change. In Miami the fighting and bickering that had always existed between her parents intensified. It reached its boiling point when her father started having an affair and was seen in public more with his mistress than with his wife. Ultimately he moved in with his mistress and abandoned his family. Marilyn's mother had packed up and moved herself and the girls to Chicago where she had family.

Marilyn never understood what went on in her father's mind that led him to abandon them without an explanation. She didn't care that he left her mother. She understood that was a personal relationship she had little to do with. But she felt as though he should have continued his relationship with his daughters regardless of what was going on between him and his wife. He brought even greater pain into his daughters' lives when he left his inheritance to his stepchildren and made no mention of his blood children in his will. That, in Marilyn's opinion, was an act that showed discontent toward his daughters, not his ex-wife.

Marilyn obviously had been deeply hurt by her father's actions. He died without ever seeing her again, and had been buried by the time she found out he had passed away. He never got to see his little girl graduate from college and earn her master's degree. Because of that, Marilyn had decided to skip the graduation ceremonies altogether. She had so many questions for him that would go unanswered, so many things to share with him that she would now have to keep to herself. After Marilyn told me about her father, we held each other for a long, long time, but she never shed a tear.

Marilyn's not breaking down in tears during what was a very emotional moment did not surprise me. I understood full well how it felt not having a father to lead you, to talk to, and to protect you. I knew what it was like to have my emotions ignored by the very ones who brought me into this world. And I knew that a million tears would not change that. Up to this moment I had always associated all my pain with my mother. Now all of a sudden I was angry at my father as well.

"My father didn't even bother to think before he brought me into this world," I told Marilyn as we separated from our embrace. "All he thought about was getting his dick wet. I'm certain he didn't think he'd be around to be a grandfather to my kids. He was a seventy-something-year-old geezer already. Who the fuck did he think was going to take care of us until we were old enough to take care of ourselves? Because of his decision to fuck a nineteen-year-old when he should have been enjoying a flower garden some-fuckin'-where, we ended up with a life full of pain, suffering, and abuse. Thanks, daddy, thanks a lot, *papi*," I said as I looked toward the sky. Our desire for both of us to have questions answered by our dead fathers bound Marilyn and me closer together. I hadn't even known, before this conversation with Marilyn, that I had that desire.

"What about your mother?" Marilyn asked. "What did she do?" I paused and thought about how I could answer that question without screaming at the top of my lungs. This was Marilyn's third attempt to get me to open up about my mother. I really didn't want to answer her question but felt that I had to, so that she would continue to open up with me. I felt a genuine trust for Marilyn and wanted her to feel the same way about me. I couldn't remember the last time I felt as though those around me trusted me. Still, I hesitated to talk to her about how I felt toward my mother. But that night I felt the need to open up about the one who had hurt me so much. Marilyn gave me that opportunity.

"Nothing, that's what she did, nothing," I told Marilyn. I told her about the physical, mental, and emotional abuse my mother had not only allowed but had also taken part in. I told her about the criminal element, how her successive lovers and husbands had been involved in all kinds of illegal activities that she ignored in order to be financially supported. I explained how I had gone from an honor roll student to a menace to society because of how my mother chose to provide for us. I told her how much I had loved to play baseball but stopped because of all the anger inside me. I explained that drugs and alcohol had replaced baseball because they masked and soothed that anger.

Marilyn slumped in her seat as I told her how I had slept in the street, shoplifted for food, and drunk liquor with bums to keep warm. I closed my eyes and became a universe of tension as I told how how I had had sex with a man for food, money, and shelter. I told her how my addiction to cocaine and sex had finally led me to incarceration. And I told her about how I thought that being locked up was the thing that had saved my life. "Being locked up made me a loner," I told her, "and that is exactly what I needed, considering those I kept company with." I waited for her to react. I had just released the deepest secrets of my life, and I waited to see what Marilyn would do or say next.

I slumped back in my seat and just stared at the steering wheel. I had never before shared the details of my relationship with my mother with another person. I felt somewhat hesitant, not sure how she'd react. I thought that maybe Marilyn would make comments in defense of my mother, but at the same time I felt relieved. Then she solidified my feeling of peace with her words.

"Have you talked to her about it?" Marilyn asked. "She left my ass on the streets, came back to find me in jail, and hasn't even taken the time to find out what happened," I responded. "Do you really think she'll talk to me about it?" "What a bitch," Marilyn said. I couldn't believe those words came out of her mouth, and even though she had only spoken the truth I felt the need to come to my mother's defense. "She's not a bitch," I said as I looked away from Marilyn. "What?" Marilyn asked. "She's not a bitch!" I looked her straight in the eyes with an angry glare. "I can't believe you," Marilyn responded. "This woman beat you, left you in the hands of a drug dealer, never cared for your well-being while you were on the streets going through hell, and you still defend her?"

I sat there quietly pondering Marilyn's words. I couldn't understand how this strong Puerto Rican woman could question the oldest of all Puerto Rican traditions—honor and protect your mother no matter what, especially if you're male. Marilyn seemed to be angered by my show of loyalty toward my mother. I wondered if we had reached a turning point in our relationship. But then she explained herself, and as always awakened a new thought process within me.

"Rey, you don't have any reason to protect your mother. It is pretty obvious that if she had cared for you she wouldn't have put you through all that suffering. She is probably in denial and will probably always deny that what she did to you was wrong. She will no doubt justify her actions by saying that she did it because she loved you and had to provide for you in any way she could. I don't think she has a clue that she was the cause of your joining the Latin Kings, and going to jail. I don't think she will ever take responsibility for how you went from an exemplary student to a violent gangbanger. And she doesn't deserve credit for how you managed to turn your life around and start all over." I couldn't believe my ears. "You, Rey, *you* are the one who deserves credit for figuring out where your life went wrong and dealing with it in a positive way. You shouldn't look at you mother as some kind of saint; you should see her for what she is, the person who made your life hell."

I sat with no reaction, soaking in every word Marilyn said. I began to wonder how my life would have turned out if my mother had not been so determined to find a man to support us. I imagined we would have lived in extreme poverty, but we would have been happy. By now I could have a master's degree with honors, too. I could have moved us out of the ghetto and never have questioned my mother's parenting. Then I looked out the window into the cold streets of Chicago and saw my reality. I would never have the opportunity to do those things. I had been robbed of my childhood and young adulthood. I was finally realizing that.

"Let's go home," I told Marilyn as I started the car and drove off. Marilyn didn't say a word as we drove; I didn't either. We avoided eye contact until we got to our destination. We looked at each other and kissed deeply, reassuring each other that everything was all right.

I went home and couldn't fall asleep until I was absolutely exhausted. I lay on the bed, then got up and watched television, and then went through that routine over and over again. Hundreds of questions went through my mind about my mother. I started to see clearly how the abuse I had suffered at home led me to stray from being a law-abiding and responsible person. The realization that I would never experience a prom or a high school graduation tortured me. And now I was finally piecing together the reasons why. I didn't like the reasons. They made me angry.

I finally fell asleep and was immediately threatened by a frightening nightmare. It was the first one I had had since I met Marilyn. When I started taking classes at UIC I began keeping a journal of the things I had done, seen, and experienced as a lost child of the streets, and that had helped me to get rid of the nightmares I had been having. I would write late into the night when the nightmares kept me up and at school as I sat and waited for class to start. My previous nightmares were about gang life. The new ones were about my mother.

In my dream I saw my mother beating me with an extension cord, but I wasn't crying or screaming. I was just looking at her. Blood flowed out of wounds on my back, legs, and arms, but it never hit the ground. My mother then sat next to me and smiled as if nothing had happened.

I woke up thinking I had slept only minutes, then realized it had been almost ten hours. I got up and rolled a joint. Then I sat and stared at the walls of my apartment. Missing were the family pictures that adorned most homes. I didn't even have a picture of myself. I looked at the joint in my hand and thought about Marilyn. I knew I would lose her friendship if she found out that I still did drugs. I got up, picked up the bag of marijuana, went to the bathroom, and flushed it all down the toilet. My affair with marijuana had finally come to an end. I then located my cigarettes and did the same with them. I was determined never to smoke again. Marilyn had become so important to me that I didn't want any of this to jeopardize our relationship.

I called her and told her about the nightmares I used to have, and that I had begun to write, and that this had reduced the number and made me feel better about them. I told her about the nightmare I had the previous night. She told me that it was probably because I was starting to deal with something I had blocked out for so long. Marilyn encouraged me to write about it and also asked to read what I ended up writing. I agreed to take my journal to her that night.

That night Marilyn and I didn't talk much. We had dinner and walked around the Uptown area, saying very little to each other. It was as if we were both too deep into our thoughts to actually share them. I drove Marilyn home and, as always, we parked somewhere near her house before we got there. This time, however, we did no talking at all. We spent close to an hour kissing and expressing our passion to each other. Then I walked her to her door and drove home.

13

Lovers

MARILYN TOLD ME that her mother was giving her grief about spending so much time on the phone, and she had decided to avoid it by making our conversations briefer. She also told me that she wanted time to read through my journal, which I had given her, so that she could give me some feedback.

During that next week I didn't see Marilyn at all. I visited my older sister every day. We hadn't spent this much time together since we were in our very early teens. We were never close. I had always thought that I bore the brunt of the abuse in our household so that she and my other sisters could be spared. I knew she had been pregnant and that she now had a baby girl, but this week was the first time I ever saw my niece. My sister was shacking up with her baby's father, a tattoo-covered Latin King, who I didn't want any part of. All three of my sisters and I were like strangers to each other, and none of us made a move to change that. My reasons for visiting her were self-serving. I planned on eventually striking up a conversation regarding the physical abuse we endured as children.

My visits to my sister's place never lasted more than an hour, basically because her apartment reeked of marijuana and cigarette smoke. She didn't smoke either, but her boyfriend chain-smoked both and didn't bother thinking about the harm it might do to his infant daughter. The few times I commented on the subject I was made aware, in no uncertain terms, by my sister and her boyfriend that I should mind my own business. Their unhealthy habits bothered me; nevertheless, I kept visiting in order to achieve my goal.

Marilyn and I continued to reveal things to each other that had caused us pain. But while I was eager to talk about the troubles I wanted to deal with, Marilyn did so only in bits and pieces. She declined my invitations to my apartment, saying that she wasn't ready to step into that part of my world yet. But we still spent most of our time together and got into some very passionate moments in the car. Marilyn was certainly mysterious, and that fascinated me. Although it seemed to me that Marilyn's main cause of turmoil was not having the opportunity to confront her father, it became obvious that her mother's overlooking her accomplishments was also an issue with her.

WE MET ONE day to talk about my writing. We went to the UIC computer center so that we could make the corrections she suggested. Marilyn began trying to convince me that I should organize what I had written into a book and have it published. She thought that my work could positively affect other people who had dealt with or were dealing with the same things I had, to help them move on with their lives. Marilyn said that she would work with me to get it together and would support me every step of the way. I was so caught up in the emotion about getting all my thoughts and feelings down on paper that I didn't even consider the generosity Marilyn was extending to me.

We were alone at the UIC computer center on a cold rainy night. I dictated to Marilyn an episode of my past to be included. I told her about the thirteen-year-old kid who had died in my arms because he worshipped my lifestyle as a Latin King. I broke down in tears as I told her the story. Marilyn stopped typing to hold me. She decided that night that the details of my life were too painful for her to read and write about, and even though she encouraged me to finish and publish it, she regretfully could not help me with it.

I didn't like Marilyn's decision to stop helping me—I thought it was something that would bring us closer together—but at the same time I understood. All too often I found myself crying my heart out about what I was writing. That night did, however, serve to get us more emotionally close. It was the first time I cried in the presence of another person for as long as I could remember and I did so without regret. I wouldn't revisit my writing until many years later.

THE NEXT DAY we cruised around Marilyn's favorite part of Chicago—Uptown. We had dinner and talked about how comfortable we felt in each other's company. We left the restaurant and sat in the car kissing and becoming strongly affectionate. I invited Marilyn back to my apartment and again she declined. She did, however, say she would spend the night with me at a hotel. Immediately I drove to an area where I knew we could get a room.

During the drive, neither of us said a word. We held hands and made brief eye contact from time to time and smiled. I was nervous. I had not pressured Marilyn into sex and I didn't just think of her as another piece of pussy. Most important of all, neither of us was under the influence of drugs and alcohol. Although

I had been with many women before Marilyn, I had never been with anybody like her. She was so different from all the others. Marilyn was the first woman I would make love to who I actually cared about.

When we arrived at the motel, Marilyn waited in the car while I went and got a room key. We were given room 222. We made our way into the room as silently as we had been on our way there. Once inside the room, we started kissing and undressing each other. Marilyn asked me to turn off the lights, but I talked her out of it by demonstrating how fascinating I found her. I was as nervous as I was excited. I kissed my way up and down her body slowly and gently. In whispers I told her how soft and beautiful I thought she was. I pronounced her the sweetest woman in the world when I performed oral sex on her and tasted her juices for the first time. I felt like a man when I made love to Marilyn. I took my time, thinking only about her needs. I looked at her with the feeling that I would be with her forever and not just until I got my rocks off, the way I had thought about all the women before her.

After we made love, I stood up and admired how beautiful Marilyn was. I told her that her ex had no clue what he had lost, and made sure she knew what a wonderful lover I thought she was. After that I jumped up and down on the bed expressing how lucky I felt to be with her. This was all meant to relieve her of the insecurities I imagined her ex-boyfriend had left her with. My sincere antics seemed to work. I turned off the lights and we made love all night. We fell asleep as the sun came up.

We woke up in each other's arms and went back into the silent mode we'd been in when we arrived. Our silence didn't stop us from expressing ourselves to each other physically. We kissed and touched each other, and helped each other get dressed. Marilyn decided to keep the key as a memento of what she called one of the most special nights in her life.

Marilyn and I went and had breakfast before we headed home. During breakfast she said that she expected her mother to be pissed off at her again for showing up in the afternoon. I kidded her by saying at least she wouldn't be upset about her coming in early in the morning. Marilyn seemed to enjoy the fact that I saw the lighter side of her dilemma, then she put me on the spot.

"Why don't you come over for dinner tonight so my mother can see who has been keeping me out all night?" she asked. "OK, but only if you cook," I responded, thinking I was putting her on the spot. "Take me to the store so I can get some things to feed you with," she replied, taking me by surprise.

We went to a supermarket and Marilyn got some things to make dinner with. We then headed to her home, joking about what might happen when we arrived. As we drove to her place, she started to prepare me for the worst. Her mother, her uncle, and his wife were all sitting on the front porch in what was an unusually warm, early March afternoon in Chicago. "You're going to have to walk me to the door," Marilyn said. "I don't have a problem with that, but you have to promise to send flowers to my funeral," I said. Marilyn laughed as I backed the car into a parking spot a couple of houses down from our destination.

We walked toward the house holding a bag of groceries each as if we were delivering a peace offering. Marilyn started greeting her family members as we approached the gate. I opened the gate, and Marilyn walked in front of me up the stairs. I followed slowly behind her. When Marilyn reached the top of the stairs, she introduced me as her friend to the members of her family, starting with her mother. I shook their hands and greeted them in Spanish.

"*¿Tu eres Puerto Riqueño?* (You're Puerto Rican?)" Marilyn's mother asked. "*Sí* (Yes)," I answered. "*Yo creia que tu eras blanco* (I thought you were white)," she said. Marilyn looked on in amazement as I carried on a conversation with her family. She finally excused herself and left me there talking to them. After sharing bits of information about what part of Puerto Rico our families originated from, I said my farewells and made my way back to the car. As I drove off, Marilyn's mother waved good-bye with a smile on her face. I left with a feeling that I made a good first impression and would be welcomed back for dinner that night.

I went home and prepared myself for dinner at Marilyn's. I was anxious to go and meet the rest of her family. The short conversation I'd had with her mother made me feel much more comfortable about going there. Marilyn called me and told me to be there at six that evening. Although it was only a couple of hours away, it seemed like forever to wait. I decided to go over to my sister's to kill time before I went to Marilyn's.

When I arrived at my sister's, she was outside with her boyfriend, her daughter, and her sister-in-law enjoying the warm weather. There were also three Latin Kings present. The group was drinking beer and smoking marijuana. I felt very uncomfortable there, as if I didn't fit in, even though I wasn't that far removed from that lifestyle. It had been almost four years since I hung with the Latin Kings, and two of those years I hung in jail. Yet it seemed like I had never been there. My sister's boyfriend introduced me to everybody as an ex-Latin King. When he did that, I knew I had to find a way to get out of there as soon as I could. The Kings began asking questions about when I was a member and the drunken sister-in-law started to make comments about my looks that seemed like come-ons. My sister saved me from having to deal with any of them by handing me her baby daughter.

I talked baby talk to my niece as I made my way away from the Kings. My sister told me that I could take my niece up to the apartment if I wanted to. I did just that. Upstairs I watched television and played with my niece, waiting for my sister to come up. I figured that if she came up by herself it would be a perfect time to ask her about our upbringing. My sister never did come upstairs, but her sister-in-law did. She went into the bathroom and then sat next to me when she came out. Then she began asking questions about my availability. I told her I had a girlfriend and then asked her to stay with my niece because I had to leave. Outside I told my sister that her daughter was with her sister-in-law and that I had to go. I said good-bye to everyone present and went on my way.

As I drove to Marilyn's house I felt proud of myself for ignoring my sister's sister-in-law's passes. I realized that, in the past, I would normally have jumped at the opportunity to have sex with a woman who was so clearly making herself available to me. Even when I did have a girlfriend, I would have at least arranged it so there would be an encounter at a later time. As I arrived at Marilyn's, I smiled at what I saw as a victory in my personality change.

As I made my way up the stairs, her uncle came out into the hallway. He stopped and chitchatted with me about the warm weather until Marilyn came down and escorted me upstairs. Her mother was in the kitchen and her little sister was in the dining room. We made our way into the kitchen, where I sat at the table while Marilyn cooked. Then Marilyn's mother began talking to me about a subject that made Marilyn uncomfortable. She talked to me about her daughter, my girlfriend.

"*Es una maravilla que Marilyn está cocinando* (It's a miracle that Marilyn is cooking)," she said. Marilyn glanced my way and rolled her eyes as if to say, "oh boy, here we go." I told Marilyn's mother that I was hoping not to be poisoned. That got her laughing. Then I struck up a conversation about a can of Puerto Rican coffee she had sitting on the counter. I asked if there was any coffee in it and if she had gotten it from Puerto Rico. This was my way of changing the subject. "*Este café se vende en cualquier tienda* (This coffee is sold at any store)," she responded. "*¿Quieres una taza?* (Do you want a cup)?" "*Seguro* (Sure)," I said.

As it turned out, I found out a few things about Marilyn over dinner that I hadn't even thought about. The first thing I noticed was that Marilyn was a lousy cook. Basically all she knew how to make was rice; everything else was an adventure. Luckily her mother hung around the kitchen talking to me and having a cup of coffee long enough to make sure Marilyn didn't burn the house down. Then, as we were eating, I realized how naïve Marilyn was about things that didn't require extensive research and scientific discussion. She told me that she ate any type of meat except pork—only what she had made for dinner was rice with pork chops. Marilyn knew the cuts of meat she had prepared by their Spanish name, "*chuletas*," but she had no clue that pork chops and *chuletas* were one and the same. "OK, well, I eat one type of pork," Marilyn laughed in her own defense.

Marilyn's little sister joined us in the living room after dinner. She was a very attractive seventeen-year-old with a quick wit. She was graduating from high school at the top of her class and was following in Marilyn's footsteps by going to college right after high school. There was no discussion about where I was from and what my background was. In fact, other than Marilyn's mother asking me what part of Puerto Rico my family was from, the subject of my life never came up. I was wondering when Marilyn's mother or sister would ask about our late nights out together, but that never happened. It was as if they went out of their way to make me feel comfortable by not bringing up certain subjects. After a little while Marilyn and I decided to go somewhere where we could have some privacy.

We ended up at my apartment, where we talked about Tish and what was going on in her life. It was the first time Marilyn had agreed to go to my apartment. She seemed very comfortable there. Tish's parents had gotten serious about her moving out, and she was practically begging Marilyn to move in with her. Marilyn told me that during one discussion they had, the idea of moving out of the city came up. They had decided to move to either San Francisco or New York City. They were going to meet sometime during the week to get their finances together and to start setting dates.

Marilyn's news saddened me. My mental turmoil about women, which had just about disappeared with Marilyn, suddenly reoccupied my mind. I asked myself why I had such bad luck around women. Here I was thinking that I had finally done everything right—allowing a woman to know me and know everything about me so that I could have a long-lasting loving relationship—just to be abandoned again. I turned to Marilyn and asked why she was abandoning me.

"You're reading too much into it, Rey, you silly goose. I'm not abandoning you; I want you to come along with us. I wanted to talk to you first before I tell Tish," she told me, cradling my face. "I don't like it here in Chicago," she continued, "but I'll stay if you don't go with us."

I told Marilyn that getting out of Chicago would probably be good for me, but that I didn't have the freedom to just get up and move that she had. She had a master's degree that pretty much guaranteed her employment anywhere she went. Me? Well, I had the experience of working at UIC and nothing more. Marilyn assured me that she had thought about that, and that she wanted me to concentrate on going to school and getting the college diploma I wanted so badly. Her words made my face light up with joy. I could not believe that I was being offered financial support while I went to school. I was filled with happiness like I'd never felt before. I immediately agreed to make the move.

The decision to move out of Chicago was a relatively simple one for me to make. Although I had family members who lived in Chicago, I had no family. Marilyn was my only source of encouragement and support. I needed to be with her; I wanted to be wherever she was.

Marilyn was the first woman I had ever had a relationship with where sex wasn't the most important part of our lives. She was a beautiful and sexy woman, yet I longed for her opinions and insights more than I did her passion. I know now that it was because I was getting doses of something I hadn't even known existed before.

14

A New Plan

AT THE BEGINNING of April I notified my sister about my plans to leave Chicago. I told her that I wanted to save as much money as possible, and I asked her if I could move in with her so that I wouldn't have to pay rent. I would, of course, help out with her rent and bills, but that would still allow me to save some money. Her boyfriend readily agreed since this would give him someone to care for his daughter while he went and hung out. My sister had a job and was going to a vocational school to learn computer skills at night, so he had been a full-time babysitter.

I thought about the temptations that being around my sister's boyfriend would create for me, but took it as a challenge to my willpower. I knew there would be marijuana and alcohol around me at all times, and I knew that the gang lifestyle would be flaunted before me. I challenged myself to overcome those vices and decided that if I couldn't resist the temptations before me, then I had no right to think about leaving Chicago. My sister agreed to let me move in and we set May 1 as the date.

MARILYN AND I drove to Tish's house to tell her about my joining the move. Her reaction was not what Marilyn expected. Tish seemed angry that Marilyn had asked me to come along without her knowledge. "That wasn't the plan," Tish told Marilyn. "You and I have to talk." Tish's words were loud and abrasive. Her attitude took Marilyn by complete surprise. Marilyn asked her to come take a walk along the lakefront with us so they could talk. "Oh, no," Tish told Marilyn. "This conversation has to be between us, just me and you."

Marilyn and I left Tish's house confused about her reaction. My conclusion was that as a bisexual female she must be attracted to Marilyn, and this was why she wanted any move made to be only the two of them. Marilyn didn't totally dismiss my claim, but said that Tish had absolutely no reason to think of her as anything other than a friend. I personally couldn't see any other reason for Tish's attitude, and I teased Marilyn about it. "You know once you go black you won't come back," I teased Marilyn. "Oh, you don't have to worry about that," she laughed. "I'll come back." I teasingly asked her, "so you have given it a thought, huh?" "No, not with Tish," she answered. Then she dropped a bomb of a question. "You had sex with a man—did it leave you with gay tendencies?"

That question blew my mind. All at once the things I had shared with Marilyn rushed into my head. I knew I didn't have any desires to be with a man, and I thought I had been clear about why I had done it to begin with, but for some reason I didn't know how to answer her question. I wondered what other questions Marilyn would ask about information I had entrusted her with. The anxiety I felt at that moment was overwhelming. Because I was unable to answer the question quickly and with conviction, I began to question my own sexuality. Did I in one way or another have gay tendencies, as Marilyn put it? "No, I'm not a fag!" I finally said angrily.

Marilyn took my answer for what it was worth. My tone of voice must have alerted her that she was pursuing a sensitive issue, and in fact she was. I was not at all proud of having had sex with a man, and shuddered at the notion that I ever would have done it had I not been in a desperate situation. The way I finally responded to Marilyn's question created a silence that lasted until we got back to her place.

At her request, we pulled over and parked before we got to her house. As soon as I turned off the engine, Marilyn reached over and kissed me. I asked her how she felt about Tish's reaction. She admitted that she was surprised, but she was sure Tish would come around and change her mind. I told her that I would be moving into my sister's apartment at the end of the month, but only because I wanted to save money for our relocation. I wanted Marilyn to assure me that we would be going through with our plans before I turned in the keys to my apartment. "What if it's just you and me?" she asked. "I don't know Tish that well, so it wouldn't make any difference to me if she joins us or not," I responded. "OK, then, do what you have to do to get prepared," Marilyn said. We kissed each other for a long time. And then Marilyn rekindled the sensitive subject.

"Well, do you?" Marilyn asked as she stared out into the streets of Chicago. I watched her, waiting for her to make eye contact, but she never looked my way. It was as if she were waiting for some kind of revelation from me. "No, Marilyn," I responded. "I have no desire to be with a man. What I did, I did only because I was out on the street, cold, hungry, and half-dead—otherwise I wouldn't have done it." Marilyn finally made eye contact with me and kissed me.

After the kiss, Marilyn went on about how she would understand if I was attracted to men. She said that my sexual orientation wasn't important to her because she would be just as hurt if I ever did her wrong with a man or woman. It wasn't sexual orientation that mattered, Marilyn pointed out. It was whether or not one was faithful to the person one was with. I didn't know how to interpret her comments. It crossed my mind that maybe she thought I was lying and that she thought deep down that I was bisexual. Only the fact that she was caressing my face while she talked kept me from blowing up in anger. Then I posed the same question to her.

Marilyn sat back on her seat and sidestepped the question by telling me that I had not answered her. I told her again that had I not been in a desperate situation, I never would have gone through with the act of homosexuality. I told her that, because of that act, I lived in fear of being found positive for the HIV virus. Marilyn took exception to that remark. She used it to lead the conversation away from my question about her sexuality.

For the first time since I met Marilyn, words were coming out of her mouth with anger. She looked me in the eye only at the end of a sentence, and went right into another before I had a chance to respond. She told me it was the drug-induced, unprotected sex that I'd had with promiscuous females that I should be worried about. She informed me about HIV not being a homosexual disease, and that she couldn't believe how many ignorant people still believed that. "That man was probably the cleanest piece you have ever gotten," she finally said.

For a long time I sat there quietly, not knowing how to respond to Marilyn's barrage. I knew she was right about the danger I had put myself into by being so promiscuous with so many women. I wanted to make her understand that I knew she was right, but that she should understand how I felt living with the knowledge that I had had sex with a man. I wanted her to see how the whole notion of having sex with a man made me sick to my stomach. I also wanted her to know that the feeling didn't come from hatred of homosexuals, it came from anger I had with myself for doing things I didn't want to do, even if only for survival.

"I think you're the cleanest piece I've ever had," I said as I started the car and began driving toward Marilyn's house. Not another word was said. She got out of the car in front of her house and left without ever looking at me. I waited until she was safely inside as I always did. Just as she was walking in, she turned to me and gave me a shy smile as if to tell me that everything was great between us.

OVER THE NEXT few weeks, Marilyn and I saw each other sparingly as we allowed the changes to take place that would eventually lead to our departure from Chicago. I moved in with my sister and put my car up for sale. The money from the car would be the bulk of the funds we would use for our move. Marilyn acknowledged that she realized Tish was sexually attracted to her, and therefore Trish was not part of our moving plans. It would be just the two of us, and we were dazzled by the whole idea.

At my sister's, I slowly began to open a dialogue with her about our lost time together. I asked about what she did in Puerto

Rico while I was in Chicago. She painted a picture of having a lot of friends and good times. She told me how she and my other sisters had become part of a group of people that went to parties, to the beaches of the island, and to nearby lakes. She said that they had become very popular and wished that my mother would have stayed there instead of coming back to Chicago. I nodded and smiled like a robot.

As I sat there listening to story after story about how good Puerto Rico had been to my family, my anger grew and grew. The very few times that I started to tell her about my life while they were in paradise I was interrupted by her boyfriend. I didn't like the guy, or trust him. He represented everything I hated about my life and wanted to change. He, on the hand, was perfectly comfortable being a gangbanging, drug-using bum who was supported by a woman. I talked very little to him and often heard him complain to my sister about my animosity toward him. She always shut him up by reminding him of the financial assistance I represented.

Marilyn and I did research to figure out where we wanted to move. We both agreed that the Bay Area of San Francisco would be a great place to go, but the unemployment rate and high cost of living there made that plan unaffordable for us. Our second choice, New York City, presented the same challenges. Although we knew that Marilyn would probably be able to find gainful employment, thanks to her master's degree, I did not want to be financially dependent on her. Marilyn was sweet in saying that it was OK as long as I was going to school, but I still declined. She understood that I was grappling with having wasted most of my life on the streets and that I felt that I had too much to make up for.

We concluded that we needed to find a place that would allow both of us to be employed. I knew that I wouldn't be able to come close to making the type of money Marilyn would make, and I was OK with that as long as I had a fair chance to contribute. With that in mind, we started to do research on cities based on cost of living and unemployment rates. We decided on Dallas, Texas, as the place we would call home. When we looked through a copy of the Dallas newspaper at the Harold Washington Library in Chicago, we found dozens of job ads offering decent pay that asked for no experience other than being bilingual (Spanish/English). We made plans to leave for Dallas at the beginning of June.

I sold my car and notified my coworkers at UIC about my plans to resign my position. Marilyn and I spent our remaining days in the city trying to tie up loose ends and getting to know each other still more deeply. We often walked the lakefront for hours, or wandered around Lakeview. Marilyn told me that her family worried about our plans, and I told her about my anger in discovering that my family seemed to have lived in joy and happiness without me.

On the same day I resigned my position at UIC and accompanied Marilyn to purchase two one-way Amtrak tickets to Dallas, I finally asked my sister about her feelings regarding our upbringing. I asked her if she remembered how Pedro would beat me, and how our mother would relieve her anger toward him by beating me more. I asked her if she remembered how our mother's way of dealing with Pedro pulling a gun on me was slapping me and scratching my neck. Then I asked if they ever thought about me or talked about me while they were having fun in Puerto Rico. My sister's recollection of our upbringing was much different than my own. She became angry.

"Mom protected us!" she yelled. "Don't you go blaming her for screwing up your own fuckin' life!" Her face turned red in anger. Her boyfriend, sensing a violent confrontation, positioned himself to step between us but didn't say a word. "I don't know how she protected you but she protected me by hitting me with an extension cord!" I yelled in response. "She loved me so much that she sent me to live in the home of a fuckin' drug dealer. She protected me so well that to this day she hasn't bothered to ask how my life was while all of you were in Puerto Rico running around with all your fuckin' little friends!" I screamed in anger before she had a chance to say anything.

My sister suddenly came at me with her hands balled into fists. I took a couple of steps back and allowed her boyfriend to step between us and grab her. "Let me go! That ungrateful son of a bitch doesn't deserve my mother! You fuckin' asshole! After all Mom went through to make sure we were all OK, this is the kind of shit you come up with?" my sister screamed as her boyfriend released her. "I was an abused child! Maybe you weren't, but I was!" I stomped my right foot on the floor as if I were kicking someone to death. "I just want to know why me, why fuckin' me!" I yelled as I began crying uncontrollably. My sister was now in tears also. She looked directly into my eyes. For the first and only time in my life I felt that my thoughts were totally in sync with those of one of my sisters. Unfortunately, that feeling only lasted a couple of seconds. "Don't blame Mom, don't blame Mom," my sister said in a low voice as she made her way toward her bedroom, still crying. I turned and headed for the streets.

IT WAS A warm May afternoon in Chicago. It was fifteen miles to Marilyn's from my sister's, but I decided to walk anyway. The danger of being recognized as I walked in and out of gang-infested streets and past corners where known rivals to the Latin Kings gathered didn't even cross my mind. Gang signs were flashed from cars and from guys standing on the sidewalk as I walked by, but no action was taken. I guess they didn't find a man walking down the street in tears a threat. I made it to Marilyn's and sat on the steps with my head in my hands, trying to collect myself before I knocked on the door. Before I could do that, Marilyn came out. We went for a walk.

We walked up the street to North Avenue and hopped on the bus to the lakefront. My face was flushed from crying. Not many words were spoken on the bus ride because I didn't want to break down again. In the time it took us to get to the lakefront I calmed down and got my emotions and thoughts together enough to be able to talk about what I was feeling without crying again.

Marilyn and I walked along the lakefront from North Avenue to Addison. I told her about the incident with my sister, and we concluded that my sister was going through the same denial that I had been fighting. I told Marilyn that I felt relieved to finally know how at least one of my siblings would react to my childhood stories. Although I would have liked it if my sister had agreed with and reinforced my feelings, I still felt I had accomplished something. I suddenly felt that the hatred I harbored for my mother had been justified, and I could express those feelings freely and rightfully. I also felt I had taken the first step to forgiving my mother. I anxiously counted the minutes to my departure from Chicago—I was looking forward to getting away from the pain and starting a new life.

ON THE DAY before we were planning to leave Chicago, Marilyn took me to meet a girl she described as one of her closest friends.

Until that day, the only person in Marilyn's life that I had met aside from her family was Tish. Marilyn's friend was a pretty, shorthaired Ecuadorian girl named Nancy.

Nancy lived in a single-family home on the Near North side of the city. Although Nancy was very polite and showed me very good hospitality, it didn't seem that she wanted me to be there. She didn't pursue a conversation with me when I attempted to talk with her, and when Marilyn tried to bring me into their conversation, Nancy only responded to her, not to me. I began to feel uncomfortable and out of place. Ultimately I ended up in front of the television watching a baseball game as Marilyn and Nancy talked in another room. After about an hour and a half, we were on our way.

As we walked down the street back toward the bus stop, Marilyn began to tell me more about her friendship with Nancy. She told me that they had met in college when they were both undergraduates and that they pretty much helped each other get through school. She told me that Nancy's mother and brother had accused them of being lesbian lovers and that they didn't like Marilyn to come around. Marilyn's presence at Nancy's house often created arguments between Nancy and her mother. Marilyn said that it used to upset her that Nancy's mother seemed to overlook the line of girls that her son was having sex with under her roof, but that she barraged Nancy with insults because of what she thought about her sexuality.

I asked Marilyn if Nancy was a lesbian and if they had been lovers. "It doesn't matter if she is a lesbian or not. She's not having sex with a bunch of different people," Marilyn said. "Were you guys lovers?" I asked. "That's not the point," she responded. "It's her brother who is showing disrespect for his mother by having sex with so many different girls right there in her house. Why doesn't she say anything about that? Why is being gay less morally acceptable than being a whore?"

The whore Marilyn was referring to was Nancy's brother, and I assumed that Nancy was the gay person with good morals. Before I had a chance to make sure that my assumptions were correct, Marilyn started to tell me a story about Nancy's mother. She told me about how Nancy's mother had once been a victim of a pigeon-drop scheme and had lost fifteen hundred dollars. She then blamed Nancy, although Nancy had tried to warn her.

Nancy and her mother were walking out of a bank when a Spanish-speaking man approached her, claiming to be the holder of the previous day's winning lottery ticket. The ticket, according to the man, was worth two million dollars, but it would take several weeks to collect the money. The man explained that his family was in desperate need and that he was willing to give her twenty-five percent of the winnings for a fifteen-hundred-dollar advance.

As Nancy's mother and the man spoke, a female passerby stopped and joined the conversation. The woman began to advise Nancy's mother against the transaction, but then changed her tune after looking into a newspaper she was carrying and identifying the numbers on the man's ticket as winning numbers. She showed Nancy's mother the numbers and offered to make the transaction with the man. The man readily agreed to her offer and began to walk away with her. Nancy's mother, not wanting to be cheated out of the opportunity to earn half a million dollars, stopped the two and told the man that he had made her the offer first and that she could give him the money right away. The man advised the woman that Nancy's mother was entitled to help him first, which made the woman yell obscenities at Nancy's mother as she walked away angrily. The man agreed to let Nancy's mother hold onto the ticket as collateral until it was paid on, as long as he could fill out his information on the back of the ticket. Against Nancy's advice, her mother went into the bank and withdrew fifteen hundred dollars, which she gave to the man. He gave her the ticket with his information filled out on the back, gave her his phone number, and insisted she give him information about where she lived and her phone number.

Nancy's mother went home a happy woman. She talked about what she would do with the money and the places she would visit. Her happiness ended when she got home and took a close look at the ticket. She realized that she was holding a ticket for a lottery drawing that had not yet taken place. The numbers were definitely the winners of the previous night's drawing, but the date on the ticket was for a drawing the following week. Upon further investigation, she found that the address on the back of the ticket didn't exist and the telephone number was out of service. Nancy's mother blamed Nancy for not stopping her.

Marilyn's story was humorous and interesting enough to make me forget about the questions I had asked but not gotten answers to. By the time I knew it, the bus was approaching and the conversation switched to our departure the next day. Instead of getting off the bus with Marilyn, I told her that I wanted to go straight home and finish packing. We agreed to meet at her place the following morning and kissed each other good-bye.

That night at my sister's house, I was left only in the company of her boyfriend and my niece. My sister never attempted to talk with me, and I didn't do anything to open a dialogue either. We hadn't spoken to each other since the night we blew up at each other. Before I went to bed I smoked marijuana for the last time in my life, compliments of my sister's boyfriend. I smoked it because it was my way of saying good-bye to the life I had lived in Chicago, a celebratory high. The puffs I took from the joints we smoked were long and hard, intended to gain the drug's maximum effect. I remained quiet while my smoking companion went on and on about how I was right about having been abused and about how my mother had spoiled my sister. After his first few sentences, I totally ignored him until it was time to go to sleep.

The next morning I woke up to the voices of my three sisters and my mother. It was the first time that I saw them all in one room in a long time. I gave them brief good mornings, then went and showered, got dressed, and prepared the two medium-sized suitcases and a backpack that I would be taking with me. I came out of my bedroom, suitcases in hand and ready to hit the road. I was going to take the bus to Marilyn's, but my sister's boyfriend talked me into accepting a ride. Our good-byes were very brief. They were the type of good-byes reserved for people who barely knew each other. In fact, although we were family, we had no clue who we were and what we felt.

I told them that I was going to Los Angeles, California, knowing very well that I was headed for Texas. For many reasons, I thought that I would be better off if no one in my family knew where I was going or what my plans were. I put my luggage in the car and gave everybody the mandatory hug. I walked away to the sight of tear-filled eyes. I didn't understand what the crying was about, nor did I react to it. I thought those tears were forced because there was neither joy nor sadness to justify them. I was thinking only of getting out of Chicago as fast and as soon as I could. Although I knew that I would probably never see the faces of my family again, I was totally emotionless about it.

I said very little to my sister's boyfriend on the way to Marilyn's, and was overjoyed when we reached our destination. At Marilyn's, I took my luggage out of the car, shook his hand, and then watched him drive away. Marilyn came out with her sister's car key in her hand and asked me to put my luggage in the trunk, then to go up to her apartment. Inside Marilyn's apartment I was confronted with another version of the scene I had just left. Only at her place it seemed more genuine. No one was crying or saddened. They busied themselves making sure that Marilyn had everything she needed for the trip and time and time again assured themselves that she was doing something she really wanted to do. They all made sure she knew that they were all just a phone call away. Marilyn had taken on an important part of the financial responsibilities in her house, yet it didn't seem to matter to them that she was leaving as long as she was doing something that made her happy.

I watched in envy as Marilyn got advice, reassurances, and money to make things easier on her. Her mother prepared food for us to eat before we left and sandwiches for us to take on the train. After we ate we walked through a barrage of hugs, good lucks, and handshakes on our way to Marilyn's sister's car. Finally we were on our way to the train station.

Marilyn and her sister sat in the front and talked while I sat in the back watching the buildings as we drove by. I remembered the first time I came to Humboldt Park from the South Side. The buildings that once told stories that fascinated me now repulsed me and left me cold and empty. Then we passed the park itself. I looked deep into the park that I once considered a city within

a city and saw a graveyard. The memories I had of Humboldt
Park and the many streets surrounding it made my hair stand on
end. I planned on never seeing or setting foot in that park again,
but I knew that I had made that plan before.

We arrived at Union Station in downtown Chicago and I went
inside to get a cart for our luggage while Marilyn said good-bye
to her sister. We checked our tickets and our bags, then waited
to board the train headed toward our one-way destination. In an
hour and a half we boarded the train and were on our way out
of the city. Marilyn and I sat cuddling each other, not wanting
to look out the window to watch the city go by. It was a little
more than six months since we'd first met. We were both happy
to be leaving Chicago for our own individual reasons. The only
thing we wanted to see was Dallas, Texas.

15

Welcome to Dallas

MARILYN AND I didn't talk much on the way to Dallas. We were just anxious for the sixteen-hour train ride to be over with so that we could start our new life. The smiles on our faces and the embraces we shared showed our desire to forget all our troubles. On a sunny early afternoon we arrived in Dallas, the city we hoped would give us that opportunity.

We arrived in downtown Dallas with our hearts in our hands for each other. At the train station we located a map of the city and a hotel guide. At the information desk sat the most helpful, sweetest information desk employee we had ever met. She was a white woman in her late forties or early fifties, and she spoke with a deep Texas drawl. We told her it was our first time in Dallas and what our plans were. "Well, bless your heart, how romantic," the lady said after hearing our story. She then told us that she knew of a reasonably priced motel that would pick us up right at the station. With our permission she called the motel, and within the hour we were in a van headed toward the motel. The driver of the bus was also a middle-aged white woman with a deep Texas drawl, who also thought that what we were doing was romantic.

She offered advice about where the bad parts of Dallas were located and where we could seek employment.

At the motel we checked in and got comfortable in our room. Thirty minutes after our arrival, the lady who drove the van knocked on our door and handed us several menus for local restaurants that delivered to the motel. She assured us that the prices were reasonable and the food was very good.

Marilyn and I were elated with the hospitality we had been shown so far in Dallas. We began to conclude that these were all signs of good things to come. Since we'd arrived on a Saturday, we decided to rest, then get the Sunday paper the next day and begin looking at help-wanted ads. We ordered some Chinese food, showered, and spent the rest of the night making love.

It had been the first time that Marilyn and I had been intimate in about a month. Other than that first time we'd made love, several months back in a hotel room in Chicago, this was the first time we'd spent the night together in each other's arms. Our first night in Dallas was the best night of our short relationship to date. We were passionate and comfortable. We enjoyed and explored each other as we had never done before.

Sunday morning we enjoyed the hotel's complimentary continental breakfast like two lovebirds. We fetched food and fed each other from our plates. At every opportunity we held hands, rubbed ourselves against each other, and expressed our love.

After breakfast we picked up the Sunday paper from the hotel lobby and headed back to our room. There we showered, made love, showered again, and got busy looking through help-wanted and apartment rental ads.

There were dozens of ads seeking employees with no skills besides fluency in both Spanish and English. We circled those as jobs we would go and apply for together. Marilyn had decided that she would not seek employment that required a degree until she was sure that Dallas was where we wanted to live.

We looked through the apartment ads and were dumbfounded by how inexpensive the rental rates were compared to those in Chicago. We started calling the numbers in the ads right away. To our surprise, we found that the vast majority of the apartments advertised were located in big apartment complexes. We were expecting the two- or three-story buildings with an apartment on each floor we were used to in Chicago. It became apparent to us that we were expecting Dallas to be just like Chicago but in a different location with different people.

The next morning we got up bright and early with big hopes for our future. We had breakfast, picked up the bus schedules from the hotel lobby, showered, and got ready to explore Dallas. We stood at a bus stop about half a block from the hotel at about 7:30 that morning. Two hours later we were still standing there. It turned out that that particular bus route only made four daily stops there, and the first wouldn't be until 10:00 A.M. It was the only bus route available anywhere near the hotel, and it only took us to one place, downtown Dallas.

Of all the things we thought we'd miss about the city of Chicago, the good public transportation system had never crossed our minds. Dallas's public transportation was nonexistent by Chicago standards. Because of the inconvenience of the bus system, we were limited to one, maybe two application submissions per day. On our second day in Dallas we got stranded in an area where the last available bus ran past as we were waiting to be interviewed at a telemarketing company. We were forced to take a cab, which cost us almost a hundred dollars, to get back to the motel. The incredibly high taxi rate was another eye opener as we remembered being able to take a cab from one side of Chicago to the other for less than thirty bucks.

With immobility being an issue, we counted on an apartment-seeking agency to get us an apartment we could afford in a good part of town. That task wasn't as easy as it sounded because of our lack of employment. By our third day in Dallas, Marilyn had become frustrated with the city and did nothing but talk about going back home. I felt the same frustration as Marilyn about the transportation situation, but I wasn't about to give up on Dallas that easily. I looked at the employment section of the local newspaper and saw that all the jobs that required little more than Spanish-speaking proficiency earned ten dollars an hour or more. I knew there was no way that I could ever get those opportunities back in Chicago. Marilyn, on the other hand, with her master's degree, could go anywhere.

I talked to Marilyn so that she would understand my feelings about the employment situation. I reasoned that we came to Dallas knowing that we would struggle at first but that we would do all it took to make it. Marilyn came around and agreed.

That evening we got a call from an agent of an apartment locator service advising us that she had found an apartment complex that would rent to us while we sought employment. She also told us that the complex was located in North Dallas where it was safe and in an area where there were a lot of employment opportunities. We were so excited about the news that we ended up making love. Afterward I sat at the desk and looked over our map of Dallas, trying to pinpoint the intersections the agent had given us. I'd located the apartment complex on the map when Marilyn threw a monkey wrench into my excitement.

"Let's go to California," Marilyn said. "What?" I responded. "I thought we had discussed this already." "No," Marilyn said, "you discussed it." Her comment made my blood boil. I became angrier than I had been in a long time. "We came to Dallas because we don't have the money to make it in California and we have less now," I yelled as I got up from the desk and faced Marilyn, who sat on the bed. "Many people go out to California penniless and make it," Marilyn replied as she made her way up the bed and sat with her back against the headboard facing me.

"Marilyn, are you crazy?" I said. "We're here, we need to make it work for a little while, get some more money together, and then think about moving again." I turned around, grabbed the pen, and prepared to start mapping companies I had called to schedule interviews. "California or Chicago," Marilyn said. "Take your choice but we are leaving."

I stood there staring as I felt a rage come over me that I knew I could not control. "I don't like it here and I'm not staying," I barely heard Marilyn say. Visions of my homeless days and nights began to run through my mind. I could hear the voices of my dear family laughing at my failure to make it on my own. I had nowhere to go, nowhere to turn to. Then I exploded.

"Fuck you, bitch," I yelled at the top my lungs as I threw the pen toward Marilyn. The pen hit the wall about two feet above her head shattered into pieces and left about a foot of splashed ink. "It's easy for you to fuckin' move back to Chicago, but where the fuck would I go?" I screamed as I paced the floor in front of the bed like a madman. "We're here and we're staying here like we planned!" I screamed as Marilyn quietly made her way off the bed and headed toward the bathroom.

I sat down, turned on the television, and fumed over Marilyn's decision. I heard the water from the shower running and decided that I would go get in the shower with Marilyn and sweetly try to have her see things my way. The bathroom door was locked, though, so I had to wait for her to come out to plead with her.

While Marilyn showered, I calmed down and collected my thoughts. I put on some shorts and went over all the apologetic words I would say to her when she came back into the room. That didn't happen until about an hour later. Marilyn finally walked out of the bathroom wearing a towel around her body and went directly to get clothes out of her suitcase. As she bent over them, I came up from behind her, took off the towel, and began caressing her back. Marilyn didn't react or say a word. She just got the clothes she wanted, then retreated back into the bathroom without the towel.

About twenty minutes later, Marilyn came out of the bathroom dressed and said that she wanted to go for a walk by herself. Before I could say a word she picked up her purse and headed out the door. I sat with no reaction or thoughts as to where she was headed. What I did think about was being homeless in California or being laughed at in Chicago. I had come to Dallas determined to make it and had nowhere else to go. I didn't have the college degree to fall back on or the supportive family who would welcome me back into their home. As far I was concerned, my decision was final—I was staying in Dallas. If Marilyn wanted to leave, she would have to go by herself.

Marilyn came back from her walk with a bag of food from a local restaurant. She didn't say a word to me, nor did I say a thing to her. We didn't make eye contact. This was the first time since I had met Marilyn when I wasn't happy being in her company, and there was no doubt in my mind that she felt the same way.

She sat the bag of food on the desk and began to pull out food. Cheeseburgers, fries, and onion rings would be our dinner that evening. I grabbed my share and sat on the bed facing the television. Marilyn did the same. We sat and ate without saying a word to each other. Finally Marilyn broke the silence.

"How long are you planning on giving Dallas a chance?" Marilyn asked. "Long enough to make enough money to be able to make it in California," I responded. "Once we get to California you're going to have to get comfortable with the idea that I will be supporting you while you go to school," Marilyn said. "I promise I will do that, but I will try to help out in any way I can," I told her. This exchange went on without either one of us looking at the other. When we finished eating, we threw the remains in the trash and lay next to each other on the bed, staring at the ceiling.

I wondered what was going through Marilyn's mind. I wondered if the thoughts of financial, emotional, and educational success occupied her mind like they did mine. I could clearly see myself in a graduation gown accepting a diploma. I could see Marilyn glowing with pride as I walked up to the podium to make the speech reserved only for those at the top of their class. Then out of nowhere the transportation problems we were faced within Dallas entered my mind and awakened me from my daydream.

"We need to get a rental car, at least until we're in an apartment," I said while still staring at the ceiling. "If we can get it early in the morning, we can go fill out applications and be able to go see the lady at the apartment locator's agency and then check out the apartment she told us about," Marilyn said. "Yeah, I have the apartment pinpointed on the map, so maybe we can look for work around there," I responded as I got up and located the Dallas telephone directory.

I sat by the phone and made phone call after phone call to rental car agencies. I found out you needed a credit card to rent a car. I had a driver's license but no credit card. Marilyn had a credit card but no driver's license. Fortunately, some of the agencies I spoke to were willing to accept her card with my license. Unfortunately, all the prices were horrendous. There was no way we could afford to rent a car for the three or four days we would need it at the prices I was being quoted. I finally found one that met our budget requirement. Appropriately, that agency was called Rent-a-Wreck.

The next morning, we got on the first bus headed to downtown Dallas, where we would take another bus to a north suburban city called Plano. According to the agent at Rent-a-Wreck, the bus would drop us off about a block from the agency.

On the bus we sat near the rear and Marilyn started a conversation with a young black guy who was obviously gay. They conversed as if they were old friends. I did little more than comment every so often. The guy told Marilyn where Plano was and that he was getting off on the stop where we would catch the bus headed there. He told her that the bus we were on would take us right to the center of downtown Dallas where there would be a lot of people coming and going. I pictured downtown Chicago where thousands upon thousands of people would be on the street all at once and traffic would be backed up and moving ever so slowly yet in a rush. The guy also explained to Marilyn how to get back from Plano to Dallas.

Marilyn's face lit up with excitement as she talked to this guy she didn't even know. She wrote down every bit of information he gave her about where the gay section of Dallas was located and the places she could visit there. Marilyn turned to me and said that maybe we should look for an apartment in the area called Oaklawn the guy was describing to her. According to Marilyn's new friend, the Oaklawn area was the only part of Dallas with any kind of culture and substance. Marilyn was anxious to go there.

When we got to downtown Dallas I was astonished at how empty the streets were compared to Chicago. As I looked around, acknowledging the differences between Dallas and Chicago, Marilyn got the black guy's number and hugged him good-bye. She then pulled me toward the bus headed to Plano, which had arrived without me noticing it.

Marilyn and the gay guy waved and smiled at each other like they would be missing each other dearly. I was just happy that she had found a reason to give Dallas a chance to be our home.

We rode the bus to Plano, Texas, looking in desperation at the landscapes that passed us as the bus crawled along Central Expressway. We were looking for both differences and similarities to a bus ride in Chicago. All we could find were differences. The scenery consisted of one building housing one business after another. Even after we had long left downtown Dallas behind, the business buildings continued until we got off the bus in Plano.

The lack of homes with family and friends hanging out in front, kids playing, a fire hydrant spraying water, which would be a heavenly feeling in the hot Texas sun, was disheartening to us. For a couple looking to work, make money, and move on to another city the view was wonderful. But for those with plans to find a place to settle down and call home, Dallas didn't look like it could offer that dream.

We got off the bus in Plano and became acquainted with the
Texas sun. It was the first time since we arrived that we had the
opportunity to walk any significant distance. Suddenly it started
making sense to me why everyone drove and hardly anyone rode
the bus. With the distance between bus stops and the inconvenience of the routes, only those without the luxury of an auto-
mobile needed to bother with Dallas's transportation system.

It was about half a block's walk to the car rental agency
from the bus stop, and the heat was excruciating, even for two
people accustomed to walking long distances. By the time we
reached the agency we had convinced ourselves that we would
have to make peace with the sun in the months to come. We
didn't care what kind of car we got so long as it had a working
air conditioner.

At Rent-a-Wreck I started a conversation with an older gentleman who wore a Dallas Cowboys baseball cap. "The Cowboys haven't been doing so good," I said as I filled out the rental
application. "Now the Bears, that's a team to cheer for," I added.
"Oh, that's because they stole Mike Ditka from Dallas," he
responded.

We sat there talking football while the Rent-a-Wreck agent
processed the application and the rental car keys were handed to
me. The older gentleman gave me very detailed directions about
the Dallas Expressway system and how to get to the apartment
locator's office and then back to the hotel. I shook his hand and
followed the Rent-a-Wreck agent to a car that certainly seemed
destined for the junkyard. After assuring ourselves that the air
conditioner worked, Marilyn and I headed back toward Dallas.

I mentioned how nice it was for the older gentleman at the
rental car agency to give me such detailed directions. Marilyn

said that the directions weren't really necessary as the directions she had written down from the gay black guy were just as detailed and accurate. I told her that I understood the directions given by the old man better than the ones she had written down.

There was a moment of silence and then Marilyn responded to my remark in a very cynical way. "The directions are the same," she said. "Maybe you understand things better when discussing meaningless subjects." "Maybe you understand things better when talking to people you have something in common with," I shot back. "What is that supposed to mean?" she asked. "You like men, he likes men, you have something in common," I said in a smart aleck tone. "Oh, yeah, that's an intelligent conclusion," Marilyn said.

Again there was a moment of silence that should have put an end to the conversation, but, unfortunately, that wasn't the case. The little exchange between us seemed destined to become an argument, at least from my standpoint. It was an argument I didn't plan on losing.

"What is it with you and gay people?" I asked Marilyn in a loud, angry voice. "Why do you insist on defending a fuckin' faggot you don't even know?" "That faggot was nice enough to give us directions on where to get this car. You didn't mind him being a faggot then, did you?" Marilyn calmly said.

My anger grew without reason. I could feel my muscles tightening and my head becoming hot. "Don't you think for one minute that you're going to be calling that fag," I told Marilyn in a voice that was more threatening than demanding. "I'll call him and anybody else I feel like calling," Marilyn responded.

I became enraged and began yelling obscenities at Marilyn at the top of my lungs. I pounded on the steering wheel violently as

Marilyn melted into the car seat like a small animal cowering into a corner to avoid danger. I continued my barrage of profanities and took to degrading gay people, particularly the black guy we'd met on the bus that morning. Marilyn just sat there, staring into oblivion, not saying a word or even attempting to look my way. I turned up the radio, smiled, and sang along with the music. I was celebrating the victory of the argument.

By the time we got to the apartment locator's office, my anger had passed. I was talking sweet and being kind and gentle as if the argument had never taken place. She ignored me. I parked outside the agency and waited for Marilyn to go inside and get the apartment information. Fifteen minutes later she came out, got in the car, handed me a piece of paper with directions to the apartment complex, and we went on our way. "The directions should be easy for you to read," Marilyn said softly as I positioned the paper on the steering wheel in front of me. "She wasn't gay." Although I was quite irritated by her comment, I remained quiet. A few minutes later we arrived at the apartment complex and I forgot all about it.

The rental agents were expecting us. I was impressed that they called us by name as soon as we walked through the door. The leasing agent who took care of us said that the apartment owner would rent us the apartment if we could provide a co-signer for a six-month lease. Marilyn asked to use the phone and called her sister in Chicago. We didn't even ask to see the apartment because we didn't have much choice. After Marilyn's sister agreed to co-sign, the agent faxed her the contract and, within half an hour of stepping into the apartment complex office, we had our first apartment as a couple.

16

Is This Love?

OUR FIRST APARTMENT was a huge empty space that was really a lot more than we needed, but we didn't have any choice. Staying at the hotel was draining our savings, so we had to take what we could get. Marilyn and I were still uncertain how long we would be staying in Dallas, so we decided not to bother with furnishing the place. The apartment was fully carpeted and came equipped with a stove, refrigerator, and central air and heat. This was more than we would ever get in an apartment in Chicago and at a fraction of the cost.

The only articles we bought for our comfort were a nice thick queen-sized comforter we used as a bed, a sheet and pillow case set of the same size, and a couple of pillows. This was our bedroom set. For the kitchen we purchased a very cheap set of pots and pans and an even cheaper set of dishes, bowls, spoons, and forks enough for two people. Our entertainment came from sex and a thirteen-inch color television set that we bought only because it was on sale for sixty-nine dollars. It was an unknown brand and the display model.

After we moved in and began going on job interviews, things went well for us. In the three days that we had the rental car, we

were able to buy our basic necessities and also locate employment. Marilyn quickly found a job as a waitress in a nearby
restaurant, which lasted for about a week until she was employed
in a professional field. Marilyn dropped her idea of not seeking
employment that required a degree and was hired as a counselor
at an abortion clinic. She was really happy to have found that job,
as it was her ultimate goal to make a career in counseling. With
my limited work history and lack of higher education, I didn't
fare as well, but I did find employment. I got a part-time job at a
children's physical therapy clinic and a full-time cashier position at
a local Kroger grocery store. I worked two jobs and still didn't
make nearly as much money as Marilyn. The need for a college
education or at least some kind of vocational training became even
clearer to me.

At the clinic, I assisted the therapist in handling children with
various kinds of physical disabilities, mostly caused by muscular
dystrophy. I didn't perform actual therapy, but I helped hold them
in place and carry them from station to station. After a therapy
session I would clean and disinfect the room and get it ready for
the next patient. Working there and seeing children struggle just
to live taught me to stop feeling sorry for myself and count every
single day of my life as a blessing.

I became attached to the children at the clinic, and they to
me. The experience I had interacting with them helped me put
my life more into perspective. I watched them struggle to walk,
talk, and do the simplest basic tasks with so much enthusiasm.
I often found myself wondering if their disabilities were caused
by abuse or drug use by their parents, or if it was just their destiny. I couldn't help but picture myself in the same dilemma as
these kids were in, and I visualized them in my life. How much

more suffering would they be enduring if they'd had a family member like my cousin who had raped me as a child. I would look into their brightly lit eyes when they looked at me. I shared their joy in the accomplishment of taking a couple of steps without help, and I wished I could give them the things I took for granted. I watched them get embarrassed when they drooled all over themselves when trying to talk, and I wanted to hold them and in some way share my motor skills with them. I thought it was so unfair that such innocent beings had to suffer without cause. That's when I realized that I had a childhood in common with them. It saddened me to realize that it had taken me so long to stop my own personal suffering, and that the children I was learning so much from would probably never have that opportunity.

As positive as my experiences around the kids were, my experiences with some of the staff were totally opposite. All too often I would go into the staff break room and hear complaints about the drooling, crying, and stubbornness of the children. The sad part was that their anger seemed to focus on how little they thought they were paid to put up with being drooled on. I would sit there, slowly drinking a soda, listening to them and wondering how the police felt when they dealt with perfectly healthy kids who were out trying to kill one another. I started to think about how a police officer must feel, knowing that he or she could be killed just for approaching a twelve- or thirteen-year-old kid with the intention of helping. For the first time in my life, I found myself respecting the police profession and, in many ways, understanding the excessive force they sometimes used. All this I gathered from hearing a few therapists complain about children who had no say in how they were born.

I started work at the clinic at eight in the morning and left at two in the afternoon. It took me about an hour to get home, where I would rest for an hour and then make the half-hour walk to Kroger. There I worked until closing at 11 P.M., and sometimes stayed to help stock shelves. I also worked there on the weekends. I sometimes worked ten to twelve hours a day if I was allowed to. I only saw Marilyn late at night when I got home during the weekdays and in the evenings on the weekend. We were working toward our ultimate goal—being able to move to California.

THE COMMON BOND connecting Marilyn and me was that we both seemed to be looking for reassurance and reasons for our existence. We were both seeking approval from others and hoped that others would not judge us for our backgrounds. Neither of us had had any control over our upbringing, and therefore we should not be judged by our past. The same love, respect, explanations, and basic acknowledgment that I yearned for from my mother, Marilyn yearned for from her father. I suffered from within, knowing that my mother and I would probably never have an intelligent, understanding conversation regarding my childhood, and Marilyn suffered because she would never have the opportunity to have that same conversation with her father.

We'd had very different traumas, yet we were equally traumatized. While I chose violence, sex, alcohol, and drugs to relieve my pain, Marilyn chose books as her way to escape. I still had hope of gaining the reconciliation and approval that I so much desired. Marilyn, however, lived with the knowledge that her questions would never be answered.

Aside from our search for answers, the only other thing Marilyn and I seemed to share that had any significant meaning was our sex life. It was very healthy and enjoyable and it seemed to provide us with an escape from the troubles we faced. Then, suddenly, Marilyn began to question our need for sex, and that part of us and our life together started to fall apart.

Marilyn and I brought out feelings within each other that we had long harbored but never had an opportunity to deal with. These feelings were now coming to the surface at different times and in different ways. I knew that Marilyn's sudden questioning of our sex life was all part of her hidden emotions beginning to erupt. It was a time when she was begging for love and understanding, but I knew of no such emotions to be able to share with her. I was selfish and blind to what was trying to come out of her. Marilyn needed someone to hold her, listen to her, and assure her that it all would be OK. I didn't know how to do that. All I cared about was me, my feelings, and my desire for sex. That's all I knew.

Marilyn's excuses for not wanting sex ranged from tiredness to the experiences of the women having abortions at the clinic where she worked taking a toll on her. She said she was not ready to be a mother and would not want to go through an abortion. She also complained that the birth control pills she was taking were making her sick in many different ways. I got some condoms and made myself responsible for our birth control, but she said that condoms could break and were therefore not a safe enough option. I told her I would use two condoms simultaneously, but she still refused. Through all this daily deliberation, it never dawned on me that the situation may have gotten better if I had just taken the time to find out what was really bothering her, and listened. I took her excuses and arguments at face value and continued pursuing sex with her, and I was often disappointed.

With Marilyn's refusal to have intercourse, I turned my attention to oral sex. Her arguments regarding unwanted pregnancy and birth control pill sicknesses were useless against oral sex. There was still much deliberation and debate about the need for it, but Marilyn finally gave in. At first we started by pleasing each other either simultaneously or one then the other. After a few days of this Marilyn suddenly decided she didn't need the pleasure. She did, however, continue to please me, albeit reluctantly. Then one night we watched a program on television that mentioned an old rumor that semen had allegedly been found in a male rock star's stomach. Marilyn freaked out. She had been allowing me to orgasm in her mouth, but after hearing that she acted grossed out by it and decided that oral sex was out of the question as well.

The night of the television show I was tired and just wanted to go to bed. I thought that Marilyn was overreacting and jesting about discontinuing oral sex. The next night however, she completely turned me down when I approached her with physical contact. She said that she didn't want me to get myself worked up for something I wasn't going to get. I, in turn, became determined to get some kind of sex from her that night.

We wrestled around on the floor as I tried to undress her and she fought me off. At one point I attempted to pin her down by sitting on her chest and holding her arms and shoulders down with my knees and, then tried to force my penis inside her mouth. At first Marilyn turned her face from side to side but then she suddenly stopped and looked straight at me with bulging, angry eyes. "What the fuck do you think you're going to accomplish?" she asked. I didn't answer. I just reached behind me and tried to put my hand down her pants. "I'm going to open my mouth and I dare you to put your dick inside," she said while still staring directly into my eyes. I got off her angrily, went into the bathroom, masturbated, and showered. I came out of the bathroom to find Marilyn pretending to be fast asleep.

From that night onward our apartment became a battleground where insults and accusations were thrown around freely. The painful secrets we had revealed to each other to find relief we were now using as weapons for attack. The difference between us was that, while Marilyn wallowed in the emotional hell we were inflicting upon each other, to me it was as if nothing had happened fifteen minutes after an argument. In that short time it took me to collect myself from the anger, I always concluded that all our problems would go away if we just had sex. I would try to plead and explain my way into some kind of sexual activity. Of course this led to rejection, which would further frustrate me to the point of explosion.

One night I came home a little after midnight from my job at Kroger and found Marilyn in the shower. She had made it a habit to lock the bathroom door whenever she took a shower, but on this night not only did she not lock it, she left it wide open. I heard the sound of falling water and entered the bathroom quietly. Through the pattern on the glass shower door I could see Marilyn's naked body, as beautiful as I remembered it. She seemed so relaxed and at peace as the water hit her body and dripped down. I thought this would be the perfect time to try and rekindle what we had lost.

I quickly disrobed, slowly opened the shower door, and entered the shower. Marilyn turned toward me and asked how my day at work went. I took the soap from her hand and began washing her as I told her about my day. Surprisingly, Marilyn allowed me to wash her and was even receptive to my kisses. I washed her whole body and kissed her passionately more than once. These were the Marilyn kisses I had fallen in love with, and her body language spoke of sexual adventure.

Marilyn got out of the shower and retreated into the bedroom while I finished washing myself. I got out of the shower and walked into the bedroom as I dried myself with a towel. I was expecting Marilyn to be there waiting for me, naked and ready to continue what we had started. I found her lying on her side pretending to be asleep. Upon further inspection I realized that she was also fully dressed in sweatpants and a T-shirt.

I sat down beside her and held my erect penis in my hand as my blood began to boil in anger. I then uncovered her and pulled her sweatpants and panties down to just below her knees. Marilyn remained completely motionless while I did this. I tried to turn her over on her back but she resisted so I lay down beside her and tried to penetrate her from behind. Marilyn tightened her legs together and made it impossible for me to get to her vagina so I began working on penetrating her anus. Just when I thought I was going to succeed, she said, "Boy, you sure the hell are determined tonight." Then she got up, pulled up her pants, and walked into the bathroom.

Marilyn stayed in the bathroom for hours while I lay staring at the ceiling, completely thoughtless. Nothing at all entered my mind. I didn't think about Marilyn or our predicament. I just watched the ceiling fan spin around and around as I fell into a hypnotic state. I don't remember hearing her coming out and lying next to me. I just remember seeing her there in the morning when the alarm clock woke me up.

We got up and prepared ourselves for the workday without saying a word to each other. It was the first time since we had been living in that apartment that we left for work without any greetings whatsoever. That prepared the topic of discussion for that evening.

"How was your day?" I asked her when I walked into the apartment about eleven that night. I walked past her as she watched television and went into the kitchen to put down some ready-to-eat food I'd brought from Kroger. "How was your day, Marilyn?" I asked again. "Are you hungry?" She got up and walked into the kitchen, grabbed a plate, and began to serve herself from the food I brought. "After last night, how do you think my day went?" Marilyn said as she carried her plate of food out of the kitchen. She sat back in the same place. The only thing that kept me from attacking her verbally was the fact that I was starving. I sat about three feet away from her, facing the television and enjoyed the silence between us, which lasted only until we were both done eating and were relaxing in front of the television.

"So everything that happened last night was my fault?" I asked without looking Marilyn's way. "Considering you tried to rape me, I would say so," Marilyn responded. "I guess what happened in the shower was also an attempt to rape you, huh?" I asked in a matter-of-fact tone. "What happened in the shower was all about you, and had nothing to do with me," Marilyn said as she got up and headed toward the bedroom. "Don't blame me if you don't know how to control yourself," she said as she disappeared into the bedroom. I got up, turned off the television and the living room and kitchen lights, and then went into the bedroom with the intention of continuing the conversation.

"I guess I'll have to find myself another sex partner," I said as I lay down next to Marilyn. I stared at the ceiling as I waited for Marilyn's response to my comment. After a few minutes Marilyn finally said that with all the strip joints in Dallas, finding another sex partner should not be a problem for me.

"What the hell is wrong with you, you fuckin' bitch? We're a couple, we're supposed to have sex!" I yelled as I sat up. "Why the hell can't you understand that sex is not what I want right now. That is the least of our problems!" Marilyn snapped back. "What the hell are you doing here then?" I yelled. "Waiting for the six-month lease to expire on this hellhole so that I can go back home," Marilyn responded. "You don't have to wait! Leave now," I said, getting angrier and angrier. "If I weren't afraid of ruining my sister's credit, I would've left a long time ago," Marilyn shot back.

An eerie silence consumed our bedroom as I lay back down breathing hard in anger. I began thinking about what Marilyn had said. The more I thought about her words, the more warped my conclusions about their meaning became. I began to envision my suffering from being abandoned by Marilyn being the same as when my mother had abandoned me. I imagined her in the arms of another man, laughing at my suffering and homelessness. I saw myself having sex with men for food and shelter and sleeping in dark, dirty hallways. My vision became blurred and I felt my body tighten as I pictured myself walking directionless in the cold, doing things out of desperation in order to survive. I closed my eyes tight as my tears began to flow and the room became consumed in darkness.

I opened my eyes to see the ceiling fan spinning unevenly until I was able to regain focus. My body felt hot, and perspiration was seething through my skin. My breathing was hard and heavy and my mouth was dry. Then, from a distance, I heard whimpers followed by uncontrollable crying. I turned to Marilyn and found that she was gone. That's when I realized that the crying was coming from the bathroom.

I got up and tried to open the bathroom door but found that it was locked. I knelt in front of the door and told Marilyn that I was sorry for saying that I would find another lover. She didn't respond to me; she just kept crying. I begged her to come out of the bathroom so we could talk about it and promised not to get upset, but she still didn't respond. Marilyn had often wept after our arguments but never as uncontrollably as this time. She cried nonstop, loudly, then softly, then loudly again. She wasn't hurling curse words at me as she usually did when she cried, and not once did she pause to try and collect herself. Suddenly the seriousness of our deteriorating relationship hit me like a ton of bricks.

"Marilyn, I promise I won't yell or ask for sex anymore. I won't curse at you anymore, and I'll look into getting therapy to control my anger," I pleaded genuinely. Finally, Marilyn forced words out of her mouth in a tone so horrifying that they even scared me. "You almost killed me!" She began to cry even louder and more uncontrollably than before.

I didn't know what to make of her words. After hearing that, my head dropped and words just would not come out of my mouth, although I tried to speak. All the things I wanted to say, all the explanations I wanted to give just would not come out of me. I got up from where I kneeled, lay down on the comforter, curled up in the fetal position and silently cried myself to sleep.

The next morning, not a word was said as we readied ourselves for work. Our eyes never met, our paths never crossed. Marilyn left the apartment before I did. I waited for about fifteen minutes, standing in one place, and stared at the walls before I left. That afternoon she came home in the company of a coworker and said she was leaving. I was on my way out to my job at Kroger. I just stood there long enough to see her packing her belongings. As I walked away from the apartment, I looked back and saw her load the last of her stuff into her coworker's car. Then they drove off. Not once did she look my way.

I wanted to ask her for an explanation about her decision to depart, but I didn't. I didn't even bother to ask how to reach her. Not because I didn't want to, but because I was still in such turmoil with myself over her telling me that I had almost killed her. I didn't remember ever putting my hands on her, but I had no doubt in my mind that something terrible came out of me that night. With Marilyn out of there I posed no danger to her, and I hoped that the time alone would allow me to figure out what had happened. Things seemed so out of control after only three months away from Chicago.

I sat in the empty apartment night after night in a confused state of mind, waiting for the phone to ring. Had I lost the need to get up and go to work every day, I think I might have committed suicide in that apartment. I felt like I was incarcerated again, but without any hope of ever getting out. I began to write poetry the same way I did when I was in prison. Just as before, the poetry was dark and full of hate, but it kept me sane.

My dependency on Marilyn made it impossible for me to even think of life without her. My past experiences had led me to believe that I could not survive on my own without entering a life of crime. My past experiences had also convinced me that as long as I was providing sexual pleasure to a woman, she should be happy and should worship me. I unfortunately had no clue that other emotions existed that were just as important. To make matters worse, what Marilyn sought from me were the same things

I yearned for but didn't recognize. That mutual need had resulted in our going around in circles trying to figure each other out.

The frustration of not understanding each other, and losing the hope that we had once held onto so dearly, made our situation extremely difficult. We denied each other basic needs and desires as ways to get something else from each other. Only neither one of us seemed to know how to go about getting what we really needed into our lives. So instead of being each other's saviors, we were each other's tormentors. In many ways we were learning the truth about the questions we needed answered, but our emotions were way out of control. We didn't know how to express our feelings, and we became completely overwhelmed by the answers we uncovered.

Four days after Marilyn left, I decided it was time we see each other again. I struggled with the idea of going to see her at her job, but decided not to because of the confrontation that would probably take place. Those four days with no communication with Marilyn helped me clarify how much she meant to me. They also made me realize that a monster was living inside me; the time I spent alone, however, strengthened my belief that her denial of sex had brought about our problems. I also correlated Marilyn's actions with those of my mother and all the other women who had come in and out of my life. Finally, on Saturday morning, I set off for the abortion clinic where Marilyn worked to try and reconcile our differences.

17

Maybe We Can Try Again

ON THE DAY I intended to go see Marilyn, I got up with a nervous feeling that I was doing something very wrong. I woke up at about five in the morning and couldn't fall back to sleep no matter how hard I tried. I finally sat in the middle of the empty living room and read all the poems I had written since Marilyn had left. They all told the same story of loneliness, worry, and confusion.

At eight o'clock I left the apartment to catch the bus that would take me to downtown Dallas, where I would get on another bus that would take to me where Marilyn worked. I was scared and sensed that only violence awaited us in the future, yet I decided to take my chances in order not to be alone.

I arrived near the clinic at about ten. The bus dropped me off two blocks away and I walked from there. I saw about two dozen people holding up signs and yelling toward the clinic. As I got closer, I realized that they were protesters holding anti-abortion signs, some with enlarged pictures of what they claimed were aborted fetuses. Everyone walking past or into the clinic was handed pamphlets denouncing abortion. Women headed toward the clinic were surrounded, first verbally and then physically, in an attempt to keep them from going in. Passages from the Bible

229

were read to the women as they fought their way through the crowd toward the clinic. When a woman reached the point in front of the clinic where protestors were not allowed to cross, the protestors quickly went from reading Bible passages to yelling obscenities. I found the whole scene fascinating and intriguing. Instead of going in and asking for Marilyn, I sat on the front steps of the clinic entrance and watched the protestors in action and the reaction of the people fighting to get into the clinic. Marilyn had told me about the abortion protestors but I never imagined that they were so fanatically aggressive.

Several couples waiting to get in also sat on the steps of the clinic. Through the glass on the entrance door, I could see that there were a lot of people waiting to be attended to. I began to think that maybe the protestors were frustrated over their failure to change the minds of so many people. As more people came to sit outside, waiting or smoking, the protestors targeted their anger at them. Insults began to be exchanged.

"You murderer—you'll go to hell!" a female protestor yelled while looking directly at a heavy-set Caucasian woman standing at the bottom of the steps smoking. "You go to hell, you stupid bitch," the woman answered. "You fuckin' whore! You should be dead, you murderer, you bitch!" the protestor responded. Other protestors hugged her and led her away in tears while the waiting woman called her a crazy bitch. Then a man with a Bible in his hand came as close as he could get to the clinic and started reading passages that he interpreted as proof that what was going on in the clinic was murder. A young black man asked him if he was willing to take care of his friend's baby financially. "Are you, as the father, not ashamed of what you're having this woman do?" the man asked. "This is not my baby. I'm here to support my friend's decision, and the last thing she needs right now is for me to turn my back on her," the black guy responded. "Then you'll go to hell with her. In the eyes of God you are a murderer, too," the man yelled. "Oh please," the black guy said as he turned away and tried to ignore the protestors.

Every so often a clinic employee would open the door to summon a patron and get bombarded with insults and obscenities. The employees' reactions made it obvious that they had become immune to the protestors' tactics. I became mesmerized by the commotion and didn't know what side of the issue I should be on. I listened to the prayers, heard pleas for mercy for the unborn, and looked at the hideous pictures of fetuses and felt compassion for the protestors. Then I heard them yell obscenities and death wishes for the patients and employees of the clinic, and questioned their motives.

The insults being thrown from both sides of the issue were hateful. I had never seen people talk to each other in such an angry fashion without violence erupting. Then a young black woman walked toward the crowd and started yelling while she broke down. "Why should I have a baby from a man who raped me?" she cried. "Do you want it? Tell me, are you going to take care of it?" "There are programs for girls like you," a protestor responded. "What fuckin' program is going to make me forget that my stepfather raped me?" the girl yelled as she took several steps toward the protestors as if to attack them. Several people sitting on the steps got up and detained her, then led her inside. "Those people don't know what the fuck they're talking about," the girl said as she was led up the steps.

That girl's words stuck in my mind. I began to remember the abuse that was inflicted upon me as a child and I wondered why

I wasn't aborted. I thought about the many gang members on the street who were products of unwanted pregnancies who were now producing kids falling into the same category. I wondered if the protestors ever thought that the suffering they were trying to save the fetuses could be intensified tenfold if they were allowed to be born. I also wondered if they took under consideration the amount of pain those saved fetuses would inflict on the world because of the environment they were going to be brought into. I was confused about the logic behind the protest, so I decided to ask someone.

I walked slowly toward the protestors and immediately was barraged with insults. "You baby killer, you'll burn in hell!" a girl about fifteen years old yelled at me. The man with the Bible walked up to me and started showing me a passage. I didn't pay much attention to him because I wanted to get my questions out. "I was raped and beaten senseless as a child. Why would you want kids to possibly be born into that?" I asked. "Those who hurt you will have to answer to God," the man said. "Are you not glad to be alive now?" he asked. The question surprised and confused me. Before I could answer, I heard my name being called from the clinic. It was the woman Marilyn had gone to live with. She recognized me and motioned for me to come toward her.

I walked away, still thinking about the question. Was I happy to be alive now? I really didn't know. What I did know was that, if given a choice, I would choose never to have been born. The protestors called me a child killer and reminded me that I would be going to hell as I walked into the clinic. At that moment I felt that they had no clue what they were talking about. They had no way of knowing that I already felt I was destined for hell. I concluded that the protestors' motives were based on religious beliefs and convictions and not on the actual desire to save lives. They were so blinded by their beliefs that they seemed to know no suffering beyond what they felt existed inside the abortion clinic. I wished that just one of them had grown up in my place.

I FOLLOWED MARILYN'S friend past the waiting room toward the back of the clinic. Judging by the number of patrons waiting to have abortions, it was obvious that the protestors' cries were falling on deaf ears. She led me into the staff lounge and told me to sit down and wait, and that Marilyn would be taking a lunch break momentarily.

The lounge was a big, comfortable room with a couple of medium-sized tables with chairs on one end and a sofa and love seat positioned behind a coffee table. On the coffee table was a big glass punch bowl filled with assorted types of condoms. The contents of the bowl took me by surprise, but then I thought it was appropriate, considering the business of the clinic. I sat on the sofa facing the door and looked at the bowl filled with condoms, debating whether to take a handful or not. Several minutes later Marilyn walked into the room.

The tension I felt was reminiscent of my days on the streets of Chicago when I was preparing to confront a rival gang. I felt very defensive, ready to protect myself. But it turned out those feelings were uncalled for. Marilyn was very polite with me, although she made no eye contact.

She sat at the other end of the sofa with a salad in her hand. I glanced at her, looking for a way to start a conversation, but I was speechless. Marilyn seemed to be consumed with the task of devouring her salad, but I knew she was waiting for me to say something. Finally I got up, went to the soda machine, and bought a couple of soft drinks. I walked back to the sofa, sat right beside her, and kissed her on the cheek as I handed her a can. "Thank you," she said softly as she took it from my hand and placed it on the coffee table in front of us. "You're welcome," I replied as I opened mine. Those few words served as a way for us to start a conversation.

"How are you?" I asked Marilyn. "I'm OK. How are you?" she answered. "I'm OK, I guess. There are some crazy people out there," I commented, referring to the abortion protestors. "Yeah, we have unique patients, and you should see the protestors once they get started," Marilyn replied in her best sarcastic tone. I chuckled and began fishing in the bowl of condoms. We didn't say much else to each other, and didn't look at each other at all. In what seemed like seconds, Marilyn's lunch was finished. She asked me to stay in the lounge until she got off work in a couple hours. She then tossed the salad bowl into the garbage can and made eye contact with me for the first time as she said, "I'll see you later."

For the next few hours, women walked in and out of the room without saying a word to me. Even when they sat for a little while, they didn't bother to try and acknowledge my presence. I felt like a freak show on display. I seemed to be good enough to look at but not to communicate with. I knew without a doubt that they saw me as a woman beater, unworthy of acknowledgment. My only fear was whether they were right.

I read just about every magazine in that room trying to keep myself occupied as I waited for Marilyn. I wanted to walk out and come back later, but my self-consciousness about what the women in the room were thinking about me glued me to the sofa. Finally Marilyn appeared at the door and said we could leave.

We walked out the back door, where a smaller, less aggressive but very verbally abusive group of protestors met us. They allowed us to walk around them and bypass the pamphlets they tried to hand us, but they yelled obscenities as we made our way toward the bus stop. I turned back slightly to make sure that we weren't being followed and met the eyes of a young man who assured me I would be going to hell. For some reason his words echoed in my mind, and I concluded that he was probably right. But at the same time I wanted to run to him and tell him the real reason why I thought I was going to hell. I wanted to let him know that if I had been aborted I wouldn't have to suffer through the trials and tribulations of going to hell. I wouldn't have all the memories of violence committed against me or the violence I had committed against others. My eyes must have said those very words for me, because I read the guy's lips as they silently said, "God bless you."

Marilyn and I rode the bus to downtown Dallas and shared only small talk regarding the clinic protestors; otherwise we were silent. Once we were walking on the nearly empty streets of downtown Dallas, our conversation finally touched on the subject of our relationship.

"I can't believe you hit me," Marilyn said softly as she stared into nowhere. "Your eyes looked so evil. I have never seen anything so evil. I didn't know the Rey who surfaced that night. I'm realizing that I don't know who you are." While she talked our eyes never met, and our bodies never touched. We walked side by side, yet we were like strangers. Within me I struggled with the desire to defend myself. I tried to ignore those thoughts by looking up and down the streets of downtown Dallas and tried to put Chicago in its place. Only when I made myself understand that something terrible had really happened that night did I finally decide to break my silence.

"I don't remember ever hitting you, Marilyn. I really don't," I said as I began to choke up. "It was dark and then I heard you crying." I stepped in front of Marilyn and looked directly into her eyes. She hugged me and held me tightly. All of a sudden, my tear-filled eyes overflowed, and I began to cry seriously. We stood there for a while until my crying had subsided. We then walked silently about half a block, crossed the street, and sat on a brick planter that housed a tree in front of an office building.

We sat there and held each other for a long, long time. We buried our faces in each other's necks and held on for dear life. When we finally released each other, I began to cry again, and at that moment everything started to make sense to me. What Marilyn had described, and my lack of memory, was the exact same way I remembered experiences with my mother. I don't know if my mother remembered abusing me, but the similarities were eerie. My mother would beat me as if she had lost control of her senses, and then act like nothing had happened just a short time later. This was exactly what Marilyn was describing to me, exactly what I had done to her.

I told Marilyn about how my mother would act after one of her violent rages. She agreed that I had done the same thing, and she said that I should seek counseling for this problem. As Marilyn spoke, I sat there wondering if my mother remembered any of the beatings she'd inflicted on me. I wondered if her decision to rid herself of me was because she was frightened of the terror I might invoke within her, and not because I was a problem child. I began to tremble and everything became blurry again because my eyes flooded with tears. I buried my face in my hands as I told

Marilyn that I was scared to know that I could unknowingly hurt someone I cared for.

Marilyn, with all her wisdom, became a listener that night. That night I should have listened to her and made promises of change. I should have been on my knees begging forgiveness. Instead I cried my heart out about myself, and she listened. Marilyn held me and wiped my tears, stroked my hair, and kissed my cheeks softly. She stared off into the city as she fought her own tears and tried to remain strong for both of us. Finally I was able to regain my composure, and we just held each other quietly.

About three hours after we got to downtown Dallas, we started walking toward the bus stop where Marilyn would catch the bus back to her friend's home. The last bus going toward my apartment had already come and gone, so I decided to accompany Marilyn on her bus ride.

On the way, we talked about how Dallas sucked as a major metropolitan city, and how its citizens tended to be very sweet and nice around you and then talk badly about you behind your back. Marilyn said she wasn't quite happy where she was staying, but that she was too scared to come back and live with me again. When we got off the bus she asked me to walk her home, then she would ask her coworker to drive me home, and if not, I could at least call a cab from there.

The coworker Marilyn was staying with was a Mexican woman in her late thirties who worked at the clinic as a medical assistant. She lived with her boyfriend, who was also Mexican and about the same age. Although both of them spoke with Mexican accents, they called themselves second-generation Texans and considered Mexicans to be only those people from Mexico who came into the United States illegally. (For the most part, this was the attitude of most American citizens of Mexican descent in the Dallas area.)

Marilyn's coworker was noticeably surprised when we walked into her house together. She was short, about five feet tall, and chubby, with short hair. Marilyn introduced me and explained how I had missed the bus so she had asked me to accompany her. "You need a car to survive in Dallas," a man's voice said from the kitchen. At that moment the boyfriend made his appearance. He was about six feet tall, with black hair and a beer gut, and he wore cowboy boots. He came over to me and shook my hand, then asked his girlfriend to come into the kitchen with him. I sat on the living room couch by myself looking at the pictures on the wall of family members and Catholic saints, and the Mexican pottery and other decor, and wondered why so many people in Texas denied being Mexican.

"Come with me to the store," the boyfriend said as he walked into the living room. "I can't eat without beer." He laughed. We walked outside and got into his pickup truck, parked in the driveway of the house. He started the truck and then said, "Why don't you hit me?"

I was absolutely startled by his words. I felt my blood rushing through my body and my face burned. "What?" I responded in a loud voice that was almost a scream. I looked at him and waited for his response. "Why don't you hit me?" he repeated.

My muscles tightened and my fists balled instinctively. I wanted so much to hit him, but I knew that any violent action I might take would solidify Marilyn's fear of me. I looked him straight in the eyes, got out of the truck, and slammed the door closed. I headed toward the house, but I didn't want to go in carrying the anger Marilyn was so afraid of. I paced the driveway like a madman. I talked to myself softly but angrily, while I stared at the figure inside the truck, who posed yet another threat to my life. I stared at him as if daring him to come after me.

He got out of the truck and walked toward the back. I watched every move he made and prepared to attack him once he got within striking distance. All the violent episodes from my days as a Latin King, when I was thirsty for violence, began to fill my mind. My body trembled, and I started to size up my opponent for the kill and my surroundings for a possible weapon to kill him with. The fact that the boyfriend was five inches taller and outweighed me by over a hundred pounds didn't cross my mind. I was oblivious to everything except the man who would become my next victim of violence.

"I'm sorry, man, I shouldn't have said that," the boyfriend said in his broken English "Texan" voice while he stood at the rear of the truck. "You don't fuckin' know me," I said in a low angry voice. "Stay the fuck away from me, I will say good-bye to Marilyn and get the fuck out of here." "No, man, don't do that. Don't leave. My old lady will be pissed off at me," the boyfriend said. "I'm sorry. Come on, let's go to the store." He made his way back toward the driver's side of the truck. I watched him as he walked and wanted to run at him and rip his throat out. My desire for a confrontation made me get into the truck with him instead of going in and saying good-bye to Marilyn. I looked at him wildly, waiting for one stupid word to come out of his mouth so I could gouge his eyes out, but it never came. He started the truck and began to reverse out of the driveway without making eye contact with me.

"I'm sorry, man, I didn't mean to make you so angry," the boyfriend said as he drove. "You told me to hit you. What was I supposed to do, get happy?" I answered. "Yeah, that was stupid," he said. "I'm sure you had a good reason to hit her." "*Pinche viejas* (Fuckin' old ladies) need a slap every now and then to put them in their place." For the rest of the drive to the liquor store and back, this man went out of his way to justify my violence toward Marilyn and the need to periodically show violence toward women. He mentioned that if his girlfriend weren't paying most of the bills at home, he would have probably kicked her ass once or twice already. I don't know what kind of impression he was trying to leave me with, but he succeeded in convincing me that he was a drunken fool with a big mouth.

When we got back to the house, I went in as calmly as I could manage. I didn't want Marilyn to see any signs of anger in my eyes or in my body language. The boyfriend's decision to go from a threat to an ally made that easy to do. What I didn't do was let my guard down with him. All his attempts at starting a conversation with me during dinner I met with an uninterested "uh huh," or a nod of the head. I agreed to let him drive me home and thanked him several times, but I think he knew that I was ready to attack him at the slightest provocation. At his request, Marilyn and his girlfriend accompanied us on the drive back to my home. It was a quiet ride. Marilyn and I held hands but didn't say a word to each other. The other couple broke the silence only to ask if they were headed in the right direction. As far as I was concerned, it was a successful evening.

Marilyn and I talked on the phone over the next couple of days. She told me that her coworker's boyfriend had bragged about how he put fear into me by asking me to hit him. Marilyn apologized on his behalf. She said she felt bad that I'd been greeted by such ignorance. I assured Marilyn that the boyfriend was just tooting his own horn and that I had been close to attacking him, but hadn't. She said she was proud of me for being able to control my anger. She was sure that I was showing obvious signs of improvement, and that made her feel safer about returning. I knew that the violence that had not taken place that night had nothing to do with my self-control, but I didn't say so. It had more to do with my fear that Marilyn would see me explode and decide that getting back together with me was not a good idea. I felt lonely and kept Marilyn falsely believing that the worst had already happened, while sensing that something was aching to come out of me.

My loneliness and feelings of abandonment had me calling Chicago, pouring my heart out to people I knew couldn't care less about my predicament. I called Marilyn's little sister and told her that Marilyn was no longer with me because I had hit her. This I did while crying like a baby. That call really did relieve some of the guilt and pressure I felt about the whole situation. It also helped to bring Marilyn back to me. Marilyn called home one evening and her sister told her about my call to her. After that, Marilyn became convinced that I was regretful for what had happened between us, and that I was safe to live with. Marilyn's renewed confidence and trust in me gave me a false sense of security. I knew I was wrestling with feelings and thoughts I could not understand and had no clue how to safely release them.

Marilyn, in her quest to understand me, unknowingly opened up wounds within me that had until then been reserved for drug- and alcohol-induced violent attacks on other gang members. The release of these demons in a clean and sober atmosphere, coupled with my paranoia about being left alone, led to situations that neither Marilyn nor I could control. I suddenly found myself totally sober, and in the presence of someone who genuinely cared for me, yet acting like the animal I had been on the streets. The big difference was the obvious afteraffects. Where in the streets I'd revel in the glory of being a badass gang member, with Marilyn I would go into deep states of depression. Where in the streets I committed violence against individuals I didn't know, didn't care for, and would probably never see again, with Marilyn I had to face the realities of my actions. The only good thing that came out of the situation was that I no longer had nightmares.

There were times when I'd stare into nothing for hours on end. I would snap out of it, telling myself I was through with these periods of nothingness, only to fall back into the same state moments later. The brunt of all my bouts with confusion fell on Marilyn, who was trying to deal with her own demons.

18

Release of Pain

ABOUT A WEEK after my visit and three days after we had last spoken on the phone, I found Marilyn waiting for me when I returned home from my job at Kroger. It was Saturday night, and she was watching television as she waited. I was so happy to see her there that I started to cry. Marilyn got up and hugged me. We kissed and held each other, then proceeded to make passionate love to each other for the first time in almost a month and a half. It was the first time since our first days in Dallas, close to four months ago, that I felt happy to be in Marilyn's company. The next morning I went in and worked at Kroger until two in the afternoon and walked back with Marilyn, who had come to the store to see me. We talked about our mistakes and agreed that we should buy a car, which would allow us to get around so I could find a better job and also get therapy. We would also use that car to move ourselves to California once we decided it was time to move on.

In the week that followed, I shopped around for a car, and our relationship seemed to be in better shape. Our sex life returned and the arguments cooled. In actuality, we didn't argue because we didn't touch on any subjects that were really affecting us. We didn't talk about the violence that had taken place, or how we felt about it. We stopped talking about my feelings toward my mother and about hers toward her father. The reality was that the things we did talk about had no substance. Our conversations always revolved around our displeasure with what we thought of as the phony sticky sweet ways of the people in Dallas, and about the moronic guests on the Jerry Springer show, which we watched religiously.

The following weekend I purchased a car and resigned from my part-time job at the children's clinic so that I could have time to search for other employment. I was excited about finding a full-time job. I decided to take advantage of the seeming lack of bilingual employees in this state where the majority of people seemed to be Spanish-speaking only. In Texas, most of the Hispanics who were born there were forbidden to speak Spanish by their parents in order to decrease their chances of being discriminated against. The result has been generations of non-Spanish-speaking Hispanics who denied their Mexican heritage, and had names such as William, Charles, and Cody with Spanish last names they pronounced as if they were English.

I took full advantage of this and applied at a local college that was in need of a bilingual clerk to work with students applying for English-as-a-second-language courses. With my background working at the University of Illinois at Chicago, I was called for an interview and then a second interview that really put into perspective the feelings some people in Dallas had toward Hispanics.

The college called on a Friday afternoon while I was working at Kroger. Marilyn answered the phone and was told that I

was one of two finalists for the job and that I should come in for
a second interview on Monday morning. I was to bring two
forms of identification so they could make copies of them to have
on record if I ended up being the chosen candidate.

On Monday morning I dressed in what I deemed acceptable,
professional attire—dress slacks, white shirt, and a tie. I dropped
Marilyn off at work and headed for the interview. The first interview was with a woman who would be the supervisor of the chosen candidate; the second was with the assistant director of the
adult continuing education department.

I walked into the office of the assistant director fifteen minutes before my scheduled interview and introduced myself to the
receptionist. The receptionist asked me to sit while she notified
the assistant director that I was there and offered me a cup of
coffee. I took a small Styrofoam cup filled with coffee from her
and sat in a chair that was located directly across from her desk
about ten feet away. Five minutes after I sat down a woman
dressed in a white skirt and jacket with a bright red silk blouse
came out of her office and greeted me. The assistant director had
white hair, which she wore up in a stylish bun, and spoke with a
deep southern accent. She spoke softly and moved in a way that
said, "I'm all woman." Diamonds sparkled from her ears, neck,
wrist, and fingers. She was the classic rendition of a southern
belle as I had always imagined them to be.

"Mr. Sanchez," she said as she stretched out her hand to greet
me. "I'm so glad you're here. If you don't mind I'd like to get
started early." "Yes, that's fine," was my response. She asked me
to give my driver's license and visa to the receptionist so that
copies could be made, and then we could begin the interview.
After that she turned around and walked back into her office.

I was puzzled why I was being asked for a credit card but hesitated to say anything. Just before the assistant director went back into her office I called out to her. "Excuse me, ma'am," I said. "I don't have a credit card," I told her as she walked back toward me. "Oh, we need a copy of your green card," she said, laughing softly. Her request only served to further confuse me. The only green card I had knowledge of was the one given to welfare recipients to get medical care in the state of Illinois. "I'm sorry, I'm not on welfare," I told her with a puzzled, worried look on my face.

There was a moment of silence. Time seemed to stand still while two very confused individuals looked at each other. Finally the receptionist broke the silence by asking me if I had not been given the message to bring two pieces of identification with me to the interview. "Yes," I said as I turned to her. "I have a driver's license, social security card, and my birth certificate." "Well bless your heart, that's all we'll need," the receptionist said as she made her way from behind her desk. The assistant director assured me that I was in good hands with the receptionist and retreated into her office.

The receptionist took my identification and reviewed it. I explained that I had not yet traded my Illinois license for a Texas license because I had not started driving in Texas until recently. She asked me about my place of birth as she looked at my Spanish-language birth certificate from Puerto Rico. I explained that Puerto Ricans were born U.S. citizens and that I had lived in Chicago since I was six. "Puerto Rico is part of the United States?" she asked. "It's a commonwealth," I told her. "It is so beautiful there," she responded. As she walked out of the office she told me that she was off to make copies of my IDs and would return shortly. I sat back down and waited. When she came back she handed me my IDs and led me into the assistant director's office so that the interview could begin.

The assistant director asked me to sit down in a chair in front of her desk. We talked about my work experience at the University of Illinois at Chicago and about my proficiency in reading, writing, and speaking Spanish. After about fifteen minutes the interview was over, and the assistant director told me that I would know by the end of the week whether I was the chosen candidate or not. I assured her that if I was hired I would be ready to start work at a moment's notice. She expressed her pleasure with my enthusiasm and eagerness and assured me that I would be called sometime that week.

I WALKED OUT of the college and drove home feeling positive about my chances of getting the job. If I was hired, I would be making the same amount of money working eight to five, Monday through Friday, that I made working ten to twelve hours, seven days a week, at Kroger. I would also get medical and dental insurance. Since I was no longer working at the clinic, I was able to go into work at Kroger earlier and sometimes get out earlier. I would take Marilyn to work in the morning and she would ride the bus back home in the afternoon. I never gave their request for a visa a second thought until two days later. We sat in front of the television watching the news, waiting for Jerry Springer to come on, when there was a story that shocked me a bit. A police bust somewhere in East Texas had taken place, where half a dozen people were selling counterfeit Immigration Service identifications referred to as visas. All of a sudden the questions at the college regarding my identification made sense. They thought I was Mexican and that I was a resident alien of the United States, not a citizen.

That evening I told Marilyn about the episode at the college, and she became enraged. For the next half hour I listened to her go over why she thought every known evil in the world was a product of white people. She went from the mass murder of Native Americans to slavery and ended with the Ku Klux Klan, who were, ironically, Jerry Springer's guests that evening.

Marilyn believed that some form of sympathy and support for the beliefs of the KKK lived in the hearts of the majority of white Americans. She felt that even those whites who preached the rhetoric of racial harmony would have no issue with returning to the days of old when whites were allowed to do as they wished to nonwhites. In Marilyn's opinion it was very easy to imagine that the great majority of white Americans would be content to see the nation return to slavery.

As I listened to Marilyn, I began to realize that she felt more contempt for white people than I had ever witnessed. I knew that, like myself, she thought that some whites gave up their stereotyped views of nonwhites only when it benefited them. But that's where the similarities between her beliefs and mine ended.

I challenged her theories with my own experiences. I asked her if she felt that my descent into gang life had more to do with racist attitudes of whites toward Puerto Ricans than the abuse I'd suffered at home. She stated that she thought it was a combination of both. She explained that no one but my mother could be held responsible for the abuse I had suffered, but that the rampant gang activity within the Puerto Rican community had a lot to do with racism. She pointed out how freely illegal drugs and guns are allowed to flow in and out of the Puerto Rican community and how police are in many ways directly involved with the trafficking. In contrast, she said, gangs would never be allowed to operate so openly in white neighborhoods. "Do you think it was just luck that you had so many suburban white customers when you were selling drugs?" Marilyn asked.

I sat quietly thinking about what she said and how much sense it made. White kids who wanted to pursue extended gang careers did end up living in the neighborhood and being just as lost as the rest of us, whereas those whites who left after fulfilling their curiosity were welcomed back and their brief forays into gang life were blamed on inner-city minorities. Still, I didn't think it was white conspiracy that explained why gangs existed, so I continued to dig into Marilyn's theory.

I asked her how she thought whites were responsible for the drug problems in the Puerto Rican neighborhoods if there weren't many whites there. "Don't be stupid, Rey. Stop thinking that just because for the majority of your life the only place in the world that existed was Humboldt Park, there aren't any outside influences there. How many Puerto Ricans do you know with gun licenses? How many of your 'homies' manufactured or had the means to bring the drugs they sold into this country? You should know more than anyone that there would never have been a war on drugs had young lily white kids not started dropping like flies from overdoses. It's ignorance like yours that keeps our communities brainwashed into believing that we are our own victims," Marilyn lectured.

I found it hard to argue with what Marilyn said—it made absolute sense to me. I could have debated her theory, but the only thing that I really heard from her lecture was that she thought I was stupid and ignorant. Maybe I was, regardless of how right I thought she was or how much sense her argument made. I still felt a need to defend myself.

"My Puerto Rican mother kicked my Puerto Rican ass, so I joined a Puerto Rican gang and got all kinds of guns from Puerto Ricans, who I freely killed. I continued to do it because I loved being considered a macho badass Latin King, and I liked the fact that others feared me. Along the way I did not run into one white person other than cops, who by the way feared me as well," I told Marilyn. I paused and waited for her reaction. When I didn't get one, I continued.

"Maybe just because you got your little diploma you think that the rest of us are stupid and ignorant. I personally don't think that Puerto Ricans are so damn stupid as to let themselves be manipulated into destroying themselves. Maybe, just maybe, it's the greed, and the widespread child abuse disguised as discipline and child neglect in our communities, that created the gang and drug problems. But then again, maybe you're right. Maybe you were one of the hand-picked Puerto Ricans allowed by whites to educate themselves in order to show that we're all not bad. If we all only just learned to conform to white ways like you did, then everything would be so much better."

Marilyn was now noticeably aggravated, and she looked at me with anger in her eyes. She questioned what she thought was my defense of white people, and reminded me that if it were up to the people at the college where I had interviewed, I would be deported to Mexico even though I was Puerto Rican. Then, out of the blue, Marilyn accused me of wanting to be in a relationship with white women because of their interest in wild sex instead of emotional happiness. I asked her where the hell she got that idea, but she ignored my question and continued her angry onslaught on white women.

Marilyn said that all cultures had been methodically brain-washed to embrace the classic European features and mannerism as the measure of beauty and grace. She said that men routinely sought out and appreciated women of all races with light eyes, stringy hair, and thin faces and bodies as a way to convince themselves that they had a white woman. Even if a man found those features in a woman of color, Marilyn thought, any man of color would drop her in a second if the opportunity to be with a white woman presented itself.

Marilyn's tirade made me chuckle and wonder what was really bothering her. I told her that the things she described as being "classic European features" were simply things that made a woman attractive. That comment did not sit well with her. She got up angrily and went into the kitchen. Then she asked why I wanted to be with her if I didn't find her attractive. I didn't answer. She came back into the room saying that she didn't have light-colored eyes, stringy hair, and a bone-thin body, so I shouldn't be with her. I realized that she had taken my comment as a personal attack, so I kept quiet and let her vent. Marilyn scanned through the channels of the television looking for women of color to show me that they had white-girl features. They were either born with them or had surgically created them, but they all had the light eyes, stringy hair, and thin faces and bodies. Finally she settled down to watch Jerry Springer, and all was quiet. I didn't tell her that I did notice that most women on television shared the same physical makeup regardless of their skin color.

Our discussion of racial biases served to further shape my way of thinking. This kind of discussion was the thing I loved most about being with Marilyn, but lately the enlightening conversations had been very few. Marilyn was still wrestling with feelings she had no one to talk to about. She therefore took my every opinion as a personal attack. After the show was over, she quietly retreated to the bedroom and suddenly wasn't in the mood for sexual contact again.

I didn't bother pursuing sex that night or for the next few nights after that. I didn't want us to get into the situation we had been in before. I instead decided to let Marilyn get over her current animosity toward sex.

On that Friday, just before I left for work at Kroger, I got a call from the college extending an offer to come work there. I readily accepted and told them that I would be there bright and early Monday morning. I went to Kroger and gave notice. Later that night I told Marilyn the news, expecting her to be happy for me and to be up for some celebratory sex. That wasn't the case.

Marilyn said that I was selling out by going to work for people who she thought obviously found me racially inferior. She asked me how I felt about being the token minority in their office. "It's a fuckin' job," I responded, "just a fuckin' job."

I reminded Marilyn of our ultimate goal and said that it shouldn't matter where or with whom I worked as long as I was making decent money. Marilyn questioned the need for us to pursue any kind of goal together and then locked herself in the bathroom.

I lay in the bedroom staring up at the ceiling with a million thoughts filling my head. I'd go from thoughts of forming a Latin King section in Dallas to getting back into the profitable drug business to working my way through college and becoming a teacher. I also had thoughts of beating Marilyn senseless for thinking of abandoning me. These were desperate thoughts. Her comments felt like a butcher knife cutting me into pieces. My head felt like it was going to explode with all the different thoughts going through it. Finally, I conjured up an imaginary woman, in whose eyes I knew all and did nothing wrong. I fell fast asleep fantasizing about her.

Saturday morning I drove Marilyn to work without saying a word to her. She had no words for me, either. The tension between us was obvious and seemed to mark the beginning of a violent storm coming our way. When we arrived at her job, she got out of the car without saying good-bye, and I drove off as if I were relieved to be ridding myself of her.

I picked her up from work that afternoon in a forced happy mood and asked her if she would accompany me shopping for business clothes to wear to my new job. I explained that we could go to secondhand stores and rummage through the clothes there. She agreed and actually seemed calmer and in a better mood than that morning. She was her old talkative self and went on and on about her day of work in the clinic. That day, she told me, they had arrested a teenage girl who came into the clinic pretending to be a patient but then started to scream out passages from the Bible and calling people murderers once she was inside.

We went to several secondhand stores and ended up with a wardrobe of eight shirts, six pairs of pants, two suits, and five ties for less than a hundred dollars. We then tried to make it back home before a nearby dry cleaner closed so we could drop the clothes off. On the way home, she brought up her day at the clinic again as if this day in particular had really bothered her.

Marilyn asked me if I had given any thought to the idea of getting married. I told her that I had not, but that I would love to marry her once we worked out all of our problems. I sensed a moment of romance developing between us. I expected to hear sweet words of everlasting love in our future, and of determination to make it together. Instead Marilyn stated that if we got married she did not want to take my last name. Marilyn suggested that we could combine both our last names and create a new, original name that would only belong to us and our children. That name would be Sancia ("San" from Sanchez and "cia" from Garcia).

I found Marilyn's suggestion laughable and outright idiotic. When I told her that I was completely happy with my current last name, she suggested that I marry a white woman or at the very least a weak Latin woman. I questioned why she thought a woman who took her husband's last name was weak. She said that it's not a man's world anymore and I just needed to get used to that idea. I began to get aggravated with Marilyn because she would not elaborate any more as to why she felt that way. I felt an instant of uncontrollable anger burning within me and tried with all my might to contain it. But then Marilyn proceeded to talk about abortion as it pertained to a child I might father.

"If I get pregnant, I'm getting an abortion, so maybe you ought to look into getting a vasectomy if you don't want that to happen," Marilyn said nonchalantly. I gripped the steering wheel with both hands, tightly determined to control my anger. I asked Marilyn if she was pregnant and braced myself for an answer I might not want to hear. "If I was, you'd never know it," Marilyn said, looking away from me.

I felt my heart begin to beat fast and my skin getting cold. I looked in all directions, desperately trying to distract myself from the growing feeling, but I just couldn't. In an instant my muscles tensed, my face got hot, and I exploded in anger.

"What the fuck are you talking about, bitch? Who the fuck do you think you are, thinking you can kill my child without my knowledge? I'll fuckin' kill you—I'll kill you and eat your fuckin' pussy for lunch, bitch. You don't know who you're fucking with!" I yelled while I drove recklessly at a breakneck speed.

Marilyn was petrified by my outburst. She sat silent and frightened. My heart was pumping hard and my breath was heavy. I envisioned pulling over and throwing Marilyn out into oncoming traffic. I realized the craziness of the thoughts running through my mind, and to keep them from becoming real I began talking to my imaginary girlfriend in my mind to calm myself down. Finally, I felt able to look at Marilyn without feeling the need to strangle her. "I plan to be a father one day, and my kids will have my last name, so I don't think a marriage between us will ever happen," I said in a calm and collected voice. After I said those words, I felt at peace with myself. For the first time I began to look at Dallas as a place I could call home on my own.

WE ARRIVED AT the dry cleaner, and Marilyn waited outside as I walked in and dropped off my clothes. I walked out of the establishment happy because they did in-house dry cleaning and would have the clothes ready for me the next day. The smile on my face and my change in attitude gave Marilyn the courage to talk to me again.

"I thought you would be more open-minded about abortion," Marilyn said. "Well, then, excuse me for sounding like a hypocrite but I don't think an abortion is necessary if at least one of the parents is willing to love and make sacrifices for the child," I responded as I drove out of the parking lot and headed home. "It seems to me that it takes two to make a child so it should be the decision of two to abort it. In the same way you are surprised about my closed mind, I'm surprised at your selfishness." "It's my body," Marilyn said in a soft voice. "Yeah, well maybe you should think about a hysterectomy so that no one else has to be burdened with your self-serving decisions made solely by you and your body," I responded. Nothing else was said until we got home.

We walked around the apartment silently getting ready for bed and avoiding each other. I lay down and tried desperately to fall asleep before Marilyn came into the room, but I ended up just staring at the ceiling fan as it went around and around in circles. Marilyn came in and lay next to me and stared at the ceiling too. "Do some research," she said. "I can do anything I want with my body and you have no say." "You're talking to the wrong person when it comes to respecting the law," I said as I turned and faced away from her.

Neither of us said another word to the other for the next couple of days. We went out of our way to completely avoid each other, knowing that the slightest provocation would create disaster. We lived like pit bulls in a cage waiting to attack and destroy each other at any moment. I knew the time would come when our thoughts would explode into words of anger. I knew it would come and I feared it.

ON TUESDAY NIGHT, the second day on my new job, all seemed to be going extremely well. I felt so good about my future at the college that I stopped by Kroger on the way home and resigned from my job there. When I got home, Marilyn was in the kitchen cooking just enough food for her. She said she didn't think I'd be home so early and that I could cook for myself once she finished. It wasn't so much that she told me I had to cook for myself that aggravated me, it was the way she said it. She snickered as if the idea of me doing something for myself was asinine.

I turned on the television and sat on the floor with my back against the wall separating the kitchen from the living room. "Oh I see, you expect me to be your housewife. I don't make a very good one of those," Marilyn said. She came into the living room with a plate of food in her hand and sat in front of the television to eat. I stared at her, wondering what had gone so wrong with us. As I watched her eat, and as she totally ignored me, I began for the first time to regret leaving Chicago. "What the fuck am I doing here," I said as I got up. Marilyn didn't look my way, or even stop eating. My blood began to boil.

I stood at the window looking out at the parking lot, filled with cars but with no signs of life. "I'm going back to Chicago when the apartment contract expires," Marilyn said. "You should stay here in Dallas. I think you'll do well. You have a decent job now and there are plenty of your type of women here." "Fuck you, Marilyn," I responded, still staring out into the parking lot. "I'm never going to be that stringy-haired Barbie with no opinion of my own," Marilyn said as she got up and went into the kitchen.

I grabbed my head tightly with both hands and ran my fingers through my hair as if I were trying to pull it out. I sat in the corner with my back against the wall and wrestled with the anger boiling inside. "What the fuck is your problem with white women?" I asked Marilyn in the calmest voice I could conjure. She didn't respond. She went about washing her dishes, completely ignoring me. "If you don't like the way you look, then do something about it and stop blaming the world. Maybe if you had blue eyes and stringy hair you'd be more of a woman and less of a bitch." I was getting more furious with every word.

Marilyn stopped what she was doing and walked out of the kitchen angrily. She stood about three feet away from me and said, "Look at you, look at you, such a fine example of a man with the nerve to pass judgment on what a good woman is or isn't. The king of Humboldt Park, God's gift to women. Well, maybe if your cousin hadn't fucked you in the ass, you'd have a clue what it means to be a man."

Marilyn's words shot through me like high-voltage electricity and made me tremble. The one and only person I had ever opened up to about that experience with my cousin had just used my own words to destroy me. If her intension was to hurt me, she had succeeded. She had also succeeded in sending me into a rage. I rushed her, grabbed her by the neck, and squeezed unmercifully. I felt the need to strangle her and beat her to death. Her eyes bulged out and began to roll back in their sockets as I felt the life in her body drain through my fingertips. I watched her face turn red as she gasped for air and realized I was about to kill her. I threw her to the floor and fell to my knees, crying hysterically. It was the first time I remembered exploding in violence without darkness accompanying my actions. I thank God for that.

That night was the first time that I actually looked into the eyes of my victim. Marilyn's eyes had a look of horror that until then I thought existed only in mine. I thought about all the people who had experienced that horror at the expense of my satisfaction and began to feel ill. I ended up curled in a fetal position on the floor, crying my heart out, begging God for forgiveness.

A couple of hours later, I opened my eyes into the darkness that had engulfed the living room. I sat up and found myself alone. I got up and took a step toward the bedroom but immediately stopped myself. Instead, I turned on the television, grabbed pen and paper, and sat in a corner of the room and wrote this poem.

In my little corner of the world, violence and pain.
In a crowd, yet lonely.
Try to rise above, but held back by those who say they
    care.
The past haunts me, but not by my own choice.
My honesty is bad, my lies are believed.
I accept myself, my faults, my strengths,
My weaknesses, my feelings.
But I'm expected to fail.
My achievements are overlooked,
My failures glamorized.
I know nothing. I'm not responsible.
A disappointment is what I'm made to be.
Loneliness is my best friend.
Dreaming is my pastime.
Understanding is my desire.
My little corner of the world is priceless.

After I finished writing it, I read it over and over and cried myself to sleep.

I awoke to the sound of Marilyn making breakfast. I went into the bathroom, showered, and prepared for work. When I came out of the bathroom I found that Marilyn had left without me. My first thought was to go after her and give her a ride to work but, after thinking about the previous night, I decided not to.

Although I was well aware of what I had done to Marilyn the night before, I also felt a certain calm. I felt that I was no longer afraid of my thoughts, no longer confused about my past actions, and no longer afraid to be alone. In fact, I suddenly yearned to be alone. I realized that Marilyn and I were not and would never be a functioning couple. The trauma I had inflicted on her was something I knew she would never forget, and neither would I. We had to get away from each other and start our lives anew. All I had to do was wait out the time left for the apartment contract to expire and she would be gone. Then, and only then, would I find out if my new sense of awareness was real.

OVER THE NEXT two months Marilyn and I continued to have our disagreements, but my feelings never went anywhere near violence. I made peace with the fact that Marilyn wasn't for me and didn't approach her for sex or any other type of physical contact. I left the satisfaction of my sexual desires to my imagination. I looked forward to Marilyn's departure and to living in Dallas on my own.

Marilyn eventually apologized for using her knowledge of my rape to hurt me. I apologized for hitting her and guaranteed her that it would never happen again. I purposely kept my vision of the night I'd grabbed her by the neck fresh in my mind. It served to remind me of the evil I was capable of, and of the person within me I didn't want to be. It bothered me to look at Marilyn and see a person who had firsthand knowledge of the terror that lived inside of me. I felt convinced that I could not be at total peace until Marilyn was gone. While I waited for her departure, I took refuge in writing poetry and becoming a hard-working and dependable employee at the college.

The lack of meaningful conversation at home led Marilyn to make a habit out of spending hours on the phone talking to friends and family in Chicago. By the time we realized it, the phone bill had grown to close to a thousand dollars, and, one month before the apartment contract expired, it was shut off.

As the countdown to the day we needed to renew the apartment contract or vacate it began, Marilyn made no secret of her intention to move back to Chicago. She gave notice at her job that she would be quitting, and to the apartment complex that the contract would not be renewed. I in turn, began looking around for a cheaper apartment where I could live after Marilyn left. Then all of a sudden Marilyn had a problem with me staying in Dallas.

As the end of the contract approached, Marilyn became more persistent in her desire for me to go back to Chicago with her. She became upset when I found a smaller, cheaper apartment and submitted a rental application. She was also displeased when I asked her to help me clear my name with the phone company by paying at least half the bill she had mostly built up herself. Finally, Marilyn began saying that she might want to stay after all. She expressed a desire to complete our journey to California in the near future.

I should have been happy to hear that, after all I had put her through, she was still willing to give life with me a chance. But I wasn't. I wanted to be alone, and I began to feel desperate when Marilyn acted as if she didn't believe me. I told her I wanted time to think, time to grow, time to assure myself that I would never hurt another human being physically or otherwise.

Marilyn thought my intentions were noble and said she would help me achieve all of my goals. What she didn't know, and couldn't understand, was that I needed to go through a growth period on my own. When I was convinced that Marilyn wouldn't be leaving, I decided to put a fear in her heart that would change her mind.

I rented an efficiency apartment, which we moved into upon the expiration of the contract of the apartment we lived in. Our new apartment was small, but it was at a price I could afford without assistance. From the moment we moved in, I began to pester Marilyn about paying the phone bill. I routinely followed that request by agreeing to pay the bill myself if she went back to Chicago without me. Marilyn countered by paying the phone bill and the deposit required to connect phone service at our new apartment. Still, I persisted in trying to get Marilyn to go back home until one day she blew up at me.

"You fuckin' asshole!" she yelled. "Now that you can afford to live without me you don't need me anymore. What happened to your fear of being abandoned? What happened to not being able to live without me? Don't fool yourself, Rey, you're no better a person now than you were when you were in a gang." Marilyn paced the floor of the small kitchen.

I walked up to the counter separating the kitchen area from the main room, reached over, and grabbed a knife. I ran the knife blade over the palm of my hand slowly as I looked at Marilyn like a maniac stalking his prey.

"I bet this knife cuts really good, but it won't cut me. Think it will cut you? I think so. You know I could chop you into little pieces, throw them in the trash compactor, and no one would know the difference? Think I'm afraid of going to jail? Been there, done that. Remember? You're right. I'm no better than when I was in a gang. Once a King, always a King, bitch. Now fuck with me!" I said these things to Marilyn while I looked her straight in the eyes and continued to run the blade of the knife on the palm of my hand.

Marilyn was in shock, unable to talk or move while I went through my routine. I felt so much pity for her, knowing it was all a ploy but not caring about the trauma I might be inflicting on her. Finally I put the knife down and walked away. As soon as I turned my back on her, tears began rolling down my face. The next day, she purchased a bus ticket back to Chicago for that same night.

We said very little to each other on the way to the bus station that evening, and there wasn't a long tearful good-bye. She looked at me sadly as she walked up the steps to the bus, and I lowered my head to try and avoid eye contact. I walked as fast as I could out of the bus station to my car and cried all the way back to the apartment. Six months after moving to Dallas, I was finally on my own.

During the first few weeks, I learned how to deal with the tragedies of my past without getting the rest of the world involved. While I was at work, no one had a clue about the turmoil I was going through. At home I was a broken mess. I thought about Marilyn every second I was in my apartment, and I cried nonstop for hours at a time. I began forcing myself to recall the abuse at the hands of my family members and the violent episodes in the streets of Chicago. Only now I wasn't angry, and I wasn't wondering why; I was rejoicing in the fact that it was all behind me. I was happy to be alive and in a position to prove to myself that I wasn't born to be the good-for-nothing monster of my past. I cried out all the pain that had haunted me for so long and enjoyed being alone more than I could have ever imagined.

I BELIEVE THAT everything happens for a reason, but I find it hard to accept that the reason Marilyn came into my life was to help me release the demons within me and to absorb them through my violence toward her. In retrospect, however, that is exactly what happened. Marilyn beckoned and allowed me to dig deep inside myself and let loose all the things that had impaired my growth. She helped me see things in terms of the truth, not through the myths laid before me by my abusers. Because of Marilyn I learned to hate—and at the same time understand—my mother for her actions, and therefore I was able to forgive her. I only regret the way I released my pain, suffering, and confusion. I don't think that in Marilyn's wildest dreams she thought that by helping me open up and deal with my demons she would become the target of unspeakable horror. I wish I could have learned about the realities of my violent outbursts without Marilyn suffering them. Unfortunately, this wasn't the case. I now fear that, in doing away with the traumas of my life, I inflicted new, lasting ones on the very person who saved me.

19

Changes

AFTER ONLY TWO months of being on my own I felt a peace of mind that completely overwhelmed me. I walked for miles sometimes for no other reason than the feeling of being able to do it without having to look over my shoulder. I knew no one and no one knew me, and I liked it like that. There was no graffiti separating gang turf because there was no gang turf. And even if there was, I was oblivious to it because I no longer recognized that lifestyle. I no longer allowed the gang life to reign supreme over the kind of person I should be and the attitude I should present. I saw gang life for what it was—a waste of time and a waste of life. I began to like living in Dallas because of the peacefulness it offered me, but it also represented the terror that I had inflicted on Marilyn. I wanted to forget about that and knew that the only way I could do so was to leave. Without research or any well-thought-out motive, I decided to pack up and move to Miami.

I submitted my two weeks' notice at the college and called Chicago to locate Marilyn with the intention of apologizing. Four days after I spoke to her sister, Marilyn called.

In the short amount of time that Marilyn had been back in Chicago, she'd found a job and an apartment. Marilyn also used this time by herself to deal with the things that had happened between us in Dallas. The distance between us allowed her to talk freely and bluntly about how she felt about what had happened to her. In no uncertain terms Marilyn let me know what a big jerk I had been. I did nothing to stop her from expressing herself; in fact, I encouraged her. From that day on we talked on the phone almost daily, and there wasn't one conversation when I didn't apologize for what had happened between us. Tears more often than not accompanied those apologies, as I would visualize her look of horror and beat myself up for having caused her pain. Marilyn said that she forgave me and wanted to see me, but not in Dallas. A little over two months from the day Marilyn left, I packed up my car and headed for Chicago. I wanted to see her one last time before I made my way to Miami. I knew that it would make my trip a lot longer but I also knew that I had to look into her eyes and beg forgiveness. Marilyn didn't know about my plans to move on to Miami. As far as she knew my permanent destination was Chicago.

THE DRIVE FROM Dallas to Chicago was long, yet it felt as if I was on the road for only minutes. I was anxious to get the trip over with, so I drove straight through, stopping only for gas. My thoughts were clear and clean. I marveled at the landscapes I drove through and wondered why I hadn't explored more of the world and what it had to offer. I looked at myself in the rearview mirror and smiled, knowing that soon I would be able to explore the country whenever I wanted.

I arrived around noon on a beautiful, sunny Saturday in the city that had once been my home. I had been gone nine months. I got off the highway on the south side of the city and made my way north, driving through the streets that shaped what Chicago was all about. At noon, the city was already alive with all the peoples and cultures that make up this city. I made my way past Humboldt Park and drove on streets that had soaked up blood spilled because of my ignorance. As I looked out the window of my air-conditioned car, I couldn't help but feel sorry for those who had crossed my path. I began to sweat and tremble but not because I was scared. It dawned on me that here I was in a city where I had lived most of my life, a city with millions of inhabitants, and there wasn't one person who would be happy to see me, not even my family. I knew then that I could never live in Chicago again, regardless of how much I loved it.

By the time I got out of the Humboldt Park area I was drenched in sweat. Again I looked in the rearview mirror and for the first time I saw my face and Humboldt Park together in one place, and I smiled in my newly felt security. My heart, already accelerated, slowed to a complete and normal calm once Humboldt Park was no longer in sight. I drove to Wrigley Field, parked my car, and walked around it, wondering if I could have ever been good enough to play for the Cubs. I remembered how I loved to play baseball as a kid and not being able to play as I grew into a teenager because of my gang involvement and drug use. A tear rolled down my face as I recalled how the abuse I had suffered at home tore me away from the game I loved so much and led me into a life of destruction. I bought a Cubs cap from one of the street vendors, then sat on the stairs of a building across the street from Wrigley and stared at the stadium. After about an hour of daydreaming, I walked away with the feeling that, if I had only had the love and support of a parent, I could have played at Wrigley. It may have been far-fetched, but it was my conclusion and it served its purpose.

I went over the words I wanted to say to Marilyn as I drove, hoping that our meeting would bring closure to the guilt I felt. My plan was to apologize to Marilyn face-to-face, then get out of town as fast as I could.

I arrived at Marilyn's and knocked on her door nervously. I heard footsteps coming toward the door and I wanted to run away before it was opened. I braced myself for the worst as the locks on the door were undone and the door opened. I saw Marilyn's face and noticed that she was just as nervous as I was. We stared at each other for several minutes before speaking. "Come in," Marilyn said softly. "How are you?" I whispered as I entered the apartment. She closed the door and we stood there silently looking at each other. I didn't know what to do. All the things I'd thought of saying to her, and the apology I had longed to give her for so long, would not come out of my mouth. Finally, we stepped toward each other and hugged. The hug turned into a kiss and from then on it seemed as though the horrors that had happened in Dallas weren't even a memory.

Marilyn and I ended up driving and walking around Chicago that whole weekend and making passionate love at every opportunity. On my first day back, we talked a little about what had happened in Dallas. Then we decided to put the subject to rest so that we could begin healing. After that weekend I started driving Marilyn to and from work and listened to her desire for me to stay with her in Chicago—words spoken between our lovemaking sessions. It seemed as if Marilyn had forgotten about everything that had happened in Dallas, and I had forgotten why I came to Chicago. Living with Marilyn again, and living in Chicago again, felt promising.

On my fifth day in Chicago Marilyn told me not to pick her up after work because she was going to run some errands with a friend. With free time on my hands I went to an early afternoon Cubs game and then decided to seek out members of my family. My older sister still lived in the same place. I found her boyfriend hanging out in front of their building, accompanied by a small group of Latin Kings and Queens. In that group was my younger sister, who was now also a member of the Latin Queens and was pregnant by a Latin King. They sat there drinking and smoking weed with infants present, including my niece. My little sister also smoked and drank even though she was pregnant. My mother looked down from the second-floor window at them as if everything were normal. For them, it was.

I felt like continuing on without stopping, but couldn't because they spotted me and called out to me. My little sister ran to me and hugged me. As I held her, all I could think about was the nauseating smell of marijuana and cigarette smoke that oozed from her clothing and hair. My "brother-in-law" shook my hand and seemed surprised and a bit irritated when I didn't follow through in forming the Kings' handshake. I simply held his hand firmly, normally, and with respect for myself. My mother appeared and hung onto my neck for dear life as she cried. Sadly, I didn't know her well enough to know whether they were tears of joy or pain. Then, reluctantly, I went upstairs to drink the cup of coffee she offered to make for me.

I sat in my sister's apartment for what was the longest, most awkward, and uncomfortable half hour of my life. There we were, mother and son, in a ten-by-ten room, sitting about two feet from each other, and we had hardly a word to say to each other. My mother told me she planned to return to Puerto Rico in the coming months. I mentioned my displeasure with the activity going on around and in front of my niece. That was all I said. I finally got up the nerve to say my good-byes and got out of there as quickly as I could. I promised I'd be back before I left town, knowing full well that I had no intention of doing so. Again, I left with everyone thinking I was living in California.

I drove off feeling sad and disillusioned. I wondered how much I had contributed to my siblings' current lifestyle and if it would take them doing jail time to finally wake up as I had done. This visit with my family served only to fortify my feeling that I didn't belong in Chicago. I could not live in the same city with the family I felt didn't care for me or love me and still be OK. I knew that sooner or later I would confront my mother about her lack of love for me. I knew that at some point I would blow up at my sister over the environment she was creating for her children. And I feared that when that day came, no one would care or listen and I'd be dismissed as an unimportant part of the family. I feared that I would eventually blow up in a violent uproar that would result in a great tragedy.

The next day, against Marilyn's wishes and tears, I left for Miami. Marilyn seemed angered about my sudden decision to leave. She repeatedly asked me why I was leaving, but I felt no need to answer her. The passion we had shared since I arrived back in Chicago was overshadowed by my memories of what had happened in Dallas. The anger I felt toward my family made me realize that a violent outburst was just a confrontation or a word away. I loved Marilyn but needed to get as far away from her as possible. Marilyn looked at me with her tear-filled and beautiful eyes and didn't say another word. It was as if she finally realized why I wanted to leave. It was as if she sensed another demon getting ready to expose itself from inside me and she wanted no part of it. Although I knew that my destination was Miami, I told Marilyn I was returning to Dallas.

As I drove out of Chicago, I began to feel calm and secure about my future. I was uncertain about the weeks and months ahead but optimistic that I could make it on my own. The drive to Miami was long but incredibly peaceful. My mind was free of the hate brought on by past memories of a life filled with violence. This violence, my mother, and Marilyn still occupied space within me, but they didn't make me angry any longer, nor did they make me cry tears of sorrow. I had analyzed these feelings and learned from them. When I did cry because of my memories, the tears were accompanied by a smile because I knew the tears were over the joy I felt for having survived.

20

Here and Now

THIS IS MY private life today. Please excuse me for being vague about details regarding my family. I do this to protect them.

I'm living my life and dealing with my God on a daily basis. I know I have a lot to make up for, and I don't allow myself to forget that for one second. I have come a long way from the kid once fascinated by a big city, and from the ruthless gang member that kid became. I survived the hardships of the ghetto streets in Chicago and prison life. Now each and every day is a struggle to survive as a normal, law-abiding citizen.

Upon arriving in Miami, I took any job I could find regardless of how menial it was. I washed dishes, slopped hamburgers, and, yes, I did get promoted to the fry station. While working at these jobs, I searched for a job where I could use the few computer skills I had learned in prison and at previous jobs. I also wanted to get back to school and further prepare myself for the future. I filled out many applications and went to dozens of interviews with no luck, but I didn't get discouraged. I knew that advancement comes by education and hard work, by being born to financially successful parents, or by kissing ass. I had no choice but to work hard and get as much knowledge as possible about anything and everything. Getting turned down for a job wasn't half as bad as dodging bullets. I had always known the rules of right and wrong, but now I was living by them. I knew the consequences of living life as a criminal and those of working hard and dedicating myself to living in peace. I decided to worship the latter with all my might.

Finally I was hired as a customer service representative for a cable company. I was on my way. The company offered a paid-tuition program as long as I was gaining skills that would help me in my job. I enrolled in computer classes at a junior college and have been working with computers in one form or another ever since.

Once I arrived in Miami I became obsessed with making myself a better person through hard work and education. I engraved in my mind that no one was to blame for my failures and no one was to be rewarded for my successes but me. My bilingual and computer skills allowed me to readily gain employment. I went from one job to another, not because I was fired or asked to resign, but because I kept moving into jobs with higher pay and more responsibilities. Ultimately I ended up with a large national company that allows me to grow within the organization while paying for my continuing education. I have been with the same company for almost ten years now.

I'm married and a father. I met my wife about a year after I arrived in Miami and married her after six months of dating. Two years later our first child was born, and my life was changed completely. I remember looking into my child's eyes for the first time and finally knowing what the meaning of true love was. Two years later our second child came along. Having been there every step of the way through the births of my children, I can't imagine what selfishness causes some parents to just abandon their kids or allow them to become victims of abuse. I have never felt love like the love I feel from my kids. And I imagine I never will.

Each and every day I worry about the activities and kids my children may get involved with, and what kind of influences and temptations they face. Because of my experiences as a child, I am very protective of them and wary of all adults around them including teachers, coaches, and other parents, and even in shopping malls they are never out of my sight. I don't want any child, especially my own, to ever go through the kind of experiences I did. This is why I am so protective. I forever keep in mind my belief that if I had had loving, supportive parents involved in my day-to-day life, then I would have been saved from the lifestyle that sucked me in. This is why I dedicate each and every day to showing my kids the importance of being a close family, and the need to work hard and get an education.

My wife and I go through the same ups and downs that every couple goes through. We come from extremely different worlds and ways of life. Her family represents everything mine doesn't. They are tight-knit, very family oriented, and have solid moral values, which revolve around her parents. Not surprisingly, they all lead pretty productive lives. Our differences do present problems that make it hard for us to understand each other's needs sometimes. Fortunately, we do have one belief in common that allows us to survive and motivates us to work on understanding each other—we both believe that our children will be happiest if they have two parents to raise them. We realize that our love for our children is stronger than any difference we may have. Knowing this has opened up many lines of communication for us. But although we are strong as a family unit, we are both aware that if it weren't for our kids, we wouldn't be together at all.

I STOPPED GOING to school when my first child was born to allow my wife to be a stay-at-home mom. This was a decision we discussed together, and we decided that it would be best for our children's upbringing. Even though I still do not have a college degree, I have been able to work myself into a comfortable position within corporate America that allows me to support my family and provide a comfortable lifestyle for them. I'm a big believer that everything is possible through education and regret not having completed mine.

I HAVE MADE great strides in creating a relationship with my own family. I visit them every now and then, and keep in contact with them over the phone. I have accepted that we will never be a tight-knit family and, considering what we've been through and our differences, it's probably better this way. When we do get together, I never bring up our upbringing with my siblings or my mother. We talk about our kids, music, supermarket-tabloid-type subjects, and find some comfort in discussing our individual accomplishments. This allows our time together to be a pleasant refuge from the anger and difficulties of the past. The ultimate compliment I have received since I began to interact with my family again came from one of my sister's coworkers. This woman had been told about my past. Upon meeting me she exclaimed that if she hadn't been told, she never would've known. Amen.

I HAVE FINALLY gained the peace of mind I long searched for. I no longer have nightmares about the violence of my past. I don't drink or smoke anything, or do drugs. I don't get angry very easily and choose to go for a run instead of expressing my displeasure through confrontation.

Very recently, however, I've relapsed into the angry, hateful ways that were once my norm. I began to feel that every question and/or constructive criticism was an attack against me. I felt I was being pushed into a corner and needed to defend myself by striking back violently. I began looking at people at work with contempt. Every time I came across a coworker with a holier-than-thou attitude, which is common in the business world, I wanted to explode on them and give them a taste of street business. I had this overwhelming feeling of wanting to beat respect and humbleness into people I thought were self-serving, arrogant individuals. Fortunately, I began to recognize these unhealthy feelings and the damage they could create. I immediately sought out a therapist and I'm taking medication. I was recently diagnosed with bipolar disorder, which explains my extreme mood shifts between manic and depressive states without ever feeling normal or at peace. I don't know how this will affect my future. Please pray for me.

IN THE STREETS, the criminal is well known and highly visible, only he or she is ignored. In the working world, the criminal comes with college degrees attached to a résumé, shakes your hand, and compliments you instead of questioning the colors of your clothes and pulling a gun. They may not destroy you and put pain in the lives of your family via violence, but they do it by ripping your job out from under you and leaving you without any means of support. And they often get others to do their dirty work for them. This is all legal; there's nothing anyone can do about it.

I often sit in meetings with people who have no clue what suffering really is and hear them discuss the futures of others as if they are God. I wish they could be stripped of everything they have and be put in the drug- and gang-infested streets so they could feel what it's like. Then I realize that if they were in that situation, they'd probably become gang leaders, because the same form of ruthlessness is rewarded there. Gang leaders make decisions that are self-serving. They, too, use others to do their dirty deeds in order to expand their wealth and power. They are willing to destroy the lives of everyone around them without losing a bit of sleep. For a gang leader, making people suffer is all in a day's work. That's why I sometimes get the feeling that I want to grab one of these people in meetings by the neck and pound them senseless. But these are just residual thoughts. I know that sooner or later my name will be the one thrown around in a meeting, so whenever I hear of a position becoming available that I think I would enjoy, I begin preparing myself for it. This is the same action I take whenever I hear of a downsizing period approaching. I begin preparing myself to go elsewhere. I make it my prerogative to prepare myself to move on at the expense of those who show me the road. This is what my survival skills have become.

ANOTHER GREAT CHALLENGE I face is the sexual problems I have resulting from the sexual abuse I suffered. My sexual problems range from days of impotence to uncontrollable lust. I have been to doctors who assure me that my periodic bouts with impotence are not physical. I go to therapy, which has lessened the occurrences, but they still surface when least expected. Sometimes it even happens while I'm in the middle of a sexual act. How embarrassing.

My sexual dysfunction doesn't seem to deter me from lusting after women. Fortunately, therapy has helped me to control the previously distasteful ways I used to express these feelings. There were times when I would blatantly undress women with my eyes and very obviously check them out even if they were standing in front of me giving me a work assignment, taking my blood, or charging me for purchases. The age or appearance of the women doesn't seem to matter—my lustful feelings target all women.

My problem with lusting often puts me in very uncomfortable situations with serious consequences that are difficult for me to comprehend. At work I was talked to regarding how uncomfortable I made the women around me feel on several occasions. One female coworker went as far as filing sexual harassment charges against me. Out in the streets, women confronted me with hostility, as they demanded to know what the hell I was looking at. Still, I had no clue what I was doing wrong, especially since there always seem to be women who like being lusted after and want to take it a step further.

I have not yet gotten total control over this problem but, because I have identified and accepted it, I take precautions that keep me from putting myself in embarrassing situations. I make sure not to put myself in situations where I'm alone with women at work, and when I'm absolutely required to, I force myself to maintain eye contact and keep the conversation professional.

Even with those precautions I have been told that I'm flirtatious. I have a long way to go.

I FEEL STRONGLY that if I had not been such a good student in grade school before the abuse started, I never would have survived. I would either be dead or in jail, or I would have made a career out of gangbanging and been a bum hanging out on the corner and terrorizing the streets of Chicago. I truly believe it was those first seeds of an education and my early success that ultimately gave me a thirst for knowledge and still give me the desire to learn all I can about everything I can. But then there are the aftereffects of the abuse.

Every so often I fall into daydreams where the beatings I endured replay in my mind. I cry when I think about how I had neither a mother nor a father to protect me from abuse by the other. But once these thoughts start to fade, I rejoice in the fact that they don't make me act violently anymore.

Another thing I suffer from is the overwhelming feeling of guilt whenever something bad happens around me even when I am not the cause of the problem. I find myself retracing my steps to assure myself that I'm not the guilty party and pray that I'm not questioned about it because of my obvious nervousness. Needless to say, I'm not a very good candidate for a lie detector test.

I have thought about how it sounds like I have blamed all the problems of my life on my mother or some other adult. The conclusions I have drawn are based on how I feel about my life in my current state of mind, and the bitterness I feel about my past. The fact is that I have led a relatively peaceful, productive life since I started dealing with the violence of my upbringing. I have always understood right from wrong and the consequences, only now I choose to do right because of me, not wrong because of others.

GANGS WILL ALWAYS exist as long as the community and the police are enemies. Gangs will run rampant as long as people in the community do not trust the police. I also know that as long as the blue wall of silence exists—the one that protects corrupt cops—there will never be trust for the police.

The tragedy of September 11, 2001, gave all the cops in the nation an opportunity to put all bad feelings about them behind and start with a clean slate. Unfortunately that opportunity was wasted. Police across the country went from being ultimate heroes back to being the cowardly, abusive assholes most citizens thought they were before the 9/11 tragedy came to pass. It is hard to believe that a profession can be forgiven for shooting an unarmed man forty-one times, confessing to wrongly incarcerating citizens, and shoving a stick up an apprehended individual's ass—all things that happened before the 9/11 tragedy—and yet they still managed to put themselves back on the public's shit list. I wonder if their indifference in any way stems from the fact that a vast majority of their victims are people of color. Being acquitted by all-white juries doesn't help solve the problem, but it does give an accurate picture of race relations in our country. I want to add, too, that I have not been harassed by any police officers since leaving Chicago. Still, it's amazing how so many good cops let a couple of assholes ruin all their reputations by not speaking out.

I DON'T UNDERSTAND why jail sentences for those who will shortly be released back into society do not come coupled with educational goals. I fail to see why educational mandates are not set as conditions for inmates regaining their freedom. For the most part gang members are people who have very little education or skills to make it outside of the 'hood. Why not make them earn a skill that will help them get out and be productive instead of allowing them to sit in the weight pile and become bigger, stronger, and dumber criminals? Getting some form of education while serving time worked for me. The only answer I can think of for wanting bigger, stronger, and dumber criminals is that it guarantees repeat offenders and keeps a billion-dollar industry thriving. So, you boys in the 'hood—which side of the industry do you prefer to be on?

I KNOW FIRSTHAND the evil that lives within individuals, and have chosen to never let myself be caught unprepared. In the streets, where you can potentially encounter someone who lives for the sole purpose of ruining the lives of others, this means packing a gun and being alert. In the working world, it means not being complacent, keeping yourself marketable, and having the same, if not a higher, level of alertness. It is unfortunate that we have to live this way, but people who thrive on creating pain in the lives of others exist in every sector of our society.

That's why I'm pissed off at the world. I'm pissed off because of all the fuckin' people who shut their eyes while others are victimized because it doesn't benefit them to get involved. It pisses me off that every-fuckin'-body is such a tough guy until a tough situation is actually presented to them. Then they become crying little pussies blaming the world and everything in it. I hate that niggers, spics, and white trash get body slammed for everyone to see on television shows like *COPS* while the real higher-stakes criminals get elected to public office.

We live in the most racist country in the world, yet this racism can't be confronted because it's not patriotic. And it drives me crazy how rich assholes get away with every fuckin' thing, including murder, while those of us who can't afford a team of high-priced lawyers have our lives scarred for shit such as smoking a joint.

This is the country with the most freedoms but you're not free to do shit unless you pay for it. You might disagree with what's wrong, and yet you can't point out the obvious and you can't be angry without getting labeled a fuckin' lunatic. So instead we blame everybody and everything else while our anger boils and until it fuckin' blows up and you start shooting every-fuckin'-body in sight. Then all of a sudden people care, but only until the ratings drop.

For Those at Risk

To THOSE OF you out there living the gang life or looking to get into it, please take a moment to let the following words soak in.

I have never met a gang member who wasn't looking out for him- or herself first and foremost. The loyalty they show you to suck you into the lifestyle disappears the moment you decide not to risk spending the rest of your life in a jail, not to be a moving target, or the moment someone who outranks you suddenly has something against you. You are not the King or Queen of the streets as you are made to feel you are. You are simply a scape-goat for dirty officials and drug dealers you'll never even meet. Don't fool yourself—there are easier ways to live the hip-hop life. I mean you can wear the clothes, enjoy the music, do the dance, but do it with those who stay in school and without getting your-self killed. All the police, judges, politicians, and suburbanites you think you are hurting by your acts of delinquency are get-ting rich at the expense of your life.

If it is abuse at home that is making you turn to gangs, seek help. Please seek help. Go to a teacher, to a school counselor, talk to anyone who you think can get you out of the abusive situa-tion. But you have to understand that extreme situations often call for extreme measures. Prepare yourself to make tough decisions that may feel as if they are the wrong things to do. Just understand that you have to get out and there is no time to be a pussy. Take control of your life before someone else makes you lose control. It's amazing how so many good kids let a couple of assholes ruin their reputations and then they turn bad when they feel they have no choice. Or they get into a situation where they are hurt by a rival gang or a cop and suddenly have a reason to accept the gang way as the right way.

I can go on and on about the dos and don'ts of the streets but I'll spare you the lecture. Bottom line is that standing on the corner acting tough does not make you tough. It makes you a stupid, ignorant asshole who fucks up everything for the rest of us. Get an education, and go live the life you think you are being denied.

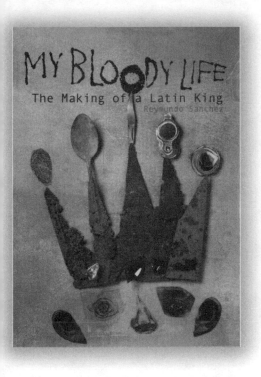

"A slow-motion riot of drugs, sex, and gunplay."
—*Publishers Weekly*

"Sanchez writes plainly and powerfully . . ."
—*Booklist*

"A viciously candid, self-deprecating memoir . . ."
—*Chicago* magazine

My Bloody Life
The Making of a Latin King
Reymundo Sanchez

ooking for an escape from childhood abuse, Reymundo Sanchez turned away from school and baseball to drugs, alcohol, and then sex, and was left to fend for himself before age 14. The Latin Kings, one of the largest and most notorious street gangs in America, became his refuge and his world, but its violence cost him friends, freedom, self-respect, and nearly his life. This is a raw and powerful odyssey through the ranks of the new mafia, where the only people more dangerous than rival gangs are members of your own gang, who in one breath will say they'll die for you and in the next will order your assassination.

CHICAGO REVIEW PRESS